THE AMERICAN EXPLORATION AND TRAVEL SERIES

[For a complete list, see page 241]

Jean-Bernard Bossu's

TRAVELS
IN THE INTERIOR
OF NORTH AMERICA
1751-1762

———

Jean-Bernard Bossu's

TRAVELS
IN THE INTERIOR
OF NORTH AMERICA
1751-1762

Translated and Edited by
SEYMOUR FEILER

UNIVERSITY OF OKLAHOMA PRESS : NORMAN

LIBRARY OF CONGRESS CATALOG CARD NUMBER: 62–10766

Copyright 1962 by the University of Oklahoma Press, Publishing Division of the University. Composed and printed at Norman, Oklahoma, U.S.A., by the University of Oklahoma Press. First edition.

To my mother, Sarah Feiler

EDITOR'S INTRODUCTION

THE FEW PERTINENT FACTS KNOWN about the life of Jean-Bernard Bossu inform us that he was born in 1720 at Baigneux-les-Juifs, a village several miles to the northwest of Dijon in Burgundy. The village even today has a population of little more than 350 inhabitants. Bossu's career as a naval officer took him on three different occasions to the French colony of Louisiana. During the first two trips, from 1751 to 1757 and from 1757 to 1762, he had occasion to travel up the Mississippi Valley and through present-day Alabama. The account of these travels and explorations was published in two volumes by Le Jay in Paris, 1768, under the title of *Nouveaux Voyages aux Indes occidentales; Contenant une Relation des differens Peuples qui habitent les environs du grand Fleuve Saint-Louis, appellé vulgairement le Mississipi; leur Religion; leur gouvernement; leurs moeurs, leurs guerres et leur commerce.* A later edition of this same work was published in Amsterdam in 1769. The third voyage, undertaken after Louisiana had become a Spanish colony, is described in another work entitled *Nouveaux Voyages dans l'Amérique septentrionale, Contenant une collection de Lettres écrites sur les lieux, par l'Auteur, à son ami, M. Douin, Chevalier, Capitaine dans les troupes du Roi, ci-devant son camarade dans le nouveau Monde* (Amsterdam, Changuion, 1777). The author returned to France, where he died in 1792.

The present work is a new translation of the account of Bossu's first two trips as related in the second Le Jay edition of the *Nouveaux Voyages aux Indes occidentales.* An earlier and rather rare English translation entitled *Travels Through That Part of North America Formerly Called Louisiana* was done by John Reinhold Forster in 1771 and was published by T. Davies in London. The present translation was considered necessary because of the rareness of the earlier English version, its somewhat archaic language, and Forster's unfortunate tendency to give a word-for-word translation. The Forster work, too, often fails to translate Indian terms into English or to give the names of tribes and places in the forms used in English. In the present translation, wherever possible, tribes, places, plants, and animals have been given their contemporary names. An attempt, however, has been made to keep the work in Bossu's style as much as possible.

Bossu himself admits that he wrote in the straightforward, simple, and often naïve manner of a military man. Although he makes no pretense to being a man of letters, the influence of the *philosophe* writers of eighteenth-century France is quite obvious in his writing. There is a fairly evident tendency throughout the account to treat the Indian as a "noble savage" and to depict him as a simple man following the "universal law of nature." In comparisons drawn between the "savagery" of the North American and the "civilization" of the western European, it is the latter which usually comes off second best. The epistolary form of the work is itself a reflection of the taste of the period.

The simplicity of style in no way detracts from Bossu's descriptions of what he saw and experienced during his travels. As a matter of fact, the straightforwardness and lack of stylistic adornment add to the impression that here was a man who recorded what he saw with exactitude and precision. Although the descriptions are often short, they seem to neglect little which bears upon the lives of the Indians he encountered. Bossu was interested in everything he observed among the tribes. Birth, marriage, death, religion, government, and war were all included in his account of Indian life. The food the people ate, the clothing they wore, the games they participated in were recorded in some detail. His insatiable curiosity led him to examine such varied aspects of native life as child rearing, medicine, magic, and the relations of the Indian and the white man.

The author's observations and comments were not limited to the human inhabitants of the continent. Vegetation, animals, and birds as well as cultivated crops, terrain, and the quality of the soil all come under his careful scrutiny. The fact that nothing concerning the people or the land they lived in seemed insignificant to Bossu makes this work a valuable contribution to the study of French Louisiana in the eighteenth century.

Evidence that the *Nouveaux Voyages aux Indes occidentales* was favorably received in France at the time of its publication is contained in a review appearing in the September 15, 1768, issue of Grimm's *Correspondance littéraire,* an important journal of the period.

> The account of these travels is written with extreme simplicity, and it is for this very reason that you will read it with extreme pleasure. The reader has no reason to doubt M. Bossu's veracity; it is so perfectly evident. The author has neither enough brilliance, artifice, nor motive to tell you anything except what he has seen. The details that he gives us of the savage nations among which he has lived agree with what we already know. We, furthermore, feel that they are true just as we know that a portrait is realistic even when we are not familiar with the model. These details are extremely interesting because of the simplicity and the naïveté of the customs they describe.
>
> We see in this work man as he was at the beginning of society, for these nations which we call savage are very civilized. . . . M. Bossu

thought that he could be as truthful in speaking about the French officers stationed in Canada and Louisiana as he could when speaking about the Indians. He called both honest men and scoundrels by name; this simplicity has cost him dearly.[1]

The article goes on to explain that Bossu, although he had met all the requirements of the French censors and had received the government's permission to publish the work, was thrown into the Bastille for six weeks because of his criticism of Kerlérec, the governor of Louisiana. The *Correspondance littéraire* adds that Bossu came out of prison just as hale and merry as when he entered, which might indicate that he did not at all regret publishing the *Nouveaux Voyages aux Indes occidentales*. We can be grateful for his decision.

SEYMOUR FEILER

Norman, Oklahoma
February 2, 1962

[1] Grimm, Diderot, Raynal, Meister, etc., *Correspondance littéraire, philosophique et critique,* ed. by Maurice Tourneux (Paris, Garnier Frères, 1879), VIII, 186.

CONTENTS

CONTENTS

xiii

ILLUSTRATIONS

Jean-Bernard Bossu's

TRAVELS
IN THE INTERIOR
OF NORTH AMERICA
1751-1762

———————

A LETTER TO THE CITIZENS OF FRANCE

CITIZENS OF FRANCE, I am offering you this collection of my observations on part of the New World, before and after the last war. You will be the judge of whether I have made it interesting enough.

The devotion that I have always had for my native land has led me to serve the interests of my Prince rather than my own. This has been my policy at all times and in all places.

I do not believe that it is enough for a member of the military merely to serve. Any practical knowledge he may have, relating to his service, should also be offered to the state. I have kept these two aims in mind in the account of my travels. I shall be only too happy if you find my work elucidating.

Because my subject warrants it, I have found it necessary to go to the source of difficulties caused by persons who have, perhaps, abused their authority in these distant lands.

Since I dislike engaging in personalities, I shall try, with all the natural frankness of my profession, not to offend the sensibility of decent people. Yet, if I encounter unjust men, guilty of irregular conduct, who oppose the Sovereign's orders and violate both divine and

3

human law, while they greedily acquire riches at the expense of the unfortunate, it is my duty to reveal to posterity their intrigues and their breaches of trust.

I shall let the reader judge the quality of my character sketches. There is just one reflection I wish to make: Those whose duty it is to govern men should make every effort to be thoroughly familiar with the ability, the character, and the intelligence of the subjects in their employ.

I sincerely hope that my readers will find both amusing and instructive information in these letters. I am vain enough to believe that my motives will gain the indulgence of real patriots, who are more concerned with truth than with an elegant style. My wishes will be fulfilled if I gain their confidence.

Foreword

THE AUTHOR OF THESE MEMOIRS spent twelve years traveling through
the vast area inhabited by the Indians. With the purpose of allying
them more closely with the French, he learned their language so he
could become thoroughly familiar with their character and their
customs. His ability to ask them all sorts of questions made his service
to the King of even greater value. He was thus able to guarantee the
accuracy of his observations.

He wrote these letters to a distinguished officer who was curious
about the life of the inhabitants of the other hemisphere. The author
has tried to reveal and explain their most secret thoughts. He was
surprised to discover the oratorical talent and order which are evident
in the speeches of these men whom we call savages. Proof of these
gifts is found in a speech given by Thamathelé-Mingo,[1] chief of a
tribe called the Alabamas, which dealt with establishing perpetual
peace among warring tribes. The résumé of this speech is found in
Letter XV.

The historical letters which make up this collection introduce

[1] *Mingo* means "chief of the area."

the reader to a series of surprising and curious facts, whose nature and variety are of great interest. The moral and political reflections which appear in the letters are natural and unaffected. There is evidence throughout of the same uprightness and fidelity which governed all the author's actions. His deeds are justly praised and are verified by the authentic papers attached to the work. Everything in it, the geography as well as the general history of Louisiana, is accurate. He has told his story by means of very interesting anecdotes.

This account contains a true summary of the events which took place in Louisiana. They are reported in chronological order from the time of the discovery of the country in 1512[2] until 1762.

The author, incapable of fooling the public and convinced that simple, unadorned truth is more impressive than fancy, tells what he has seen and learned during his travels. He could have gone on at greater length, but he preferred a restrained, succinct style to a rambling one. He relates only the most interesting facts.

Although this description contains amusing as well as useful information, you can be sure that it is not written in the Romanesque style used by most travelers,[3] who invent stories and substitute ingenious fables for the truth to make their work more interesting. Important anecdotes concerning the Indians' way of life are lacking in the works of such authors. Knowledge of the Indians can be acquired only after a long period of residence among them.

Everything reported by this author might appear to be fictitious were it not for the verification of a number of distinguished people now living in France who accompanied him on his travels.

It was considered necessary to add historical, geographical, and other notes to explain certain symbolic expressions used by the Indians in their speeches.

[2] Louisiana was first called Florida. Juan Ponce de Leon discovered it on Palm Sunday, March 27, 1512. He must have named it Florida because of the beauty of the country with its orchards and its flower-covered countryside. [Bossu was mistaken here.—ED.]

[3] This is evident when you read these edifying letters.

It is with extreme distaste that the author mentions several matters of a personal nature. He was forced to do so because they are closely related to his topic. His principal motive, however, for presenting to his compatriots the virtues and vices practiced in this foreign land was to fill them with horror of prevaricators and admiration for honorable men.

The fairness and the wisdom of the Ministry, whose efforts are directed toward the general good, will do much to counteract the corruption which is obscured by war and distance. The Ministry's maintaining of order in the colonies, its zeal and devotion to the navy, in addition to the Family Pact which is responsible for the good will among the subjects of the two crowns, guarantee that France will share the riches of the New World with her good ally, Spain.

May heaven fulfill our wishes and grant long life to the Bourbon family.

A Letter from the Marquis de l'Estrade to the Author

Sir:

I have received in duplicate all the letters you have sent me during the years 1759, 1760, 1761, and 1762. Since the first letters did not reach me, they must have been intercepted. You can rest assured that I would not have failed to answer them. I am, nevertheless, very happy to learn that you have arrived safely at Corunna, despite the hardships of your extremely rough crossing.

Let me get back to your historical letters, which I have read with a great deal of interest and pleasure. Everything in them, sir, indicates that you are an honest, intelligent, diligent, and enlightened officer. The account of your travels bears such an indelible stamp of truth that no plagiarized version can imitate it. It is quite obvious throughout the letters that you are a keen observer, a loyal citizen, and a friend of mankind.

Your account, sir, of the life of the Indians pleased me a great deal. I must admit that your description fascinates me as much for the important and strange facts it contains as for the natural style in which it is written.

8

The thoughts you express are simple, wise, and true. They have the additional quality of being stated sharply and precisely. Your style is quick, sometimes warm, and always clear. Reading the letters is a fascinating, effortless, and delightful experience, since almost everything in them is interesting. The story of the old man who sacrifices his life for his son and the one about Monsieur de Belle-Isle's four unfortunate companions who die of hunger are very touching.

It is, moreover, impossible to praise highly enough an officer who has faced the greatest danger for his country and has enriched the reading public with a thousand useful, new, and curious observations which have resulted from his research.

I do not at all doubt that if this collection were published, the public would receive it favorably. This is especially true because the work has been written with military candor, which is certainly preferable to the correct style of so many of our clever writers.

Such recent events will be of interest to politicians, citizens, and philosophers, who are the friends of humanity.

Personally, sir, I cannot fully express to you my admiration and my gratitude for your kindness in choosing me for your correspondent. I shall long remember the pleasure your letters have caused me. My sons have read your work with great attentiveness, and they, as well as I, have found that it inspires in them the manly virtues which should be an integral part of the profession for which they have been destined since birth. In their imaginations, they have already traveled through those vast regions which you have courageously visited in reality, while serving your country.

I am, sir, respectfully yours,

The Marquis de l'Estrade de la Cousse

Château de Boux, near Vîteaux, Burgundy
December 15, 1762

Letter I

To the Marquis de l'Estrade.

The author's departure for America; a description of the town of Cap François; the Spaniards' cruelty toward the natives of the island of Santo Domingo; work in the mines; the true origin of the disease of Naples.

Sir:

When I had the honor of bidding you farewell, you asked me to inform you of everything that might appear noteworthy in this new world. You insisted, too, upon my giving all the interesting details of the trip. I am happy that my stay at Cap François offers me the opportunity to fulfill this obligation which is dear to me because of the pleasure it brings you.

I was at Belle-Île-en-Mer in 1750, where the Chevalier de Grossolles was in command. He gave me a letter from Count d'Argenson notifying me that His Majesty had just given me a lieutenant's commission in the marines. This minister ordered me to leave for Rochefort without delay. I, therefore, set sail on the first fishing boat which was carrying to La Rochelle sardines caught off the coast of Brittany. This is the main source of revenue for the inhabitants of Belle-Île.

In November we set sail off Le Palais, the city situated on Belle-Île. The very first night we encountered such a violent storm off the coast of Poitou that we thought our little ship, which was battered, tossed about, and surrounded by waves, would go down at any mo-

11

ment. The crew consisted of a pilot and three sailors from lower
Brittany, who are commonly called sea wolves. They are so used to
the sea that they go out on it in the severest weather. Since the wind
had increased, our captain was forced to anchor at Île Dieu, between
Poitou and the region of Aunis. After eight days the sea became calm,
and we set sail once more, continuing until we reached the Île de Ré.
I crossed a sea channel three leagues wide, which separates the island
from the continent, and arrived at La Rochelle; I got to Rochefort
the next day. Upon my arrival, I was ordered to report to the commanding naval officer, Monsieur le Normant de Mési,[1] a man of true
merit who is worthy of his post because of his intelligence and his
kindness. He told me that, after I had obtained all that was necessary for my trip overseas, I could sail from La Rochelle aboard the
four-hundred-ton *Pontchartrain du Port*. Monsieur le Normant had
equipped this ship for His Majesty, and it was to be used to transport
four marine companies, whom we picked up at the citadel on the Île
de Ré. These troops were to reinforce the garrison at New Orleans.
We set sail from La Rochelle on December 26 and had contrary winds
off the coast of Spain for two weeks. We were about to put in at
Corunna to seek shelter, but fortunately the winds suddenly shifted.
At the end of January, we were within sight of Madeira,[2] a Portu-
guese possession which is called the "Queen of Islands" because of
the fertility of its fine soil. The island, about twenty leagues in circumference, produces excellent wines and beautiful, delicious fruit.

On February 15, we were at the Tropic of Cancer. On the six-
teenth, we had some amusing ceremonies which sailors hold for
those who have never crossed this line. The novices are baptized with

[1] Attached since then to the Naval Ministry, with the title of Intendant General
of the Navy and of French Colonies. I am pleased to take this opportunity to ac-
knowledge publicly my gratitude for his warm welcome and the many favors he has
done me.

[2] An African island in the Western Sea north of the Canaries, which were discovered in 1417 by a Norman nobleman, Jean Benthencourt, who was called King of
the Canaries. He helped the Spaniards conquer these islands, which belong to them
today.

sea water but can be spared this generous and uncomfortable bath by paying off the chief mate. Finally, two months after leaving La Rochelle, we were happy to arrive at Cap François[3] on the coast of the island of Santo Domingo, the first land in America in which the Spaniards built cities and fortresses.

The cape is located at the foot of a mountain and is protected by a fort cut into rock at the mouth of the port. This fortress, which is well supplied with artillery, juts out into the sea and forms a promontory or cape, from which the city gets its name. Its inhabitants are European merchants, Creoles, and Negroes, whom the settlers use to grow sugar cane, coffee, indigo, cacao, cotton, cassia, tobacco, and other products.

The Spaniards and the French share this country; the latter occupy the western part. Santo Domingo, the capital of the island, is the residence of a bishop kept there by His Catholic Majesty to oversee religious matters.

This island has become famous as the place of origin of the disease of Naples, or syphilis. There is so much disagreement on this point, and there are so many different stories, that I believe I should report the truth to you.

Nicolas de Obando was the governor of this country toward the end of the fifteenth century, under the reign of Ferdinand of Aragon and Isabella of Castile. Having been given explicit orders to convert the subjugated Indians, he parceled them out to the Castilians, giving one hundred to one, fifty to another. He called this system *repartimiento* (separation or division). You will doubtless agree that that is a peculiar way to gain converts in the New World. Such actions are certainly opposed to the true spirit of Christianity.[4]

---

[3] Now called Cap Haïtien.—ED.

[4] King Ferdinand was notified of these irregularities, and he tried to correct them. He was particularly concerned with the Indians, whom he wanted to protect and attract to the Faith. This has always been the primary concern of Catholic kings. Indeed, he gave several orders and published laws asking that they be taught gently through good examples and selflessness. All of these good intentions lost their strength

13

These gold-hungry Spaniards forced the wretched Indians to work in the mines and to spend eight to nine months almost buried in the bowels of the earth. This hard work, the sulphurous fumes of the mines, and the famine caused by the inability of the Indians to work their lands caused their blood to become so bad that their faces turned saffron yellow. Unbearably painful boils broke out on all parts of their bodies. Soon they passed on this contagious disease to their wives and, consequently, to their enemies. Since there was no cure, both the Indians and the Spaniards died of the disease.

The despairing Spaniards thought that this disease would not follow them to Europe where they went for a change of climate. They were wrong; when they returned, they gave the Europeans the disease they had received from the Americans. God, however, pitied these wretched islanders; some time later, the Indian wife of a Castilian discovered a certain wood called guaiacum which can cure the disease.

It is only too true that evil gives birth to evil. The Spaniards have sacrificed millions of men in the New World and have laid waste to vast countries to steal the Indians' gold, but as a famous poet says so well:

> *By our laws, it's true, America is ruled,*
> *But her disease ruins us, it's we who are fooled.*
> VOLTAIRE

Gold and silver cause their miners as much grief and fatigue as they give pleasure and ease to their possessors. A Spanish engineer told me that it took twenty-nine years of searching to find, at Potosí, Bolivia, the Crusero vein, which is 250 yards deep. Power and greed are responsible for this sort of painful and taxing labor; it is because of poverty and servitude that men dig gold out of the bowels of the

---

with distance, just as an arrow falls short of the target which is too far from the archer's arm.

14

earth. The unfortunate men who work the mines give up the air of our atmosphere and sunlight to bury themselves in the deep, foul, gold pits. The fumes are so unhealthful that they cause dizziness and sudden nausea from the moment the workers enter the mines. They use candles to light their way in these underground passageways and hammers to break the ore, which is quite hard. They bring the metal up to the surface on their shoulders. The ladders they use are made of three poles, twisted beef hide, and wooden rungs, and are so constructed that while some workers can climb up one side, others can come down on the other side. Each ladder is separated into ten lengths. A man usually carries on his back two arrobas[5] of metal, wrapped in a cloth. The first man has a candle attached to his thumb, and all of them hold onto the ladder with both hands and climb up 250 feet.

We know from the general history of the West Indies that the people of Florida used to throw away sacks of silver as though they were of no value. This was not true of the people of the Mexican kingdom, who valued gold. Here is what Joseph d'Acosta reports in his *Histoire universelle des Indes*: "It is true that their avarice was not as great as ours, and although these people were idolatrous, they never worshiped gold and silver as much as did some bad Christians who committed the greatest crimes to obtain these metals."

The same author tells an anecdote which demonstrates perfectly man's stupid greed:

A Spanish monk, who was looking at the famous high volcano of Guatemala, was convinced that what he saw burning could be nothing but a mass of gold, since it had been burning without having been consumed for so many centuries. With this false idea in mind, he invented some kettles, chains, and other instruments to draw off the supposed liquid gold from this well-like formation. But the fire thwarted his attempt; as soon as the chain and the kettle got close to

[5] The arroba weighs about twenty-five pounds, *poids de Marc*.

that mouth of hell, they melted. Yet he insisted on inventing new ways to draw off the gold which obsessed him. Just when he thought that his fantastically strange plan would succeed, he got too close, and the fumes of the volcano killed him. In a similar manner, blind mortals rush to their death by seeking after the pleasures of life.

To get back to the Indians of Santo Domingo, we learn from the history of the country that a chief named Poncra, being harassed by the Spaniards, decided to flee from his village. The enemy, finding the village deserted, pillaged it of three thousand gold marks which had been left behind. Vasco Núñez de Balboa, Nicolas de Obando's successor, sent some of his people after the chief to tell him not to be afraid to come back and to assure him that they would be friends. If not, the Spaniard would go after him with his dogs, who would devour him.[6]

Poncra, frightened by this threat, did not dare disobey and brought with him three other chiefs, who were his vassals. Núñez de Balboa tried unsuccessfully every imaginable means to make Poncra tell where the gold came from in that land which reputedly produced a great amount of it. Neither kind treatment nor torture could make him reveal the secret, which perhaps he did not even know himself. As far as the three thousand gold marks were concerned, Poncra said they had been amassed by people who had died in his father's time, and that he himself had never considered it worth while to look for

[6] The Spaniards had brought with them leashed dogs trained to hunt Indians. As soon as they were turned loose on their unfortunate victims, the dogs tore out their entrails and devoured them. One of them, called Baromel, was especially feared on the island. Although a shield protected the dog against arrows, the Indians succeeded in killing him by piercing his eyes with darts. The Indians considered this a great triumph.

Antoine d'Herrera reports in his first *Décade* that this awful animal, whose instinct was remarkable, guarded the entrance to a mountain pass in Santo Domingo. One day an Indian woman who wanted to pass spoke these words to him: "Sir Dog, do not hurt me; I am carrying this letter to the Christians." The author added, "The dog sniffed her, pissed against her [these are his words], and let her pass without harm."

16

more, since he had no use for gold. This poor chief and his companions were fed to the dogs.

Sometime later, a Spaniard fell into the hands of Indians belonging to poor Poncra's tribe. They reproached him for his nation's greed for gold and the injustices that this greed had made them commit. It was for that alone that the Spaniards had left their own country, had suffered hardship on the sea, and had come to this island to trouble people who lived peacefully in their cabins under the protection of the Great Spirit.[7]

After that short harangue, they melted some gold and poured it into the Spaniard's ears and throat and said, "Since you want it so much, drink your fill!"

It must be admitted, though, that if Mexico's history brings to mind only horrors, that of Santo Domingo, on the other hand, is filled with examples of generosity.

One day during a famine, an Indian gave two live doves to Don Pedro de Magaratit, the King of Spain's former commander. The General took them, paid the Indian well, and asked part of his garrison to climb to the highest point of the city with him. He held the doves in his hands and said, "Gentlemen, I am very sorry that I have not been given enough to feed all of you. I cannot bring myself to satisfy my appetite while you are dying of hunger." Having said these words, he let the two birds fly free.

An infinite number of other anecdotes can be added to this one, which would serve as well to demonstrate the honor of the inhabitants of this island. There are several which deserve to be set down in history. Among those which have been told me is one that I cannot keep from passing on to you. An old inhabitant of Santo Domingo had made a considerable fortune through commerce, work, and industry. This fortune in no way changed his habits or conduct; he valued it only so far as it enabled him to help others.

As soon as a ship arrived from France, he would go to the port

[7] This is what the savages call their Supreme Being.

to watch the passengers land and, generally, he would take them home with him. One day he saw several young men who thought that their fortunes would be made as soon as they arrived in the country. They had letters of recommendation upon which they counted so heavily that they hardly paid any attention to the colonist who approached them. He left them wishing them all sorts of good fortune. He met them a little while later and found that they were quite sad and not at all happy with the reception given them. "Gentlemen," he said to them, "you were not recommended to me and were not counting on my help, but I am a man and you need assistance. Come home with me and you will be given food and lodging. In the meantime, maybe something will come along which will suit you." The delighted young men accepted the offer. They followed him to his home where they found a table set for twenty people with as many Negro servants to wait on them. One of the newcomers asked if they had been invited to a wedding reception and was astonished to learn that this was just an ordinary meal. The master of the house kept them there for some time, and through his advice and his care they soon became well established.

You can well imagine that a man with so kind a heart was loved and respected by all his slaves, who considered him their father. This settler was far removed from the barbarous greed of some colonists who force their wretched slaves to do such frightful work that they refuse to marry in order not to give birth to new slaves for their masters. When the slaves are old and sick, they are treated worse than the masters' horses and dogs.[8]

As for the inhabitants of the French islands in America, I can assure you that they are very generous to strangers. One can even

---

[8] I saw a colonist named Chaperon place one of his Negroes in a hot oven, where the poor man died. Upon seeing that the victim's jawbones had drawn back, the barbarian Chaperon remarked, "I think that he is still laughing." He picked up a poker and stirred the fire. From that time on, this colonist has become the bugbear of the slaves. The masters threaten disobedient slaves by telling them, "I am going to sell you to Chaperon."

travel in the interior of these countries without any expense. All that you have to do is look frank, decent, and honest to be received favorably on all the plantations.

It is with good cause that in France the Creoles are considered noble. They are noble in thought, in their handling of arms, and in the other arts which they practice so successfully.

Man is the same everywhere; he is equally capable of good and of evil; education corrects his vices but does not give him virtues. The same Creator has made the civilized man and the savage and has endowed them with equal qualities. That is what you will see in the course of my correspondence. If I cannot make it pleasant by means of a charming style, at least I shall make it interesting through the unusualness of the facts that I shall report. I have the honor of remaining, sir, . . .

Cap François
February 15, 1751

Letter II

To the Marquis de l'Estrade.

The author leaves Cap François for Louisiana; a short description of the port of Havana, the famous Gulf of Mexico, and New Orleans.

Sir:

We set sail for our destination on March 8, and on the fifteenth we were within sight of the island of Cuba, the most temperate of the West Indies. Havana is the storehouse of America's riches because of its site and its large and convenient port, which can accommodate more than one thousand ships. It is the usual meeting place for Spanish fleets returning to Europe, and it is defended by three forts. Sixteen years after its discovery, it was finally determined that Cuba was an island, two hundred leagues long by twenty-five to thirty leagues wide, and not part of the mainland. It is situated on the Tropic of Cancer at 23.5 degrees North latitude. Almost halfway up the southern coast of the island are a number of smaller islands, called the Queen's Garden.

During the equinox, we ran into a violent storm between Cape Catoche and Cape San Antonio, on the western point of Cuba, which we passed on the twenty-third. I was quite seasick, since I had never made long ocean voyages, but my desire to serve my country in a new land more than made up for all the hardship encountered on the trip. The winds shifted, the sea became calm, and several days later we entered the famous Gulf of Mexico, where we encountered a great amount of drift wood which came down the Mississippi from Louisiana. This wood, seen more than two hundred leagues out to sea, helped us during misty or foggy weather to find the mouth of the river. This is very difficult because of the rocks and the shallow water of the region.

At the beginning of April, we sighted Balize, a fort at the mouth of the Mississippi.[1]

In 1698,[2] Le Moine d'Iberville, a Canadian gentleman, discovered the mouth of the river which La Salle had missed in 1684. Our ship ran aground on a bar; we fired a cannon to summon the pilot, and at the same time the captain unloaded the artillery pieces and landed the two hundred regular troops who had been sent to serve in the colony of Louisiana. This lightened the ship enough to float her again.

On April 4, eighteen officers landed at Fort Balize,[3] where Monsieur de Santilly is in command. He entertained us as royally as possible during our stay at his post, which is isolated and surrounded by swamps filled with snakes and alligators.

The Marquis de Vaudreuil, having heard of our arrival, sent out several boats to get us and to bring us refreshments. After having assigned our soldiers to the ships, we sailed and rowed until we arrived at New Orleans on Easter Sunday. The Marquis de Vaudreuil is supposed to receive twenty-four more naval companies in Louisiana. These troops are to arrive on merchant vessels outfitted by the King. There are also girls, recruited in France, coming to populate the land. Industrious soldiers who want to marry them are discharged

[1] Balize was a pilot village and a fortification at the mouth of the Mississippi, half a mile from the Gulf of Mexico and about 110 miles from New Orleans.—ED.

[2] Monsieur d'Iberville, the governor of Louisiana, led the first colony of settlers there in 1699. After his death, the country had no governor for a long time. The second one was Monsieur de la Motte Cadillac, the third was Monsieur de Bienville, the youngest brother of the first.

[3] It is thirty leagues from this post to New Orleans because of the bends in the river.

from the service. The King grants them a certain number of acres of land to clear and supports them for three years. He also has them furnished with a rifle, a half pound of powder and two pounds of lead each month, an ax, a pick, seed, a cow, a calf, chickens, a rooster, etc.

The Marquis de Vaudreuil has assigned the twenty-four new companies to different parts of the colony, without favor to anyone, so that everyone can share and share alike. Lots were drawn for the Illinois post, which is five hundred leagues from New Orleans, and the company to which I was assigned received that assignment. I have the honor of being among those officers whom Monsieur Rouillé, the naval minister, has recommended to the Marquis de Vaudreuil, and I am fully aware of the benefits of such a recommendation. I can assure you that the General's table is of great comfort to me at the present time, as it is to all those who have just arrived and have not yet had the time to find permanent lodging. There is such abundance that we are served too well. The Governor does the honors of his table with such nobility and generosity that he has gained the esteem and admiration of all the officers, who rightly call him the Father of the Colony. Monsieur Michel de la Rouvillière, the director of markets, has contributed to making life agreeable for us by his fine control over staple products as well as everything else with which his office is concerned.

We expect to leave for the Illinois post August 20; Monsieur de Macarty, who will go with us, has been named commander by the Court. My visit to the different nations during this long trip will enable me to give you a detailed description of the beautiful Mississippi and of the people who inhabit its shores.

In the meantime, I shall describe the capital of Louisiana, but I do not think that it is necessary to speak of the city at length, since you are doubtless familiar with most of the maps and articles published on it. I simply want to call to your attention that New Orleans, with its well-laid-out streets, is bigger and more heavily populated today than formerly. There are four types of inhabitants: Europeans,

French Louisiana in the 1750's

Indians, Africans or Negroes, and half bloods, born of Europeans and savages native to the country.

Those born of French fathers and French, or European, mothers are called Creoles. They are generally very brave, tall, and well built and have a natural inclination toward the arts and sciences. Since these studies cannot be pursued very well because of the shortage of good teachers, rich and well-intentioned fathers send their children to France, the best school for all things.

As for the fair sex, whose only duty is to please, they are already born with that advantage here and do not have to go to Europe to acquire it artificially.

New Orleans and Mobile are the only cities where there is no *patois*; the French spoken here is good.

Negroes are brought over from Africa to clear the land, which is excellent for growing indigo, tobacco, rice, corn, and sugar cane; there are sugar plantations which are already doing very well. This country offers a delightful life to the merchants, artisans, and foreigners who inhabit it because of its healthful climate, its fertile soil, and its beautiful site. The city is situated on the banks of the Mississippi, one of the biggest rivers in the world, which flows through eight hundred leagues of explored country. Its pure and delicious waters[4] flow forty leagues among numerous plantations, which offer a delightful scene on both banks of the river, where there is a great deal of hunting, fishing, and other pleasures of life.

The Capuchins were the first monks to go to New Orleans as missionaries in 1723. The superior of these good monks, who are concerned solely with their religious work, is vicar of the parish. The Jesuits settled in Louisiana two years later, and these shrewd politicians managed to exploit the richest plantation in the colony, obtained through their intrigues. The Ursulines were sent over at about

[4] When Monsieur le Normant de Mési was naval commander at Rochefort, he had this water served at table. This water also has the power to increase fertility in women.

the same time. These pious women, whose zeal is certainly to be commended, educate young ladies; they also take orphans into their school, for each of whom they receive fifty crowns from the King. These same nuns were in charge of the military hospital.

I have been here such a short time that I am not yet able to give you an account of the customs of the people who live in the vicinity of the river. By means of an anecdote, however, I shall try to inform you of the character and the nature of the Chitimachas, who live on a river or tributary bearing their name west of New Orleans. I am sure that this anecdote will interest you even though almost all of these people have been wiped out.

In 1720, one of these people, hiding in an isolated spot on the banks of the Mississippi, killed the Abbé de Saint-Côme, a colonial missionary. The governor, Monsieur de Bienville, held all the Chitimachas responsible for the murder. In order to spare his own people, Governor de Bienville had his allies among the tribes attack the Chitimacha nation, who sued for peace after they lost their best warriors. The Governor demanded the head of the murderer. The Chitimachas carried out this order immediately and then presented the peace pipe[5] to Monsieur de Bienville.

Here is what I have learned about these solemn emissaries. They arrived in New Orleans singing in cadence the song of the calumet. They waved the pipe in the air, announcing their mission. On these occasions, they are dressed in their most beautiful clothing.

The chief of the envoys said, "I am happy to be in your presence. You have been angry with our nation for a long time. We have learned with joy what your heart has been saying, that it wishes to grant us happy days." They then sat on the ground, resting their heads in their hands. The spokesman must have done this in order

[5] The calumet is a long red, white, or black marble pipe with a two- or three-foot-long reed stem. The savages send it with deputies to the nations with which they wish to make treaties or renew alliances. This symbol of peace and friendship is decorated with white eagle feathers. With the calumet, one can travel everywhere without fear, since there is nothing more sacred among these people.

to recover his breath before beginning his speech; the others, to help them remain silent. In the meantime, everyone was warned not to talk or to laugh during the speech, since the Indians would consider that an affront.

After several minutes, the spokesman and two others arose; one of the two filled the pipe with tobacco and lighted it with fire supplied by the other. The spokesman smoked; then he wiped the pipe and presented it to Monsieur de Bienville. The Governor smoked as did all his officers, taking their turn according to rank. After the ceremony, the old orator took the calumet and handed it to Monsieur de Bienville to keep. The spokesman was the only one to remain standing, while the other emissaries sat near the presents they had brought for the Governor. There were skins of deer and other animals, all colored white as a peace symbol.

The spokesman was dressed in a robe made of several marten skins sewed together, fastened over his right shoulder and passing under his left arm. He wrapped the robe around his body, and with a great deal of majesty he began the speech which he addressed to the Governor.

My heart laughs with joy because I am in your presence. We have all heard the words of peace which you have sent us. The hearts of all our nation laugh with joy. Our women, forgetting for a moment all that had happened, danced and our children leaped like young deer. Your words shall never be forgotten. They fill our hearts and our ears, and our descendants will remember them as long as the ancient word[6] will last. Since the war made us poor, we had to have a great hunt to bring you skins, but we did not dare wander too far in case the other nations had not yet heard your words. We came trembling on the path until we saw your face.

How happy are my heart and my eyes to see you today. Our gifts are small but our hearts are big and ready to obey your words. When

---

[6] This is what the savages call *tradition*.

you command us, you will see our legs run and jump like the legs of stags to carry out your orders.

Here the orator paused. Then, raising his voice, he continued gravely.

Ah, how much more beautiful the sun is today than when you were angry with us! How dangerous a bad man is! You know that just one man killed the prayer chief,[7] whose death caused our best warriors to fall with him. There remain only the old men, the women, and the children who stretch out their arms to you as to a kind father. The gall which formerly filled your heart has been replaced by honey. The Great Spirit is no longer angry with our nation. You asked for the head of the evil man. We sent it to you in order to have peace.

The sun was red before, the paths were full of thorns and brambles, the clouds were black, the water was troubled and stained with our blood, our women wept constantly over the loss of their relatives and did not dare to go off in search of firewood to prepare our meals, our children cried out in fright. All our warriors jumped up at the slightest cry of the night birds, they slept with their arms within reach, our huts were abandoned and our fields lay fallow. We all had empty stomachs and drawn faces, game fled from us, the snakes hissed in anger and showed and bared their fangs; the birds, perched in trees near our villages, seemed to sing only songs of death.

Today the sun is bright, the sky is clear, the clouds are gone; the paths are covered with roses; our gardens and our fields will be cultivated, and we shall offer their first fruits to the Great Spirit. The water is so clear that we can see our faces in it; the serpents flee or, rather, have changed into eels; the sweetness and harmony of the birds' song charm us, our wives and our daughters dance and forget to eat and drink. The hearts of the entire nation laugh with joy to see us walk on the same path with you and the French; the same sun will light us, we shall speak with one voice, and our hearts will be one. We shall kill those who will kill the French; our warriors will hunt food for

[7] This is what they call our missionaries.

27

them, and we shall all eat together. Will that not be good? What do you say to this, Father?

This speech, delivered in a firm and assured tone with eloquence and propriety and even, if it can be said, with all possible majesty, was answered briefly by Monsieur de Bienville, who spoke the Indians' language rather fluently. He told the spokesman that he was very pleased that the nation had come once again to its senses. He had the emissaries fed, and, as a sign of friendship, shook hands with the spokesman. The Indians were sent off satisfied. From that time on, they have always been unswervingly loyal to the French and supply New Orleans with game.

My third letter will be more interesting. Until now, I believe I have fulfilled my mission and assure you, sir, . . .

New Orleans
July 1, 1751

Letter III

To the Marquis de l'Estrade.
Description of the religious ceremonies of certain people who live on the banks of the great Mississippi River; the plot of the Natchez against the French.

Sir:

I have arrived at the spot that used to be the home of the proud Natchez nation, which was so much in the public news. It is said that this formidable nation dominated the others because of the extent of its territory. These people inhabited all the land from Bayou Manchac, 50 leagues from the sea, to the Ohio, which is about 460 leagues from it. On August 20, we began our trip to the Illinois. We set out in six boats and had aboard the four companies commanded by Monsieur de Macarty, about which I wrote you in my last letter. This trip is made by rowing against the current of the winding Mississippi, which flows between two great forests of timber trees as old as the world.

The first things encountered are two German villages dating back to the grant which the King gave Law in 1720. This group was to consist of 1,500 Germans and Provençals. Their four square leagues of land, forming a duchy, was in the territory of an Indian nation called the Arkansas. Enough equipment for a company of dragoons and merchandise worth more than one million pounds had already been brought there. But Law failed, and the India Company, which owned Louisiana at that time, took possession of all the equipment and merchandise.

The colonists separated, and the Germans settled ten leagues above New Orleans. These very industrious people supply the capital with food. The two villages are commanded by a Swedish captain.[1]

Two leagues farther there are the Acolapissas, who are well known for their loyalty to the French. The true name of this small tribe is *Aquelon Pissas,* meaning "nation of men who hear and see."

Then there are the Humas, who are sun worshippers. Like almost all the other American nations, these people believe that the Supreme Being lives in the sun and wants to be worshiped in this life-giving star as Author of Nature. They say that there is nothing on earth which can be compared to the wonderful sun, which lights up the universe, spreading joy and abundance. They have dedicated a cult to the sun as the visible symbol of the greatness and goodness of a God who deigns to make himself known to man by showering him with blessings.

Fifteen leagues upriver from the Humas is Pointe Coupée, a post which is about forty leagues from New Orleans. The land here is very fertile and is covered with fruit trees. There are many Frenchmen in this area who raise tobacco, cotton, rice, corn, and other products. These colonists also sell building timber, which they float down to New Orleans on rafts.

On the left bank of the river when going upstream, at some distance from Pointe Coupée, is the village of the Tonikas, an Indian tribe which has always been very friendly to the French. Their chiefs have always eagerly joined us in war. The last one, a very brave man, was seriously wounded in an expedition against the Natchez. When His Majesty heard of this, he honored the chief by granting him a commission as brigadier of the Indian armies and decorated him with

---

[1] He is Monsieur d'Arensbourg, who was at the battle of Poltava in 1709 with Charles XII. This former officer is the head of a large, well-established family in Louisiana.

a blue ribbon from which hung a silver medal representing Paris; he also received a gold-headed cane.

After the massacre of the French at the hands of the Natchez, about which I intend to tell you in due time, part of the tribe pretended that it wanted to make peace with the great chief of the Tonikas. He notified the French commanding general, with whom he was very friendly. The Natchez, anticipating the answer to their offer, slaughtered the Tonikas, beginning with the great chief. Many of the chief's subjects were quickly destroyed by the enemy, who feared our advice to the Tonikas and our military strength. We, as well as these good Indians, shall always regret the loss of this chief whose qualities would do honor to a civilized man.

After sailing eighty leagues from the capital of Louisiana, we arrived at the Natchez post, which was an important one twenty years ago but is insignificant today. The fort is situated on a high point overlooking the Mississippi, which is only a cannon shot away. The steadily rising land of this area would be extremely fertile if it were cultivated, since tobacco, cotton, and corn grow very well here. I have spent some time at this post, which is commanded by the Chevalier d'Orgon, the illegitimate son of Prince de Lambesc, of the house of Lorraine.

The Natchez, who lived here formerly, were a very important people. They had several villages ruled by individual chiefs, who in turn were governed by the great chief of the entire nation. All of these chiefs were called "Suns," and all five hundred of them were related to the Great Sun, their sovereign, who wore on his chest a picture of the sun from which he claimed descent. *Ouachil*, the name under which the sun was worshiped, means "very great fire" or "supreme fire."

The ceremonies of this sun cult were rather august. The high priest arose before sunrise and walked solemnly at the head of his people. He carried a calumet, and, in order to honor the sun, blew the first puff of smoke in its direction. Staring at the sun's first rays and extending his arms towards the sky, each worshiper howled in turn after the high priest. Then they all prostrated themselves. The women brought their children to this ceremony and made them assume the positions required by the rite.

At harvest time in July, the Natchez had a very important celebration. They first blackened their faces, took purifying baths, and fasted until three in the afternoon. The oldest man in the nation then offered God the first fruits of the harvest.

They had a temple in which burned an eternal flame. The priests, who were very careful to keep the fire going, were permitted to use the wood of only one type of tree. If, by chance, the fire went out, the horrified nation put the responsible priests to death. This happened very rarely because the guardian priests, pretending to light their pipes, would ask for "profane" fire, since they could not use the "sacred" fire for this purpose, and would then rekindle the flame.

When the sovereign died, his wives and several of his subjects were put to death so that they could accompany him to the grave. The lesser Suns carefully followed the same custom. According to the law, when a female relative of the Suns died, her husband was put to death too. Here is the story of an Indian named Etteacteal, who was unwilling to submit to this law. He had married into the Sun family, an honor which almost ended in disaster for him. When his wife fell sick and seemed to be dying, he fled down the Mississippi in a pirogue and arrived in New Orleans. He gained the protection of Governor de Bienville by becoming his hunter. The Governor interceded for him with the Natchez, who stated that Etteacteal had nothing to fear since the funeral ceremony had already taken place without him and he was no longer of any use.

Etteacteal, thus reassured, dared to make several trips to his nation without taking up permanent residence there. He happened to be there at the time of the death of Bitten Snake, a relative of his late wife and brother of the Chief Sun. It was decided that he would have to pay his debt. Since Monsieur de Bienville had been recalled to

France, the Natchez chief decided that the letters of reprieve granted to Etteacteal were null and void, and he had him seized. In the war chief's cabin, where he was put with the other victims to be sacrificed to Bitten Snake, Etteacteal gave way to his feelings of grief. The dead man's wife was to be sacrificed, too, but she watched the preparations for her death calmly and seemed eager to join her husband in death. Hearing Etteacteal's groans, she said to him, "Aren't you a warrior?" He answered, "Yes, I am." She replied, "Still, you are crying. Life is dear to you! Since you feel that way, it's not right for you to come with us. Go off with the women." Etteacteal said, "Certainly life is dear to me. I should like to walk upon this earth until the death of the Great Sun; then I would die with him." The woman answered, "Go away, I tell you. It is not right for you to come with us and for your heart to remain behind on earth. Again I say, go away so that I shall not have to look at you."

Etteacteal did not wait for her to repeat her order; he took off like a bolt of lightning. Three old women, two of whom were relatives of his, tired of life because of their age and their infirmities, offered to pay his debt. None of them had been able to walk for a long time. Etteacteal's two relatives had hair which was no grayer than that of 55-year-old French women. The other woman was 120 years old and had very white hair, a rarity among the Indians. None of the three had very wrinkled skin. They were put to death early in the evening, one at Bitten Snake's door, the other two in the temple square.[2]

The generosity of these women redeemed Warrior Etteacteal's life. His honor, which had been blemished by his fear of death, was restored to him. He lived in peace from that time on, and, profiting by the education he received during his stay among the French, he

[2] They place a noose around the victim's neck, and eight male relatives, four on each side, strangle him by pulling the rope. That many men are not needed, but since they acquire nobility by performing these executions, there are always more volunteers than is necessary. The operation is over in an instant.

became a witch doctor[3] and used his knowledge to fool his fellow tribesmen.

The day after this execution, they began to prepare the procession. At the appointed hour, the leader of the ceremony, dressed in the ornaments appropriate to his rank, appeared at the door of the cabin out of which came the victims who were to accompany the prince to the Land of the Spirits. These were his two wives, his chancellor, his physician, his favorite servant, and some old women who had volunteered to be sacrificed.

The favorite wife went up to the Chief Sun, who was with several Frenchmen, to say good-by to them. She ordered that the Suns, who were her children, be brought to her and she spoke these words to them: "My children, this is the day when I must tear myself from your arms to follow the footsteps of your father to the Land of the Spirits. If I were to yield to your tears, I would fail in my duty and my love. I have done enough for you by bearing you next to my heart and nursing you at my breasts. Should you who were formed of his blood and fed with my milk be shedding tears? Rejoice in the fact that you are Suns and warriors. You must set examples of firmness and valor for the entire nation. I have provided for all your needs by obtaining friends for you. My friends and the friends of your father are also yours. I leave you among them. They are the French, who have tender hearts and are generous. Be worthy of their esteem by not disgracing your race. Always deal with them honestly and never ask their help for base reasons."

"And you, Frenchmen," she added, turning toward our officers, "I leave my orphaned children in your hands. They will know no other father but you; you must protect them."

She then arose and, followed by her group, entered her husband's cabin with surprising firmness.

A noble lady, who decided to accompany Bitten Snake to the

[3] The witch doctors in this country act as priests, doctors, and oracles. They try especially to pass themselves off as sorcerers.

other world because of her friendship for him, voluntarily joined the number of victims. The Europeans called her Gloria because of her majestic bearing, her proud look, and the fact that she would bother with only the most distinguished Frenchmen. They felt her loss keenly. She was familiar with many herbs which she used to save the lives of a good number of our sick. This moving sight filled them with grief and horror. The dead man's favorite wife then arose and said to them with a smile on her lips: "I die without fear; my last moments are not marred by grief. I leave my children in your hands. When you see them, noble Frenchmen, remember that you loved their father and that to the very grave he was a sincere and true friend of your nation, which he loved more than his own life. It has pleased the Master of Life to call him, and in a little while I shall go to join him. I shall tell him that I saw your hearts grieve at the sight of his body. Do not mourn, for we shall be friends in the Land of the Spirits for even a longer time than here. There is no death there."[4]

These sad words brought tears to the eyes of all the French. They did all that they could to keep the Chief Sun from killing himself. He was inconsolable at the death of his brother to whom he used to delegate the burdens of government.[5] He became furious when his attempts were resisted. He held his rifle by the breech, while the Sun who was his heir held it by the lock, causing the powder to spill out. The cabin was full of Suns, Nobles, and the Esteemed,[6] all of whom were trembling, but the Frenchmen reassured them by having all the

[4] At the appointed time of the ceremony, the victims swallowed balls of tobacco to numb their senses. Then they were strangled and laid out on mats, with the favorite on the right, the other wife on the left, and then all the other victims according to their rank.

[5] Bitten Snake was the great war chief of the Natchez, generalissimo of the armies.

[6] These distinctions were recognized by the Natchez:
The Suns, related to the Chief Sun, were of the highest rank.
The Nobles were of lower rank.
The Esteemed came after the Nobles.
Last were the common people, who were scorned.
The nobility was rapidly increased because it was passed on through the women.

Chief Sun's arms hidden and by filling the barrel of his rifle with water so that it could not be used for some time. When the Suns saw that their chief's life was assured, they thanked the French by shaking hands with them without saying a word. There was deep silence, for grief and respect restrained the great number of people who were present.

During this ceremony, the Chief Sun's wife was seized with fear. When she was asked if she were sick, she answered in a loud voice, "Yes, I am." She continued more softly, "If the French leave, my husband and all the Natchez will die. Please stay, brave Frenchmen, for your word has the force of arrows. Who would have dared do what you have done? You are true friends to him and his brother."

According to the law, the Chief Sun's wife would have been forced to follow her husband to the grave; that was doubtless the reason for her fear and her gratitude to the French who wanted him to live.

The Chief Sun held his hand out to the officers and said, "My heart is so heavy that my eyes, although they are open, did not see that you were standing. My mouth did not open to tell you to be seated. Excuse my deep grief."

The French replied that it was unimportant, that they were going to leave him alone, but that they would no longer be friends if he did not give the order to light the fires again,[7] first lighting his own in their presence. They also said that they would not leave him until his brother had been buried.

He shook hands with all the Frenchmen and said, "Since all the chiefs and the noble officers want me to remain on this earth, so be it; I will not kill myself. Let all the fires be lighted again immediately. I shall wait for death to unite me with my brother. I am already old, and until my death, I shall walk with the French. If not for them, I

---

[7] The Chief Sun had given the order to extinguish all the fires. This is done only when the sovereign himself dies.

would have gone off with my brother and the paths would have been covered with dead bodies."

This prince, who survived Bitten Snake by only one year, was succeeded by his nephew. This young prince's reign was quite unfortunate for the colony. You will see, sir, in the rest of this account, that the colony owes its safety to this young chief's mother. She managed to get from him the secret of the general plot against our nation, which she dearly loved.

In all fairness to the Indians, it must be said that their plan to kill all the French was not the result of treachery or instability. It was the bad conduct of an officer who insulted and infuriated the very people he should have been handling gently. Free and peaceful people, who were living in a land settled by their ancestors, could not permit themselves to be tyrannized by foreigners whom they had welcomed. Monsieur de Chepar, commander of the Natchez post, did not win the friendship of either the French or the Indians in his care. He mistreated everyone who was unwilling to go along with his criminal ideas, and he gave important posts to sergeants and corporals who were personally devoted to him. You can easily understand, sir, that such favoritism would subvert all military discipline.

Monsieur Dupont, the second in command, registered official complaints which were not heeded. The only answer he received was to be thrown into irons. As soon as he was freed, he went down to the capital to bring his charges before Monsieur Perrier, the governor of Louisiana. Monsieur de Chepar was recalled to explain his conduct. He was to be broken in rank, but his intrigues and his influence saved him. He was reinstated and sent back to his post.

This humiliating experience had no influence on him. He behaved in exactly the same way that he always had and was equally detested by the French and the Indians, whom he irritated to such a degree that they were forced to take extreme and terrible measures. Monsieur de Chepar, who was eager to make a fortune as quickly as possible, ordered the Sun of a village called Pomme to move out with all his people. The land, which Chepar was to turn into a plantation, would bring him a handsome profit. The Chief explained that the bones of his ancestors were buried there, but his arguments were useless. The French commander ordered the Chief Sun to evacuate the village and even threatened to send him to New Orleans in chains if he did not obey promptly. Perhaps the officer thought that he could treat this chief like a slave. It never occurred to him that he was speaking to a man who was accustomed to giving commands and whose authority over his subjects was absolute.

The Chief Sun listened to him and went off without becoming angry. He assembled his council, and they decided to inform Monsieur de Chepar that, before Pomme could be abandoned, plans for a new village would have to be drawn up. That would take two moons.

The decision was made known to the Commander, who rebuked the messengers and threatened them with the severest punishment if Pomme were not turned over to him within a very short time. When this answer was delivered to the council, the elders concluded that the best policy was to try to gain enough time so that they could think of a way to get rid of these disagreeable guests who were becoming tyrannical. Since they knew that Monsieur de Chepar was very greedy, they thought up a scheme whereby he would grant them a delay of several moons, during which period each cabin would pay him in corn, fowl, and skins. The Commander fell into the trap because of his greed. He accepted the proposition, pretending that he was doing it only to oblige this nation which he loved because of its long-standing friendship for France.

The Sun, who was not taken in by this false altruism, assembled his council once more and announced that the time requested had been granted. During this period of grace, they were to think of a way to end the burdensome tribute they were paying and, especially, to put a stop to the domination of the tyrannical French. He pointed out to them that this enterprise required the profoundest secrecy, well-founded plans, and, especially, a great deal of strategy. He advised them, in the meantime, to redouble all their outward signs of friendship and confidence in dealing with the French, while thinking of what had to be done. They were to come back to the council as soon as they had thought of some plan whose success could be assured.

For five or six days the noble elders conferred with each other, and they concluded once again unanimously to destroy all the French. After having greeted his chief, the oldest member of the council reported the decision in this manner:

> We have noticed for a long time that having the French as neighbors has done us more harm than good. We old men see it, but the young men do not. The supplies from Europe please them, but of what use are they? To seduce our women, to corrupt our nation, to lead our daughters astray, to make them proud and lazy. Our boys are the same. Young married men must work themselves to death to keep their wives in luxury. Before the French came into our lands, we were men, we were happy with what we had, we walked boldly upon all our paths, because then we were our own masters. But today we tread gropingly, fearing thorns. We walk like the slaves which we will soon be, since they already treat us as though we were. When they are strong enough, they will no longer treat us with consideration. They will put us in chains. Has not their chief already threatened ours with this affront? Is not death preferable to slavery?[8]

The orator paused to catch his breath and then went on:

> What are we waiting for? Are we to let the French grow in numbers until we can no longer resist them? What will the other nations say? We are considered the wisest of all the red men.[9] They will rightly say that we have less intelligence than the other peoples. Why wait

[8] Nature alone has taught these people to respect their sovereign and to cherish freedom.

[9] This is what the Indians call themselves to distinguish themselves from the Europeans who are white and the Africans who are black.

longer? Let us free ourselves and prove that we are real men. Let us start this very day to get ready for it. Let us have the women prepare food without telling them why. Let us carry the peace pipe to all the nations of this country and tell them that the French hope to dominate our continent. Since they are stronger in our region than any place else, we shall be the first to wear their chains. When they are powerful enough, they will do the same to all the tribes. Let us convince the others that it is in their interest to prevent this misfortune. This can be done only by exterminating the French. Let all the nations join us in the task of wiping out the French, wherever they may be, in the same hour of the same day. Let the massacre take place at the end of the period of time granted us by their chief. In that way we will be free of the burden of our self-imposed tribute and we will get back the products which we have given him. On that great day of freedom, our warriors will carry their firearms. The Natchez will go among the French, and, in each house, we shall outnumber them three or four to one. Our warriors, pretending to go out on a hunt in preparation of a great feast, will borrow firearms and ammunition and will promise to bring back game. The shots fired at the Commander's home will be the signal for attacking the French. The other nations must help us by carrying out similar massacres in their territories at the same time. To succeed in this, we shall have to prepare bundles consisting of equal numbers of twigs, one bundle to be given to each nation. Each morning of the waiting period, one twig will be cut up and thrown into the fire. When there is only one left, they will know that the time for the slaughter has come. It will begin at the first quarter of the day [at nine o'clock in the morning], and we shall all attack the tyrants at the same time from all directions. Once these are destroyed, it will be easy to keep others who may come from the Old World across the great lake from settling among us. It is extremely important that one twig be removed every day without fail. The slightest error can bring dangerous consequences. We shall give this duty to a wise man and shall ask our neighbors to do likewise.

When the orator had finished, the elders gave their approval.

The Sun of Pomme was particularly pleased with this suggestion; since he was the one most hurt by Monsieur de Chepar's injustice, he considered this a matter of personal vengeance. He was so eager to have this scheme succeed that he warned the council not to be indiscreet and even made the members promise not to reveal it to the female Suns. As much as he wanted to get rid of the French, the Chief Sun, who had to give his approval, felt that the plan called for too much violence. The Sun of Pomme, considered a just and intelligent man by his people, determined to win the Chief Sun over to the plan. He did this by making the Chief realize that his very own safety depended upon this course of action. The French commander had, after all, threatened to chase him from his village. The Chief Sun was weak because of his youth; the man speaking to him was clever; the plan was approved. The next day, when the Suns came to greet their chief, they were told for one reason or another to go to the village of Pomme and did not suspect that they were under specific orders to do so. Everything went according to plan. Charmed by the Sun of Pomme's engaging wit, they all agreed to take part in the conspiracy. They immediately formed a council of Suns and noble elders, which accepted the plan unanimously after it had once again been explained. The elders, accompanied by warriors, were sent out as envoys to the other nations. They were forbidden, under pain of death, to speak to anyone about their mission. Without the French knowing it, all these groups immediately set out together.

Although the secret of the Natchez was well guarded, the meeting of the council of Suns and noble elders worried the people. It is a well-known fact that the people of every country manage to learn court secrets. In this case, however, their curiosity was not satisfied. Only the female Suns, or princesses, had the right to ask why something was being kept secret from them. The Chief Sun's wife was only eighteen years old and was not too much concerned, but Stung Arm, the Chief Sun's mother, a woman well-aware of her intelligence, was not pleased that a secret was being kept from her. When she complained to her son, he told her that the envoys were sent out to renew friendly relations with the other nations, who thought that they were being scorned because the peace pipe had not been smoked with them for so long a time. This excuse seemed to calm Stung Arm, but she was really still troubled. Her worries were increased when she saw the Suns meet secretly with the returned envoys to find out how they were received by the other nations. Such meetings were usually public.

The Princess was furious at the idea that they were hiding from the nation and even from her what they had a right to know. It was only prudence that kept her from breaking out in anger. It was fortunate for the French that she thought she was being treated with contempt. She was right in thinking that the secret would be more closely guarded and she would find out nothing if she showed her anger. She slyly thought of a sure way to satisfy her curiosity. She got her son to visit a sick relative who lived in the village of Pomme. She took him the long way by telling him it was more beautiful than the other. Her true reason was that they would meet fewer people on the path. She very shrewdly thought that this mystery concerned some sinister plot against the French. The coming and going of the Sun of Pomme supported her belief. When she and her son came to a lonely spot, she spoke to him.

"Let us sit down here. I am tired, and I also have something to say to you." When they were seated, she added, "Open your ears and listen to me. I have always taught you not to lie. I have always told you that a liar is not worthy of being considered a man and that a lying Sun deserves even the contempt of women. I think that you will tell me the truth. Tell me, are not all the Suns brothers? Yet all the Suns are keeping something from me as though my lips were cut and could not keep a secret. Have you ever known me to speak in my sleep? I am deeply hurt by my brothers' contempt for me, but even more by yours. Did I not give birth to you? Did I not feed you at my breast? Did I not give you the best blood I had? Does not that same blood flow in your veins? Would you be a Sun if you were not my child? Have you already forgotten that, without the care I gave you, you would have died a long time ago? I have told you, and so has everyone else, that you are the son of a Frenchman;[10] but my own blood is dearer to me than that of strangers. Today I walk beside you like a dog, without being looked at. I am amazed that you do not shove me aside with your foot. I am not surprised that the others avoid me, but can you, who are my son? Have you ever seen a son distrust his mother in our nation? You alone behave this way. There is all this activity in the nation, and yet I do not know the reason for it, I who am the Chief Sun's mother. Are you afraid that I shall oppose you and make you the slave of the French, against whom you plan to take action? How tired I am of being scorned and of dealing with ungrateful men!"

The Chief Sun was deeply touched by the words he had just heard. He wept and listened to these reproaches with the usual calm of the Americans and with the respect due a mother and a princess.

Then he answered her, "Your reproaches are like arrows which pierce my heart. I do not think that I have ever rebuffed you or scorned you. Have you never heard that the decisions of the council elders are not to be revealed? Is not the keeping of a secret the duty of every man, and should I not, as chief, set the example? This was kept from my wife just as it was from you. Even though everyone knows that I am the son of a Frenchman, I have been trusted. We all knew that with your intelligence you would discover the secret, but since it was kept from my wife, was it right to tell you of it? Since you have guessed it all, what do you want me to tell you? You know as much as I do. Just keep your mouth closed."

She replied, "It was not very difficult for me to figure out against

[10] The Princess had loved a French officer for a long time. That he was undoubtedly the father of the Chief Sun in no way lessened the subjects' respect for their sovereign. As I have already said, it was the women who passed noble rank on to their children. As long as a man's mother was known, it made no difference who his father was.

whom you were taking all these precautions. Since the French are involved, I am afraid that the measures you have taken to surprise them are not good enough. I know that they are very intelligent, even though their commander seems to have lost his mind. They have enough wealth to turn the warriors of the other nations against us. If your quarrel was with red men, I would sleep more peacefully. I am no longer young,[11] and an old woman's life is not worth much, but yours is dear to me. If the elders think that it is as easy to surprise the French as it is the red men, they have made a serious mistake. The French have resources that we do not have. You know that they have cloth that speaks [paper]."

Her son told her that she had nothing to worry about as far as the plans were concerned. After he had told her everything that I have reported, he informed her that the bundle of sticks was in the temple on the flat wood (table).

When the Princess felt that she had learned enough, she pretended approval of all that had been done, and then leaving her son alone, she set about trying to find a way to thwart this barbarous plan. Time was short; the day for the massacre was not far off.

Unwilling to see the Natchez carry out their plan to kill all the French in a single day, the Princess decided to warn them. For this purpose, she used Indian girls who had French lovers, but she cautioned them never to reveal under whose orders they were working.

Ensign Macé, stationed at Fort Natchez, was advised of the plot by an Indian girl who loved him. She cried when she told him that her people were going to kill all the French. Astonished by this information, Monsieur Macé questioned his mistress. Her frightened, straightforward, and naïve answers convinced him that she was telling the truth. He went to report this immediately to Monsieur de Chepar, who had him arrested for spreading a false alarm. Seven colonists who found out about the plot the same way as the ensign asked Chepar for arms to forestall a surprise attack. The Commander

[11] Her lover had been dead for quite some time.

threw them in irons and called them cowards for trying to stir up trouble against a nation which had proven itself so friendly to him. The promptness with which the Indians paid their tribute gave him a feeling of security. Blinded by his contempt for them, he did not suspect them of subterfuge. He did not think that men of that kind were capable of being so shrewd.

When Stung Arm sadly realized that all her measures to save the French were useless, she decided to help them in spite of themselves. Since she could not save them all, she tried to find a way to reduce the number of victims. She sneaked into the temple and, without the knowledge of the priests, she pulled some of the twigs out of the fatal bundle. In that way, the day set for carrying out the plot would be advanced. She felt that the news of the massacre which would occur in Natchez territory would spread rapidly. The French who lived among the other nations would thus be warned and would prepare against attack. This was the only thing she could possibly do, and she succeeded. When the Natchez, not realizing that they had been tricked, saw that they were down to their last twig, they began the slaughter according to plan, persuaded that their allies were acting at the same moment.

On December 28, 1729, at 8:00 A.M., shots were fired in front of Monsieur de Chepar's residence, giving the signal to the Indians who had infiltrated among the French. The attack began everywhere at once. The Kollys, chief clerks of the India Company, were the first to be killed. Monsieur de la Loire des Ursins' household was the only one that offered any resistance; his servants killed 8 Natchez before they were overcome. Monsieur des Ursins, who had just ridden out on his horse, started to turn back as soon as he heard the first shot, but he was stopped by a band of Indians. He defended himself courageously and killed 4 of them before he died. That is about all the casualties the Indians had in this surprise attack. They slaughtered about 2,000 men; only 20 of them and about 5 or 6 Negroes escaped, most of whom were wounded. About 150 children, 90 women, and as many Negroes were taken as slaves, in the hope that they could be sold to the English in the Carolinas.

During the massacre, the Chief Sun was seated in one of the sheds of the India Company. First he was brought the commanding officer's head, and around it were placed the heads of the most important Frenchmen. The others were heaped up in a pile. The unburied bodies were eaten by the vultures. Pregnant women were disemboweled, and almost all those who were nursing children were killed because of their annoying cries and tears. The others were all made slaves and were treated with the greatest indignity.

Some claim that Monsieur de Chepar, being unfortunate enough to die last, witnessed this horrible slaughter and realized too late that the advice given him had been wise. The Indians told him that dogs such as he were unworthy of dying at the hands of warriors. He was turned over to the "stinkers,"[12] who killed him with arrows and then chopped off his head.

That was the end of the man who was guided only by his own decisions, cruelty, greed, and ambition. Since none of the French escaped alive, we cannot know how this officer really died. It is enough to know that he was dealing with naturally barbarous people and that he had antagonized them. Under a decent administration these people would have become the allies of the French and would have been very useful. This is how one man's faults can sometimes cause a whole colony to be lost. The greatest of caution must be used when we choose a commanding officer for these territories. Regardless of what we think of the Indians, they are not always easy to manage. Strategy and wisdom are needed to gain their good will. This story proves that you cannot insult them without suffering the consequences. Nothing could have been better carried out than this Natchez conspiracy. How much worse the situation would have been

[12] In the Natchez language, the common people are called *miche-michequipi*, which means "stinker."

An Indian Chief of Louisiana

From Jean-Bernard Bossu, *Nouveaux Voyages aux Indes occidentales* (1768)

"Medicine Man Administering to a Patient"

From a water color by Seth Eastman

without the help of Providence! The French owed Princess Stung Arm a great deal. I do not know how this debt was paid.

The nations who were in the plot with the Natchez thought they had been betrayed, since they were not aware of the trick which had prematurely touched off the attack. The Choctaws thought that the Natchez did not want them to share in the booty. To prove to the French that they had nothing to do with the plot, they joined the punitive expedition against the Natchez. The French women and the Negroes taken as slaves were returned by the Natchez, whose fortified camps were attacked. The Natchez escaped during a storm and left the territory. About one thousand of them were captured, taken to New Orleans, and sold as slaves on the island of Santo Domingo. Among the prisoners were the Chief Sun, his wife, and his mother. The Chief Sun denied that the massacre was his idea. He said that his nation had taken advantage of his youth, that he had always liked the French, and that it was really Monsieur de Chepar's outrageous behavior toward a freeborn people which had caused them to act in desperation. The French, satisfied that he was not guilty, treated him, his wife, and his mother with consideration. They soon died of grief, however, because they could not return to their people. The territory has been uninhabited since that time. The Natchez, too weak to resist the pursuing French, have found refuge among the Chickasaws.

We still have a fort here, but the colony is hardly a thriving one. The way to revitalize it would be to attract other Indians to settle here. That is all I can tell you of interest about this country, sir. I shall leave soon to continue my travels. In finishing this letter, let me assure you of my sincerest regards. I am, . . .

Natchez territory
September 10, 1751

Letter IV

To the Marquis de l'Estrade.

The author arrives among the Arkansas; the tragic death of Ferdinand de Soto's men; reflections on the folly of those who searched for a mountain of gold; the origin of the famous El Dorado; a synopsis of the account of La Salle's tragic death.

Sir:

After having sailed up the Mississippi about 120 leagues north of the Natchez territory, without coming upon a single habitation, we arrived among Indians well known for their allegiance to the French. This nation had been discovered by Ferdinand de Soto's expedition. The old chief to whom I spoke told me he had seen Monsieur de la Salle here in 1682, when he discovered the great St. Louis River, known as the Mississippi and called by the Indians *Méschaseppi*, which means "all the rivers" or "the great river."

Monsieur de la Salle passed through this nation on his way down the Mississippi. He became friendly with the people and claimed their lands in the name of Louis the Great, whose glory has lived on. After planting a cross and a French banner, he continued down the Mississippi, which empties into the Gulf of Mexico. He found the latitude of the mouth of the river to be twenty-nine degrees North. He went back up the Mississippi to Illinois territory, from there to Canada, and then returned to France.

When he arrived at the Court, he announced his discovery to

Colbert and to Ségnelai, who obtained an order from the King stating that all the land La Salle would discover from Nouvelle Biscaye[1] to the land of the Illinois and all its inhabitants, French or Indian, would be under his orders.

After the death of La Salle, Monsieur Joutel set out with guides to find the Mississippi and came upon these same people, the Arkansas. This officer is the only one who has left a trustworthy account of these people. I believe I should give you a synopsis of the story of La Salle and his ill-fated expedition.

I shall say just a word about Ferdinand de Soto's travels. We learn from the general history of America that, after having soaked his unholy hands in the blood of the Inca royal family, De Soto and his bravest soldiers wanted to come into this country to subjugate the people who live near the river, which I shall describe later. He was, however, unfamiliar with the interior of this vast continent. If he expected to find effeminate people like those of South America, he was sadly mistaken. The Indians killed some of his soldiers with clubs, flayed the most important officers among them, and hung their skins on the temple door. This so frightened the Spaniards that they set sail for Europe immediately.

History tells us that Ferdinand de Soto died in 1543, of shame because of his failure, and Europeans did not occupy this beautiful country from that time until 1682.

La Salle's fate was no happier than that of De Soto. Man's virtues are generally accompanied by vices, and to add to our humiliation, the greater the virtues, the worse the vices. You will easily see the truth of this statement in a short account taken from the diary of Monsieur Joutel.

Monsieur Robert Cavelier de la Salle left La Rochelle July 24, 1684, with a squadron of four ships commanded by Captain de Beaujeu. Two hundred and eighty-five people embarked with him at

[1] La Nouvelle Biscaye was the name of a region now included in the Mexican province of Durango.—ED.

Rochefort; they consisted of thirty volunteers,[2] some nobles, and a number of indentured servants, workmen, and girls. La Salle traveled aboard the ship directly under the command of Beaujeu, whom he did not at all trust. Every time the Captain made a suggestion, La Salle answered in a haughty tone, "That is not the King's intention." He took absolutely no steps to win over this man whose assistance was vitally necessary if the enterprise were to be successful. Everyone began to predict that the expedition would turn out badly, since its leaders were at loggerheads. Unfortunately, time proved the prediction to be right.

On December 28, 1684, the squadron discovered Florida. Since La Salle had been assured that the current of the Gulf of Mexico flowed eastward, he was certain that the mouth of the Mississippi was far to the west; this error was the basic cause of all his misfortune. He had the squadron turn to the west and proceed very slowly. From time to time, sailing landward and then following the coast, La Salle tried to find the mouth of the river.

On January 2, 1685, the ships must have been rather close to the mouth of the Mississippi, which they passed, without realizing it, on January 10. La Salle, convinced that he was just south of the Appalachians, sailed on without even sending a launch ashore.

It is even said that the mouth of the river was pointed out to him but that he did not take the trouble to verify it because he was sure that it could not be the right spot. His stubbornness could neither be conquered nor justified. He obviously did not know that the greatest men in the world have often been somewhat indebted for their success to men of lesser ability. The wisest men are those who take advantage of the knowledge and advice of less intelligent people.

Some time later, after having received information from the Indians, he wanted to turn back, but Monsieur de Beaujeu refused to

[2] There were three priests of Saint Sulpice among them, one of them La Salle's brother, another, a relative named Chedeville, and the third was Majulle. There were also four Recollect monks who were to establish missions among the Indians, and two of La Salle's nephews, Moranget and the fourteen-year-old Cavelier.

show him that much consideration. They continued on their west-ward course until, several days later, they came to Saint Bernard's Bay,[3] without knowing it. This bay is one hundred leagues to the west of the mouth of the Mississippi. The launches were sent out on reconnaissance, and a very beautiful river was discovered, at the mouth of which was a sand bar covered by about ten or twelve feet of water. This discovery was made after a great deal of bustling about and at the conclusion of several conferences, where nothing was de-cided because any suggestion made by one of the leaders was auto-matically vetoed by the other.

Because La Salle thought he was near the Mississippi and because Beaujeu's presence was more of a hindrance than a help to him, he decided, on February 20, to have all his people land at that spot. He ordered the commanding officer of the *Flute* to unload the heaviest things aboard his ship and to sail up the river. He wanted to be pres-ent at that operation but could not because he had to go to the rescue of the Marquis de la Sablonnière and five or six other Frenchmen who had gone for a walk in the woods and had been carried off by the Indians. He was still quite close to the shore when he looked out to sea and noticed that the *Flute* was being battered up against the sand bars and the rocks. He was prevented from going back to ward off this new disaster because of the unfortunate set of circumstances in which he found himself. He went on towards the village to which his men had been taken. As he drew near, he heard a cannon shot and supposed correctly that he was being informed that the *Flute* had gone down.

The witnesses were sure that the accident was the result of a premeditated plan carried out by Aigron, the ship's commander. The consequences of this loss were serious because the ship had been carry-ing arms, tools, and equipment necessary for the establishment of a new colony. La Salle rushed to the place where the ship had sunk and

[3] St. Bernard's Bay, now known as Lavaca Bay, is on the Texas coast between Corpus Christi and Galveston.—ED.

found that no one was doing anything about the situation. He asked for a launch and a rowboat, which Beaujeu willingly gave him.

First he rescued the crew. He then went after the powder and flour, and finally brought to shore about thirty casks of wine and brandy. If the *Flute*'s launch had been able to help the one sent out from the *Joli*, almost everything would have been saved, but it had been sunk intentionally. They had to wait to unload the *Flute* until the next day because of darkness. After several hours, the wind blowing in from the sea became stronger and stirred up the waves. The *Flute* was hurled up against the rocks and was smashed. A great deal of the cargo fell into the sea and floated off. This was not noticed until daybreak. Thirty more casks of wine and brandy, several barrels of flour, of meat, and of vegetables were rescued; all the rest was lost.

To make matters worse, they discovered that they were surrounded by Indians, who made off with several things saved from the wreck, despite all the precautions taken to prevent this. The theft was not even noticed until the Indians had disappeared with their haul. The French seized several canoes which the Indians had left on the shore. This was indeed small payment for things which were of much greater value. The Indians came back in the middle of the night and surprised those who had captured the canoes. The attackers killed two sleeping volunteers, whose loss La Salle sorely regretted, and wounded his nephew and another man.

All these misfortunes occurring one after the other discouraged several members of the expedition, among them the engineers Dainmaville and Mignet, who wanted to return to France. La Salle's enemies added to the discontent by denouncing his conduct and calling his plan rash and mad. La Salle, on the other hand, was never more resolved and determined. He built a storehouse with trenches around it and got ready to sail up the river, which he was convinced was a branch of the Mississippi.

They immediately began to build a fort. As soon as the construction was under way, La Salle left Joutel in command of one hundred men with orders to finish the job, while he himself, determined to sail as far up the river as possible, took with him the remaining sixty men. Joutel did not stay at the partly built fort long after that. The Indians roamed around the area every night. The harassed French fought them off, but were weakened by their losses. On July 14, Joutel and his men were ordered to join La Salle.

Several good men had been killed or captured by the Indians, others died of hardship and fatigue, and more and more of them fell sick every day. In short, La Salle's situation could not have been worse. He hid the grief which gnawed at him and became harsh and stubborn. As soon as his party was all together again, he started in earnest to build a settlement and to fortify it. He himself was the architect of the fort, and since he was always the first to get to work, everyone followed his example and worked to the best of his ability.

All he had to do was encourage this spirit of co-operation, but La Salle could not always control his temper. At the very time when his men were working themselves to the point of exhaustion, with hardly enough food to stay alive, he could not prevail upon himself to relax his severity a little or to control his vile temper, which is never appropriate in any circumstances and is certainly of no help in establishing a new settlement. Courage, health, and vigilance are not enough to assure the success of an undertaking; many other talents are needed, such as moderation, patience, and unselfishness. It is sometimes necessary to look the other way or to shut your eyes in order not to make things worse. The best way to lead troops is with gentleness.

La Salle punished the slightest infractions with unheard of cruelty. He rarely uttered a kind or a comforting word to those who suffered with the greatest of loyalty. He, therefore, had the misfortune of seeing almost all of his men fall into a state of lethargy, which was the result of despair rather than of overwork or the lack of good food.

Deciding to move inland, he gave his last orders at the fort, and on January 12, 1687, he set out on foot with his brother Monsieur Cavelier, his nephews Moranget and young Cavelier, the Recollect

53

Father Anastase, Joutel, Duhaut, Larchevêque, Marle, a German named Hiens, a surgeon by the name of Liétot, the pilot Tessier, Saget, and an Indian who was a good hunter. I have named all of these because they will be mentioned later.

The farther they advanced into the country, the more heavily populated they found it to be. When they were no more than forty leagues from the Caddoes, they learned that there was a Frenchman among those Indians. He was a Breton sailor who had been lost the first time La Salle had sailed down the Mississippi. Since 1682, this poor man had been living among the Caddoes, who had adopted him. Since his chances of ever seeing Europe again were most unlikely, he had given up all hope. Joutel, who had gone to look for the man among the Indians, left them just in time to witness a crime.

On May 17, Moranget was out hunting after having insulted Duhaut, Hiens, and the surgeon, Liétot. These three men, determined to get rid of their companion as soon as possible, decided to begin with La Salle's servant and the Indian hunter, Nika, since they were both with Moranget and could have helped him. The three told their scheme to Larchevêque and to the pilot, Tessier, who gave their approval and offered their assistance. They did not tell Marle, who was with them but whom they would have preferred to shake off. The next night, while the three unfortunate victims slept peacefully, Liétot struck them over the head several times with an axe. The Indian and the servant died immediately. Moranget sat up without uttering a word; Marle was forced to finish him off, when the murderers threatened to kill him, too, if he refused to do so. They wanted him to be an accomplice to keep him from denouncing them.

The first crime is always followed by worries, which even the worst criminals do not find easy to dispel. The murderers knew that it would be difficult to escape La Salle's just vengeance. After having deliberated on the various means of preventing this, they came to a decision. They thought that it would be best to meet La Salle and attack all those who were with him. The parricide which they had planned could be more easily carried out this way.

So strange a decision could be inspired only by the blind despair which hurls criminals into the pit which they themselves have dug. An unforeseen incident helped deliver their prey to them. A river which separated them from the camp had risen considerably since they had crossed it and delayed them two days. This turned out to be a help rather than a hindrance. La Salle, surprised when his nephew and his two companions did not return, started to look for them himself. He appeared to be troubled when he started out, and when he asked whether Moranget had quarreled with anyone, he showed a degree of anxiety, which was not in keeping with his character.

He then called Joutel and turned the command of the camp over to him. Joutel was ordered to keep guard, not to allow anyone to leave, and to light fires so that La Salle could use the smoke as a reference point if he had difficulty returning to the camp. He left on the twentieth with Father Anastase and an Indian. As he approached the place where the murderers had stopped, he noticed buzzards circling about and imagined that something must have died in the vicinity. He fired his rifle, and the three plotters, who had not yet spotted him but suspected that it was he, got their arms ready. Duhaut and Larchevêque crossed the river and stopped when they saw La Salle approaching slowly. Duhaut cocked his rifle and hid in the tall grass. Larchevêque advanced a little more. A moment later, La Salle recognized him and asked him where Moranget was. Larchevêque answered that he was farther downriver. At that very moment, Duhaut fired. La Salle was hit in the head and fell dead.

> *Oh, you inhabitants of this land,*
> *Wandering through forest, cave, and strand,*
> *You, the objects of Europe's scorn,*
> *For your mean and savage ways inborn,*
> *Speak! Has the sun which rises in your clime*
> *Ever seen among you such a monstrous crime?*
> ANTOINE-LÉONARD THOMAS, *Jumonville*

This murder occurred on May 20, 1687, in the territory of the Caddo nation. Father Anastase, who saw La Salle fall at his feet, expected to be next since he had witnessed the crime. Duhaut drew near to reassure him and told him that they had chosen this course of action in a fit of despair. They had been planning Moranget's death for a long time because he had been out to get them. Father Anastase informed Monsieur Cavelier of his brother's death. Cavelier told the murderers that if their plan also included his own death, he forgave them in advance. All that he asked of them was a quarter of an hour to prepare for death. They answered that he had nothing to fear since no one had anything against him.

Joutel was not in camp at that time. Larchevêque, who was his friend, ran to tell him that his death was certain if he showed the slightest resentment of what had happened or any intention of using the authority which La Salle had given him. If he were amenable, he would have nothing to fear. Joutel, who was a very gentle person, answered that they would be satisfied with his conduct, just as he believed they had been up until then. After that, he returned to camp.

As soon as Duhaut saw Joutel, he shouted that everyone should take his turn as commander. Duhaut had already taken over all authority, and the first use he made of it was to put himself in charge of the storehouse. He later divided its content with Larchevêque, but claimed that it was really all his. There were about 30,000 pounds worth of merchandise and about 25,000 pounds in coins and plate.

The murderers had strength and boldness on their side. Having proved themselves capable of the greatest crimes, they met no resistance at first. Soon they began to quarrel among themselves. They had trouble dividing the treasure and came to blows. Hiens shot Duhaut in the head with his pistol; the wounded man took four steps and then fell dead. At the same time, Rutel, the Breton sailor whom Joutel brought back from among the Caddo Indians, fired at Liétot, who lived for several miserable hours with three bullets in his body. Thus the two men who had killed La Salle and his nephew Moranget were themselves the victims of the madness they had unleashed in the colony.

The scandalized Indians did not know what to make of these murders. They are more justified in thinking of us as savages than we are in referring to them by the same term. In any event, that was the tragic end of Robert Cavelier, Sieur de la Salle, a man with the ability, the intelligence, the courage, and the steadfastness which could have carried him to great heights, if, with these good qualities, he had been able to master his black, sullen temper and the harshness of his character and to check the haughtiness with which he treated not only those who depended entirely upon him but even those who were his associates. What is even sadder is that no one felt sorry for him. Because of the failure of his enterprise, those who judge only by appearances considered him an adventurer. Unfortunately this type of judge is in the majority and represents public opinion. He was also justly reproached for never taking anyone's advice and for having ruined his own undertaking through sheer stubbornness.[4]

Many things contributed to the failure and the tragic end of the expedition. If, as many people thought, the only purpose was to establish a colony at the mouth of the Mississippi, there might have been some degree of success. It is certain that La Salle, after having been left at Saint Bernard's Bay by Beaujeu, very quickly learned that he was west of the river. If all he really wanted was to find it, the Caddoes would have given him guides on his first visit among them, just as they later did for Joutel. His real purpose was to head toward the Spaniards in order to discover the location of the Santa Barbara mines and to look for an El Dorado too. Because he wanted to do too much, he accomplished absolutely nothing except to cause the death of his men, as well as his own. He was mourned by no one.

[4] In an attempt to make Duhaut's crime less horrible, it was even said that La Salle had killed Duhaut's son and several other people with his own hands and that the plotters, fearing that they would die because of La Salle's injustice and harshness, were moved by desperation and vengeance. We should be quite careful when dealing with this type of calumny, since it is quite usual to exaggerate the faults of a man who is down and even to attribute to him some which are not really his.

Before I finish this letter, allow me to make several remarks on human madness. The greed of the Spanish captains must have been great indeed for it to have inspired them to look for a mountain of gold or an imaginary El Dorado while the country they lived in overflowed with that metal. That just proves that all the treasure in the world cannot satisfy man when his heart is filled with greed.

The Spaniards were not content with the wealth of Peru; they set out to find El Dorado, a country whose rocks and stones were made of gold. The Indians, taking advantage of the greed of their enemies in order to get rid of them, kept talking of the gold, the silver, the diamonds, and the pearls of El Dorado. In order to get them to leave, the Indians did everything in their power to make the Spaniards believe that that imaginary country really existed. The Spaniards believed these interesting reports, and it is thought that that is the origin of the famous El Dorado, which made such a stir throughout the world.

Rumor had it that El Dorado, a heavily populated country, was situated on a vast plain beyond a snow-covered mountain chain. Quesada and 250 brave soldiers set out immediately to find it. From the top of a mountain, they discovered a vast plain which, from afar, looked like the sea. At the foot of the mountain, they founded a city which they called Santiago to commemorate the day on which they had discovered the plain. They also called the city Las Atalayas[5] to indicate the purpose of their travels, the discovery of El Dorado. This city, which still exists today and can be seen on the map, seems to stand as a challenge to posterity to go out and discover this unknown treasure. After suffering unbelievable hardship in the Ayrico forest and losing all his men, Quesada arrived at Timana in 1543.

Orellana, who set out on the same trip that year, left Peru, went down the Maragnon, or Amazon, River, got to the coast, and did everything possible to find the mountain of gold. All his troubles were in vain. His only distinction was that of having made one of the most

[5] *Atalayar* means "to spy" or "to discover" in Spanish.

horrible trips ever heard of. At the same time, fearing that Quesada might alone discover El Dorado and become rich, Philip de Ure took off from Coro in Venezuela with Aquito, Lieutenant Velalcazar, and 120 men. Because an Indian chief had told him that most of Quesada's men had died, Ure decided to head south along the Guabari River. He reached the first Omagua village in pitiful condition, according to the account of Father Simón y Piedrahita. What would one not do for gold? *Auri sacra fames quid non pectora cogis?*

A Spanish author has said, "Let us question the most important captains of our nation and let us ask the same question of the Englishman Keymise[6] and the other captains of his nation: My friends, what is the reason for your travels? Why do you take such chances on the high seas? Why do you run such risks and wreck your ships? Let us inquire of the two Pizarros, Quesada, Orellana, Barrio, and other famous captains in such places as Quito, Bogotá, Meta, and the Amazon. Why do you go to so much trouble? What good does it do to muster troops and travel in such savage countries?" They answered, "We are looking for famous and rich El Dorado. Why should our determination surprise you? Is it not natural for us to be willing to suffer to gain the greatest treasure in the world? Even Peru, which did not need this wealth, sacrificed many lives in its search for it."

It is not difficult to judge an enterprise when its sole aim was to send men off at great risk and expense to look for treasures which they already had safely at home.

What is the use of so much philosophizing? During my stay here, I shall have the opportunity of sending you another letter, which will contain any interesting information I can gather about the politics and the form of government of the people who live here. I am, sir, . . .

Arkansas territory
October 29, 1751

[6] Less than one hundred years ago, Keymise tried to discover the land of gold.

Letter V

To the Marquis de l'Estrade.
A description of the customs of the Arkansas nation; their religion; their warfare; the richness and fertility of their land.

Sir:

By describing this Indian nation and its particular characteristics, I hope to give you a general idea of all the peoples of North America. There is, as a matter of fact, very little difference among them in custom and in thought, especially in regard to the Supreme Being whom they call *Coyocopchill*, which means "Great Spirit" or "The Master of Life." The Arkansas live along a river bearing their name, which has its source in New Mexico and empties into the Mississippi. These tall, well-built, brave Indians are good swimmers and skillful hunters and fishermen. They have given proof of their devotion to the French on several occasions.

I spoke to you in my last letter of an old Arkansas who said he had seen La Salle. This good Indian added that from that time on he has had a great deal of esteem for the French, who were the first white men he had ever seen. As chief, he had always urged his nation to have no European allies but the French. These Indians, following the Chief's advice, wanted no part of the Natchez' plot to massacre the

French. I must give credit to these good Indians, who are still at war with the Chickasaws among whom the Natchez found refuge.

The land of the Arkansas is one of the most beautiful in the world. The soil is so fertile that, almost without cultivation, it produces European wheat and all kinds of fruit and vegetables which are unknown in France. There are all kinds of game such as wild cattle, deer, bears, tigers,[1] leopards, foxes, wildcats, rabbits, turkeys, hazel grouse, pheasants, partridges, quails, doves, wood pigeons, swans, geese, bustards, ducks of all kinds, teals, loons, marsh hens, golden plovers, woodcocks, snipes, thrushes, starlings, and other birds which are not seen in Europe.

When I arrived among the Arkansas, the young warriors welcomed me with the calumet dance. I should tell you, sir, that these people dance for many different reasons; there are dances dealing with religion, medicine, joy, ritual, war, peace, marriage, death, play, hunting, and lewdness. This last dance has been abolished since our arrival in America.

The lewd dance was held secretly at night by the light of a large fire. All those who joined this lustful group were supposed to strike the post[2] and swear never to reveal what they had done or seen at this dissolute dance. Both men and women danced completely nude, accompanying their obscene poses and gestures with lewd songs. You will excuse me if I refrain from translating them, although they are merely light and witty in the original Indian language.

There are skillful men among the Arkansas who would probably astound our magicians. I saw one, in my presence, do a trick which will seem unbelievable. After going through some of the usual magician's motions, he swallowed the seventeen-inch rib of a deer, hold-

[1] The author frequently used Old World names for American animals.—ED.

[2] When the Indians swear or take an oath, they hit a post with a tomahawk to remind them of the blows they have struck in war. They promise to keep their word religiously. An oath taken in this way is irrevocable. When a brave becomes a chief, he cannot assume his new rank until he has struck the post as a promise that he will lead his nation well.

ing on to one end, and then pulled it up out of his stomach. This Arkansas went to New Orleans to show this trick to the governor and all the officers of the garrrison. This is what the Indians call "making magic."

Here is the way the Arkansas declare war. The chief's cabin is the scene of a feast at which dog is the principal dish. The warriors believe that this meat will make them brave, since dogs will sacrifice their lives to defend their masters. A man who kills a dog belonging to the enemy is made a warrior, but he has to bring the dog's scalp as proof, as though he were dealing with a man, or no one will believe him. The Indians have a great number of hunting dogs and watchdogs.

After the meal mentioned above, the chief calls a war council. The powwow is held in a large council cabin built for this purpose in the middle of the village. The chief and the most important men take their places according to rank on mats or wildcat skins. When everyone is seated, the chief or the orator takes his place in the middle of the gathering and makes his speech in a loud voice. He tells the people of his nation that it would be disgraceful if they did not seek revenge for the insult they have received from one of the other tribes. If they did not get satisfaction, they would be considered women.[3] The entire assembly shows its approval by saying, "Ugh, ugh!" The chief then holds out a bundle of twigs to the assembly, and all those who want to fight enlist by taking one.

The next morning the women go crying through the village, "Young men and warriors, you have received your twigs. Leave! Go to war! Avenge the death of our relatives, our allies, and our friends. Do not come back until you are covered with our enemies' blood and have their scalps."[4] Then all those who have received twigs go to their assembly point.

[3] Calling an Indian an old woman is the same as calling him a coward.

[4] It is the custom among Indians to rip the skin off the head of all enemies killed in war. They keep count of their kill by the number of scalps they bring back. These

Worshiping the Manitou

From Joseph-François Lafitau, *De Zeden der Wilden van Amerika* (1731)

"Worship of the Sun"

From an engraving by R. Hinshelwood after Seth Eastman, in Schoolcraft,
Indian Tribes of North America

Then a young Indian carefully paints a club red. This weapon, called a "head-breaker," is taken to the edge of enemy territory where a notch is cut in a tree and two crossed arrows are drawn in red. This is their symbol of war. Red means that the nation wants revenge and will not be satisfied until enemy blood is shed.

Before setting out, the chief of the nation holds another council and usually follows it with a war feast to which he invites his allies. He presents them with twigs to get them to go along as auxiliary troops. After the meal, they sing and do a war dance.[5] The war dance is very interesting to see. All the young men are painted red. The one who does the discovery or surprise dance remains in a crouching position as he spies on his enemy. He jumps up suddenly, club in hand, and utters piercing screams as he attacks his foe in simulated battle. The dance partner falls as though struck by lightning and stiffens his arms and legs like an epileptic. After this, the victor does a scalping dance. He pretends to make an incision in the forehead and around the neck of the enemy. He then goes through the motion of digging his long fingernails into the cut and places his knees on the victim's shoulders. He then pushes forward quickly with his knees as he yanks back with his hands, removing the dead man's scalp, hair and all. All this dancing and singing is done to the beat of a drum and a rattle.[6] The Indians never go off to war without consulting their "Manitou."[7] They attribute both their good and their bad fortune to it. If the Manitou is not good to them, they abandon

trophies are attached to a pole. We usually give them ten crowns' worth of merchandise, at the King's expense, for each scalp of our enemies.

[5] These are the words of the war chant: "I am going to war to avenge the death of my brothers. I'll kill, exterminate, rob, and burn the enemy. I'll bring back slaves, I'll eat their hearts, I'll roast their flesh, I'll drink their blood, I'll take their scalps, I'll make cups of their skulls." There are other such words dealing with vengeance, cruelty, and murder.

[6] This rattle is a calabash, or type of gourd, which the Indians fill with glass or enamel beads. They also attach bells to their legs.

[7] A false god of the Indians. Sometimes they use a dried crow, snake, amphibian, or quadruped.

it unceremoniously and take another. Before leaving for war, the chief goes through a period of severe fasting and paints his body black. After the fast, he washes and paints his body and face red. He then harangues his warriors in the presence of the false god. After this, they prepare the belongings they are to take with them. Sometimes they wage war as far as four or five hundred leagues from their own territory.

Their equipment consists of a bear skin, which they use as a bed, a buffalo hide, which serves as a blanket, a cat skin, in which they keep their pipes, and a little ax, which is useful for building shelters in the woods.

Their arms and ammunition consist of a rifle, a buffalo horn for powder strung across the shoulder, and a small skin sack in which to keep bullets, flints, and a wad-extractor. In addition, they carry a bow and a quiver full of arrows which they use when hunting. They never use their rifles for this purpose when they are on a war trip, because the noise might alert the enemy. They agree among themselves as to how to go about surprising the enemy. The Indians are famous for their skill in this type of warfare which is almost always fatal to the foe.

They do not worry too much about food supplies. Everyone is provided with a little sack of corn flour or maize roasted in just about the way we roast our coffee. When they are hungry, they mix some of the flour with a spoonful of water, but generally do not eat it until they have come close to the enemy.

Indians can travel for three or four days without eating and suffer no ill effects. They just tighten their belts and go on their way.

When the Indians have attacked and defeated their enemy, young warriors leave immediately to carry the news of the victory to their village. Even before their arrival, they announce, through a system of cries, how many prisoners have been taken, how many have been killed, and the number of scalps that have been brought back. The women prepare to greet the prisoners or slaves by beating them with sticks. Whether these captives, who are bound and painted black,[8] will live or die is determined by the women. Those who have lost a husband or a son have the right to choose a prisoner to replace him. Those chosen are adopted as husbands or sons and are immediately set free.

Those who are not adopted are burned alive over a slow fire. The young men of the tribe take out their anger on these unfortunate victims, who are scalped and tied to a wooden frame[9] where they undergo the most frightful torture without complaining. As a matter of fact, they sing until they die, declaring that they are not afraid of death or fire. They even taunt their executioners by saying they are not suffering enough. If things were reversed, the victims would know how to make the executioners suffer even greater torment. The prisoners even point out where the fire should be built up more and which parts of their bodies are most sensitive.

It should be mentioned that when they get ready to go on the warpath, they very carefully paint their bodies and faces red. With their red bodies and their mad cries, they resemble a troop of demons who have come straight from hell.[10] They are kind to their friends but very cruel to their enemies.

In matters of religion, they believe in a Great Spirit, whom they worship in the form of an alligator or a snake. They fear the devil, called the Evil Spirit, and worship the sun and the moon. When it thunders, they think the Master of Life is speaking to them in anger.

Before ending my letter, I should like to tell you about an event which will seem strange to you, but which, in spite of its insignificance, could be very useful to me during my stay in America. The

[8] Those who are painted in this manner are destined to be burned in the middle of the village, unless the women adopt them.

[9] This frame consists of two posts, which are stuck in the ground, and a crosspiece. The captives are forced to sing and dance around these posts.

[10] Usually both male and female Indians have no hair on their bodies, except on their heads. In that respect, they say we resemble animals. They think this, too, when they see us eat herbs and salads.

Arkansas have just adopted me. A deer was tattooed on my thigh as a sign that I have been made a warrior and a chief. I submitted to this painful operation with good grace. I sat on a wildcat skin while an Indian burned some straw. He put the ashes in water and used this simple mixture to draw the deer. He then traced the drawing with big needles, pricking me until I bled. The blood mixed with the ashes of the straw formed a tattoo which can never be removed. After that, I smoked a pipe and walked on white skins which were spread under my feet. They danced for me and shouted with joy. They then told me that if I traveled among the tribes allied to them, all that I had to do to receive a warm welcome was to smoke a peace pipe and show my tattoo. They also said that I was their brother and that if I were killed they would avenge my death. I am now a noble of the Arkansas nation. By adopting me, these people have shown me the greatest honor they can pay to a defender of their land. I consider it similar to the honor received by Marshal de Richelieu when his name was inscribed in the golden book among the names of the nobles of the Republic of Genoa.

It is true that there is some difference between having your name inscribed in a book and having to undergo the operation which the Indians performed on me. I cannot tell you how much I suffered and how great an effort I made to remain impassive. I even joked with the Arkansas women who were present. The spectators, surprised by my stoicism, cried out with joy, danced, and told me that I was a real man. I was truly in great pain and ran a fever for almost a week. You would never believe how attached to me these people have become since then. This is all that I can tell you about them.

We are planning to set out for Illinois territory at the beginning of November. Since it is late in the season and we still have three hundred leagues to go, we run the risk of being stopped by the snow and of having to spend the winter en route. We have to stay here for a while until we can prepare enough biscuits for a trip made long by the currents and the north winds which we shall have to buck at this time of the year. It looks as though I shall not be able to write to you until next year. I am sending this letter off on a boat which will reach a warship just before it sails for France. I hope that my letter finds you in good health. A letter from you would give me the greatest pleasure. I am, . . .

Arkansas territory
November 6, 1751

P.S. I found a half-blood among the Arkansas. After questioning him, I learned that he was the son of Rutel, the Breton sailor who got lost at the time of La Salle's expedition down the Mississippi in 1682. I have had the honor of mentioning him before.

This half-Indian said that his father had been found and adopted by the Caddo Indians. He was made a warrior and was given an Indian girl as his wife because he had frightened and routed the enemies of the Caddoes by using his rifle, which was still an unknown weapon among them at that time.

Rutel then taught the Indians how to sail and row their canoes. Through these skills they were able to defeat an enemy "naval" force. Rutel's instruction in this type of navigation, completely new to the Indians, earned him the gratitude and the veneration of these people. They considered him the greatest man in the world. The famous Ruyter, who rose from sailor to lieutenant and admiral of the United Provinces, was perhaps less esteemed than was Rutel among the Caddoes.

LETTER VI

To the Marquis de l'Estrade.

An account of the author's trip from the Arkansas to the Illinois; the wreck of the King's ship *St. Louis*, on which he was sailing; he falls into the Mississippi and is saved by an Arkansas.

SIR:

Here I am at last, thank God, at Fort de Chartres, after a long, hard, and dangerous trip. We left the Arkansas Indians on November 7 and traveled three hundred leagues to get here without seeing a single village or house. Since this stretch of land is absolutely uninhabited, it is fortunate that there are herds of buffalo and many deer, especially in this dry season. We often killed many buffalo, deer, and bear as they crossed the river to which they had come in flocks for water. When the French are on the march, they usually hire Arkansas Indians to keep them supplied with game. These hunters go out in their canoes in the morning and kill buffalo along the river's edge. The meat is left along the shore and is later picked up by the boats of the convoy.

The Indians carefully cut the tongues and the steaks from the animals they have killed and offer them as gifts to the commander and the officers of the convoy. After this, a sergeant or a corporal distributes the meat to the soldiers in each boat. Sometimes they have so much that they make a consommé soup out of it. The pleasure we get from hunting makes up for the hardships encountered on the trip. Game is so plentiful near the St. Francis River that, when we camped on its banks, we found it impossible to sleep because of the constant coming and going all night long of swans, cranes, geese, bustards, and ducks. Near the territory of the Illinois Indians, there are doves, which are a type of wild wood pigeon, in such thick clouds that they eclipse the sun. These birds, which live only on beech tree seeds and acorns, are excellent in the fall. Sometimes you can kill up to eighty of them with a single rifle shot. It is too bad that only a few savages inhabit such beautiful country.

Monsieur de Macarty, the Irish leader of the convoy, had an attack of the gout and did not want to spend the winter en route. He decided to set out before the others when we were still at the juncture of the Ohio and the Mississippi, thirty leagues from the Illinois. He took with him the best rowers without worrying the least about those he left behind, contrary to the orders of the Marquis de Vaudreuil. Yet the law of nature requires every man to lend his assistance in case of enemy attacks or other misfortunes, such as the one which occurred to my ship, the *St. Louis*. It got stuck on a sand bank, and we had to unload it almost entirely before we could get it afloat again. I lost two days and was not able to rejoin the convoy.

To make matters worse, three days after the accident, when I had only fourteen leagues more to get to the Illinois, my ship struck a tree which emerged from the water like a flying buttress. The Mississippi is full of such trees, especially in the dry season. Water rushed in through the large hole caused by the accident, and the ship sank in less than an hour. I lost everything that I owned and came close to dying. I jumped into a canoe so loaded down with things that had been salvaged from the wreck that it overturned. Several soldiers drowned and I would have too if a brave Arkansas, disregarding the severe weather, had not jumped into the water and seized me by the hooded coat I was wearing.

A short time after my arrival at Fort de Chartres, I was present at an incident which almost ended in tragedy. At the instigation of the English, the Piankashaws and the Weas planned to wipe out completely five French villages which were established among the Illinois. Monsieur de Macarty sent me on ahead to prepare lodgings for some troops which were coming by convoy. The Indians had thought out their strategy and planned to head off the convoy. At that time I was in Kaskaskia territory where Monsieur de Montcharvaux was in command. He did not know exactly what the Indians were up to, but, remembering the Natchez massacre, he suspected them of some treachery because of their great show of affection during their too frequent visits to the homes of the French.

It is at such times that a commanding officer feels the full weight of his responsibilities. Montcharvaux, assisted by Gruise, an intelligent and brave officer, did not become discouraged. He held a secret meeting with the most important and the oldest inhabitants of the area. He honored me by asking my advice, although he did this through kindness rather than necessity since I had just arrived and knew very little about the local situation. I must say, however, that he was quite pleased with the simple advice I gave him. It was my opinion that the best way to find out what the Indians were plotting was to remain on the defensive without giving any indication of our suspicions. I suggested that we send out several colonists, mounted on their horses and armed with rifles as though they were going hunting. After roaming about for a while, they were to come galloping back to the settlement as though they had discovered something new. All we would have to do then, in the midst of this general alarm, would be to observe the Indians carefully; the expressions on their faces would betray them. My advice was taken, and the Indians thought that the French had discovered their plot. The massacre was to have taken place on Christmas Day right after High Mass. The Indians had found out when Christmas would be by asking on what day the Great Spirit's Son had been born.

When they thought that their plot had been discovered, they

tried to flee. We opened fire and killed twenty-two of them. La Jeunesse, a Creole sergeant, who was a good hunter, killed four of them in my presence. Monsieur de Gruise attacked those who were in the Jesuits' house. He wounded several of them and took five prisoners, among them an Illinois, who were thrown into chains.

Monsieur de Macarty rushed messengers to the Marquis de Vaudreuil in New Orleans to give him an account of the expedition. The Governor ordered the prisoners to be returned to their people, who came crying, peace pipe in hand. They disclaimed all responsibility for the plot and said that the English were the cause of their madness. They were very grateful when they were granted peace, and all is quiet at present. Nevertheless, as a precaution, the settlers have been ordered to carry their rifles to Mass, and the officer of the guard will post two sentinels at the door of the church during the service.

I must not forget to mention, sir, that all of this happened without our having a single man killed or wounded. In order to run faster, the Indians threw aside their blankets, their clubs, and their tomahawks. The vigilance of Commander de Montcharvaux and of Major de Gruise headed off the plot at the very moment when it was to be carried out.

I have come back to Fort de Chartres where we lead a rather peaceful life. I do not have much news, but I shall tell you several anecdotes which may amuse you. At least they will give you some idea of the character of the Indians. During the winter I hired an Indian hunter from a Michigamea village. One day, when he had killed a great deal of game, instead of bringing it to me, he traded[1] with some Frenchmen for brandy and became roaring drunk. When he came to my lodging in that condition, I received him coldly, took away the rifle which I had given him, and pushed him out. In spite of all that I could do, he came back into my kitchen, lay down, and refused to leave. When he regained his senses, he realized that he had

[1] Trade consists of exchanging merchandise made in Europe for skins which the Indians obtain by hunting.

committed a serious blunder. Wishing to make up for it, he left, taking his rifle, some powder, and shot. The next day he came back, loaded down with game. Around his naked body he wore a belt to which he had tied by the heads the wild fowl he had shot. He undid the belt and dropped the birds in the middle of my room. Without saying a word, he sat down near the fire, lit his pipe, and handed it to me. He then said, "It is true that I lost my senses yesterday, but I have regained them. I admit that I deserved the treatment you gave me when you put me out of your cabin. You did well to let me come in again, because the other Indians would always have thrown up to me at the slightest provocation that I had been thrown out of Chief Big Nose's[2] cabin."

Many Europeans, thinking that the Indians cannot reason and have no common sense, consider them as brutes. Yet the anecdote that I have just told and a great many others show that these people have a sense of honor, know how to punish themselves when they have done wrong, and realize full well when they have acted badly. There are people in Europe who act as ridiculously and as barbarously as the Americans.

To get back to my hunter, you know as well as I that drunkenness places man on the same level as the animals, and that this vice is difficult to overcome even among the French. The Indians imitate them easily in this respect, and they point out that the whites taught them to drink firewater.[3]

One day my Indian found the door to the King's storehouse open. He sneaked in like a snake, opened the spigot of a cask of brandy, and spilled half of it while trying to fill a bottle. I was forced to dismiss him because of this accident. Since he was a good hunter and had only this one fault, when his wife asked me to make medicine to keep him from drinking, I was willing to try it if she and their rela-

---

[2] A name which the Indians had given me to distinguish me from the other officers. They give each one a name depending on the good or bad traits they have noticed in him.

[3] This is their name for brandy.

tives would help. One day when the hunter was drunk and wanted still more to drink, I had someone tell him that I had some brandy but was very stingy with it. He came immediately to ask me for some, but I told him I wanted to be paid. He answered that he was very poor but that he would lend his wife to me for a moon if I wanted to accept her. I explained to him that the chiefs of white warriors did not come among the red men to take advantage of their wives. I would, however, accept his son as a slave if he wanted to sell him to me for a cask of brandy. We concluded the sale in the presence of witnesses, and he turned his son over to me.

I felt like laughing from the very beginning of this farce. I also had him drink some brandy into which I had put long pepper. After he had drunk, he was bound and permitted to sleep. When he became sober, his relatives and the chief of the village, who knew of the scheme, went to see him in his cabin, where he was stretched out on a mat. They explained to him the horrible and unnatural thing he had done when he had sold his own flesh and blood. The Indian came to see me immediately, wailing,*"Indagey wai panis,"* which means, "I do not deserve to live; I am unworthy of the name of 'father.' " He blamed the brandy which I had given him and which had set his body on fire; he called it the urine of the Chief of Hell, the Evil Spirit who was to blame for all of this.

His wife, who had a sense of humor and who was enjoying herself at her husband's expense, asked him with a straight face where his son was. He asked to be forgiven again and said that he knew that I would return his son to him, since I was kind. He also knew that the Chief of the French[4] and the Father of the Red Men had no child slaves in his empire. I answered that that was true but that I had adopted the boy as my son and was going to take him to France and make a Christian of him and that all the skins of his nation could not buy him back.

His relatives pretended to weep and advised the drunken Indian

[4] This is what they call the King of France.

to get the prayer chief, or the man who talks to the Great Spirit. This is what they call the priest. I told him that I would do what the prayer chief[5] advised, that I would give his son back to him but that he must be baptized, and I would be his godfather. I also demanded that the boy's father swear off drinking, which had been so harmful to him. He said that my words were strong and that he would remember them as long as he lived. He asked me to adopt him as a brother[6] and said that he was going to strike the post immediately. From that time on he has never drunk wine or any other alcohol. He has refused even when I have offered it to him and says that since he has struck the post, the Master of Life, who I myself said could not be fooled, would be angry with him. He reminded me that once I had told him how many glasses of brandy he had drunk, although I had not seen him do it. I had been right, and the Great Spirit who sees everything must have told me. This is how I went about finding out how many glasses of brandy he could drink. I left a clean glass near a cask of brandy. Every time he took a drink, I washed the glass and put it back where it had been. In this way it was easy for me to know how many glasses he had drunk. The astonished Indian thought I was a sorcerer.

I have frequently noticed that the Indians are delighted when the French caress their little children. I took advantage of this in order to have them welcome me and, at the same time, fear me when I had reason to be displeased with their stupidity. The angrier I seemed to be with the fathers, the more I pretended to love the children. I lavished caresses and European trinkets on them. The Indians understood that since I had nothing against their wives and their children, I liked them as much as ever and that I was angry only with those who had wronged me and not with their families. This touched them, and, as a result, they went out to hunt small game, which they threw on the ground in front of me. They would say, "This is to calm you. Do not be angry with us." I answered immediately, "I am willing to

---

[5] Abbé Gagnon, Sulpician and chaplain of Fort de Chartres.

[6] Adoptions are frequent among the Indians.

forget the past when I see you return intelligently, when you do not come to me with empty hands."

Fathers' hearts are the same throughout the world. Parents are pleased by the friendship shown to their children, who respond affectionately.

You understand that it does not take much for me to gain the friendship of these people; you just have to know how to go about it. That is enough for the present. Let me remind you, sir, of the plan that I intend to follow. I examine only the situation that prevails in the places that I visit. I try particularly hard to learn something of the character of the people with whom I can spend just a short time. I think this is a worthy study for a traveler to undertake. Since you are a military man and a philosopher, I am sure that you will be pleased with the things I shall have to tell you. You can rely on the accuracy of my accounts. I will tell you absolutely nothing which I have not seen with my own eyes. Invention and exaggeration are completely foreign to me. I am, . . .

Fort de Chartres, in Illinois territory
March 28, 1752

Letter VII

To the Marquis de l'Estrade.
  Eyewitness account of the war between the Fox nation and the
Illinois; how the French settled among these people.

Sir:
  I have learned how the French came to settle here. The hunters
and trappers who first discovered the Illinois country remained there
and formed an alliance with the natives because they found the
climate at forty degrees North latitude very much to their liking.
Several of the men married Indian girls, most of whom became
Christians. After the discovery of Louisiana, the India Company sent
into the Illinois territory several families which remained and multiplied so that there are now five French villages.[1] The largest of these
settlements is called Kaskaskias, after an Illinois tribe which is situated about half a league away.[2] In accordance with instructions from
the Court, the engineer, Saussier, has drawn up plans for a new fort
to bear the same name as the old one, Fort de Chartres.
  This country, which is the most beautiful in the world, supplies
flour to the southern part of the colony and deals in furs, lead, and

---

[1] The India Company owned Louisiana; it was turned over to the King in 1731.
[2] The five French settlements are Kaskaskias, Fort de Chartres, Saint Philippe,
Cahokia, and Prairie du Rocher. There is now a sixth one called Sainte Geneviève.

76

salt. Buffalo and deer are particularly fond of the grazing lands surrounding the great number of salt licks in the area. The salted meat and tongues of these animals are sold to New Orleans. The hams are every bit as good as those of Bayonne. The local fruit is as good as that grown in France.

Except for their language, the Illinois have more or less the same customs and habits as those Indians whom I have already described. They marry and, after the hunt, leave each other without ceremony or fuss. Indian marriages, governed entirely by natural law, depend only upon the consent of both parties. Since they are not bound by civil contract, the couples merely separate when they are no longer happy together, claiming that marriage is a matter of love and mutual assistance. I have seen very happy marriages among these people; divorce and polygamy, authorized by law, are not common. If an Indian is a good hunter, he may have two wives. Some of them marry sisters in the belief that they get along better than strangers. Indian women generally work hard, since they are warned from childhood that if they are lazy or clumsy, they will have worthless husbands. The Indian father, whose natural sentiment is not stifled by greed, ambition, or other well-known European characteristics, does not force his child to do things against his will. With natural understanding, which we would do well to imitate, children are married to those whom they love.

The Illinois were formerly the most powerful Indians in Louisiana, but continual wars waged against the tribes to the north have reduced them to a very small number. The hatred between the two groups has arisen because of the Illinois' invasions of Canadian Indian territory, plus the fact that, in their war and hunting expeditions, the Illinois have killed or carried off both male and female beavers. This is considered criminal and cowardly among the tribes who trade beaver skins for supplies with the Europeans.

In 1752, the Cahokias, out on a hunting trip, met six Fox Indians.[3]

[3] The real name of these people is the Outagamis; they live just west of Lake Michigan.

They captured the six, although they were not at war, and decided to burn them to keep them from talking. One of the Foxes was fortunate enough to escape from the stake to which he had been tied, and eluded his executioners by jumping into a lake and swimming under water. He remained hidden in the reeds and showed his head above water just often enough to breathe. He had the stamina to remain in this position all the time his comrades were being burned. During the night he escaped the vigilance of the Illinois, who thought that he had drowned or had been eaten by the "armed fish."[4] Since he was naked and without arms, he was forced, while traveling, to eat grass like an animal in order to live. When he got back to his tribe, he told them what had happened to him among the Illinois and described the terrible fate of his traveling companions. Their relatives went into mourning immediately as is the custom. The chief assembled his men, for nothing is done without a council, and they decided to send bundles of twigs[5] to the chiefs of allied tribes, among whom were the Sioux, the Sauks, and the Kickapoos, who marched as auxiliary troops under the standard of the Foxes, forming a thousand-man army. When everything was ready, the Fox general set out by river to attack the Illinois, especially the Michigameas, among whom the Cahokias had found refuge. The warriors set out in 180 birchbark canoes and went down the Wisconsin, which empties into the Mississippi. With the aid of the river current as well as their oars, they were soon carried into the territory of the enemy, the Illinois. They passed safely in front of Fort Cahokia, which was commanded by the Chevalier de Volsei, an officer of my detachment. The *avant-garde* of this Fox army was composed of the best runners, who were to land first and act as scouts. They landed at a spot about a quarter of a league from the enemy village, which was surrounded by woods and a ra-

[4] This is the most voracious fish in Louisiana. It cuts fishhooks in two with its teeth.

[5] The Indians, who are illiterate, use these twigs to count the number of warriors and to indicate the assembly date.

vine, permitting the invaders to come within musket shot of the unsuspecting Michigameas.

The Foxes intentionally chose the holiday of Corpus Christi for their attack. They knew that the Illinois would go to see the French religious ceremony held at Fort de Chartres one league away. When everything was ready for the attack, the Fox chief told twelve of his fastest runners to expose themselves to the enemy. The young men immediately rushed upon the village, shouting a death cry, and killed everyone in their path. When they had fired their weapons, they left the village as quickly as they had entered it. The Illinois took up their arms and gave chase, but the main body of the Fox army, hidden in tall grass, fired a volley which killed twenty-eight of the enemy. At the same time they attacked the village, set fire to it, massacred men, women, and children, and led the survivors off as prisoners.

On that glorious day, the Foxes lost only four men, among whom was a bemedaled[6] chief of the Sioux, who had come along as allies.

From a height overlooking the plain and the village of the Michigameas, I saw this massacre which took place on June 6, 1752. I even had occasion to save a fifteen-year-old girl who was bringing me some strawberries when the attack began. She came running into my arms, and the pursuing enemy did not dare fire for fear of hitting me.

You can judge for yourself, through this account, that there is nothing more dangerous than having these people attack you without warning. Only those Illinois who were curious enough to go to Fort de Chartres to see the procession escaped the vengeance of the Foxes. The victors, with their bound captives in the vanguard, set out in their little boats. As they came up to the French fort of the Cahokias, they fired a salvo with their muskets. The Fox chief flew the French colors from his canoe and could not have been prouder of his victory if he had conquered an entire empire.

---

[6] I have already mentioned this honor ordered by the King and granted by the General to those Indians who are bravest and most loyal to the French nation.

Monsieur de Macarty has just written to the commanding officers of the Canadian posts concerning ransom negotiations for the Illinois taken by the Foxes. The latter had been so shrewd in conducting their affairs that we had no notion of their plans until the attack was over. They kept their plans hidden from us, knowing that we would have insisted upon intervening between them and the Illinois, who are our friends and allies. The offended nation wanted full vengeance. In this unfortunate affair, about eighty Michigameas were killed or taken prisoner.

On June 16, 1752, the commander of Fort de Chartres ordered me to assemble the remaining members of the defeated Cahokia and Michigamea tribes, and I spoke to them through the King's interpreter.

"I speak to you, my children,[7] on behalf of your father, Monsieur de Macarty, who shares in your misfortune. He asks you to end the present famine through the careful planting of your corn. Because his heart suffers to see you weak with hunger, he has sent you some corn. He has asked me also to give you powder, shot, and flints. We can do nothing more, considering that we too have enemies, and we do not know when the boats will arrive from the big village [New Orleans]. Your father suggests, too, that you go out hunting, that you take your families with you so that you can feed them, and that you leave a few men behind to protect the fields against animals. It would also be wise for you to send some of your people back from time to time to see what is going on here."

This is the reply of the chief of the tribes:

"My father, it is good that the great chief[8] pities us. You know that we were taken by surprise, since you were an eyewitness and saved one of our daughters. The Foxes and their allies massacred us, burned our cabins and our supplies, and plundered our village while we were sheltered by the Kaskaskias. You can understand that we

[7] The Indians usually call the officers "father."
[8] These people refer to the chief officer of a province or territory in this manner.

cannot leave men here, since they would starve and would continue to mourn those of our relatives who died during this horrible surprise attack. Tell our father, through the talking paper, that, to show our allegiance to him, from time to time we shall send some of our people to him with game. They will come also to see and know what is going on here.

"We hope that the great French chief will defend us and will help protect us against the enemy. Please ask him to inform several families of our people, who have remained among the Kaskaskias, that they are to join us in defending the fort which we are planning to build on the banks of the Mississippi."

Speech of Chikagou, a medal chief:

"I ask you, father, to have our arms repaired. We shall leave immediately afterward. Tell the great chief not to listen to the bad words which our enemies will certainly use against our nation. Let him remember that I have given him my word and that it shall be kept. I keep the word he has given me in my heart."

Answer:

"If you are telling the truth, you will always be welcomed by your father. All the other French chiefs will try to please you if your heart agrees with your mouth. It is good that you are leaving soon. Consider the damage that the dogs of your village have done to the livestock belonging to the French settlers.[9] If they have not complained until now, it is because they are touched by your misfortune and are pained to see you reduced to such dire straits. But since they are beginning to be annoyed, you had better take care of the situation. Your father will be happy when you are once again on your hunting grounds. His heart is sad because you are hungry, and he feels pity for his children.

"I wish you happy hunting and a good harvest upon your return. I hope that the Great Spirit will pity you; do not slight him. Tell your

---

[9] The Indians have many hunting dogs. During the food shortage, the hungry dogs ate the livestock of the French settlers. The Indians' dogs are half wolf.

young men not to do foolish things such as destroying female beavers in the lakes and the hunting grounds of your enemies, who will certainly, as you have sadly learned, seek vengeance.

"Your father has written to Monsieur Adamville, who is the commanding officer in Peoria Territory, and has asked him to negotiate peace between you and the Foxes. He will also discuss the ransom for your women and your children. The necessary merchandise will be supplied by the King, your father, the Great Chief of white men and red men."

Among the Indians, those who run away or desert in an action concerning honor or the defense of the tribe receive no physical punishment, but they are considered a disgrace to the human race. They are called old ladies, and even the women scorn them. The ugliest girls do not want them as husbands, and, if by some chance, a girl did want to marry one, her parents would oppose it for fear of having in their family cowardly men who would be of no use to the tribe. This type of person is forced to let his hair grow and to wear an *alkonan*[10] like the women. I knew one of them who, ashamed of his status, left all alone to wage war against the Chickasaws, our enemies and theirs. He approached them by crawling on his stomach like a snake and remained hidden in the tall grass for three or four days without eating or drinking. Our Illinois killed and decapitated an Englishman who had wandered off from one of the supply convoys which the English habitually ran to the Chickasaws. After that he mounted on his horse and fled. This exploit took him three months. Upon his return, the Indian nation rehabilitated him and gave him a wife so that they could produce warriors. I should tell you that, before leaving, he had eaten dog meat, in keeping with the belief which I have already had the honor of describing to you.

The great chief of the Illinois is a member of the family of the Tamaroas princes, formerly the sovereigns of this territory. This chief, or Indian king, is the son of the one who went to France with his

[10] A short skirt worn by the women to cover their nakedness.

entire retinue in 1720. He was presented to the French king, who decorated him with a medal bearing His Majesty's portrait. Now his son wears it around his neck. There was also among them a woman who was called the Princess of the Missouris.[11] Sieur Dubois, a sergeant and the interpreter for these American ambassadors, who was promoted by the King to the rank of officer, married this Missouri lady upon his return from France. She became a widow and then married Marin, captain of the militia. Their daughter is still alive.

The Indian princess told her compatriots of the splendor she had seen at the French court, where she had been welcomed and showered with presents. She was given, among other things, a repeater watch set with diamonds, which the Indians thought was a spirit because of its apparently supernatural movement. I have spoken to an old Indian who was a member of Princess Tamaroas' party. I questioned him about France and asked him what he thought was beautiful in Paris. He replied that the *Rue des Boucheries* was beautiful because of the quantity of meat he had seen there and that the *Rue Saint Honoré* pleased him, too. When he told his fellow tribesmen that he had gone to the opera, where all the people were magicians and sorcerers, and that he had also seen, on the *Pont Neuf,* little men who spoke and sang,[12] they would not believe him. When he told them that he had seen in the great village of the French (Paris) as many people as there are leaves on the trees of their forests (a figure of speech used by the Indians to indicate a great number, since they have no numbers beyond one hundred), they answered that, since such a thing was impossible, the Europeans must have bewitched his eyes and must have shown him the same people over and over again. He added that he had seen the cabins of the great French chiefs, Versailles and the

[11] She was the daughter of the great chief of that nation. It is said that she was the mistress of Monsieur de Bourmont, who, when he was commander of the Missouri territory, talked so much of the marvels of France that he got several Indians to go back with him. Their daughter became a Christian and was baptized at Notre Dame.

[12] These were obviously puppets.

Louvre, and that they held more people than there were in all the tribal lands. He said that he had also seen the cabin of the old warriors, l'Hôtel Royal des Invalides. Since the old man was beginning to be senile, he agreed with the other Indians that the French must have bewitched him.

Another Illinois, who had also gone on the trip, told the Indians that he had noticed at the Tuileries and in other public places men who were half women, with curled hair, earrings, and corsages on their chests. He suspected that they wore rouge, and he said that they smelled like alligators.[13] This American spoke with the great scorn of these people, whom we call *petits maîtres*. They are born with the natural weakness and coquetry of women. Nature seems to have started to make them women and then forgot and gave them the wrong sex. This Indian had also noticed the enormous height of the headdresses of the women of that time[14] as well as the height of their heels. I wonder what he would have said if he had seen the exaggerated width of their hoop skirts and the narrowness of their waists, strangled by that piece of armor called a whalebone corset? These coquettish women are made just as ridiculous by these artifices as are their stupid admirers. You have noticed, just as I have, during your travels through Europe, that foreigners and people from the provinces become insufferable to their compatriots when they try to imitate our *petits maîtres* and our *petites maîtresses*. Our Indian said that such effeminate manners dishonor a respectable nation.

I have received a letter from the Marquis de Vaudreuil, who expresses his sympathy because of my sad experience in losing my ship. This naturally generous governor wanted to lighten as much as possible the misfortune of an officer who has lost everything he possessed in the service of his king. He has given me permission to go to New Orleans and has offered me money and food. I am afraid that I shall

---

[13] The Mississippi alligator has pouches filled with a musk which is stronger than that of the West Indian alligator. Its odor is so vile that the alligator can often be smelled before it can be seen.

[14] This was during the Regency.

find that he has left for France. I can truthfully say that he has earned everyone's esteem and loyalty. The Indians constantly compare him with his predecessor, Monsieur de Bienville. When the tribes do not speak of a governor with praise, but, on the contrary, join all the inhabitants in detesting him, that is the strongest accusation against him.

Before finishing this letter, I should like to say a few more words about the Missouris. Baron de Porneuf, who was the commander of Fort d'Orléans in their territory, is very well acquainted with their character. He assured me that they had at one time been warlike and honest but that they were corrupted by the bad conduct and the constant fighting of the French hunters, who were contemptible because of their fraudulent dealings in business affairs. These Frenchmen committed the greatest and the most unforgivable crime of all in the eyes of the Indians—they seduced and carried off native women. Because of the disorderly conduct of these Frenchmen, the Missouris were not very kindly disposed towards them. That is why, under the administration of Monsieur de Bienville, they massacred Sieur Dubois and the little garrison under his command. Since not a single soldier escaped with his life, we have never been able to determine who was right and who was wrong in this affair.

The story which I am going to tell you will prove that these people are savages in name only and that the French who tried to deceive them fooled themselves instead. Here is the proof. Forty years ago, when these Americans still knew no Europeans, a hunter came into their country, taught them to use firearms, and sold them rifles and powder. As a result, their hunt was successful, and they had a great quantity of furs. Another hunter arrived some time later and tried to sell them ammunition. Since the Indians still had quite a supply on hand, they were not very eager to deal with this French adventurer. He thought up a rather strange trick to sell his powder without worrying too much about what the consequences might be to his fellow countrymen. He thought he had accomplished a clever piece of work in fooling these poor natives.

The Indians, who are naturally curious, wanted to know how France came by this powder, which they call grain. The hunter told them that it was sown in fields and harvested like indigo and millet in America. The Missouris, happy with this discovery, sowed all their powder and had to buy a new supply from the Frenchman, who made a considerable profit in beaver, otter, and other furs. He then went down the river to the Illinois country, at that time commanded by Monsieur de Tonti.

The Missouris went to the field from time to time to see if the powder was growing. They carefully placed a man on guard to keep the animals from destroying the future crop. They soon, however, discovered that the Frenchman had tricked them. It should be remembered that Indians are fooled just once and that they never forget it. They promised to avenge themselves on the first member of our nation who would come among them. A short time later, the lure of profit tempted our hunter to send his partner out with an assortment of merchandise to sell to the Missouris. The Indians discovered that this man had been sent by the one who had fooled them. They made no mention of the trick played on them, and they even lent the trader the public cabin, located in the middle of the village, as a storage place for his packages of merchandise. When he had displayed his wares, the Missouris entered in great confusion, and all those who had been simple enough to sow their powder walked off with some of the merchandise, so that the poor trader was done out of all that he had brought with him. He complained bitterly about this treatment to the great chief of the nation, who answered in a serious tone of voice that the Frenchman would receive justice but that he would have to wait until the Indians had harvested the powder planted upon the advice of his countryman. The trader could count on the chief's word as a sovereign that a general hunt would then be ordered and that all the furs taken would be given to the Frenchman as a reward for the important secret he had imparted to the Indians. It did the traveler no good to argue that perhaps Missouri soil was no good for the growing of powder, that the chief's subjects had misunderstood, and that powder could be grown only in France. All of his reasoning was in vain; he left weighing much less than when he arrived and was quite embarrassed over being taught a lesson by savages.

This lesson, however, did not discourage other Frenchmen from visiting the Missouris. One decided to play a trick on them. He armed a pirogue, which he loaded down with trinkets and with a barrel of ground ashes and coal covered with a layer of powder. When he had arrived at the village, he displayed all his baubles in the large cabin in order to tempt the Missouris to steal them. This is, indeed, exactly what the Indians proceeded to do. The Frenchman shouted and insulted the Indians. He ran to the barrel of powder which he had prepared, broke it open, grabbed a burning stick, and cried, "I have gone mad! I am going to blow up the cabin, and you are all going with me to the land of the spirits!" The frightened Indians did not know what to do. The Frenchmen who were outside the cabin said that their brother had gone out of his mind and could not be brought to his senses unless his merchandise was returned or paid for. The chiefs and all those who had relatives in the cabin begged the villagers to comply. The people were moved, and each one brought to the cabin all the furs he owned. The Frenchmen then informed them that he had regained his senses. The chief handed him a peace pipe, which he smoked. The trader then poured water on the powder to show that it could never again be used, and incidentally, to conceal his trickery. He carried off more than one thousand crowns in good furs. From that time on, the Indians have thought highly of him and have given him the name of "True Man" or "Man of Valor."

I shall finish my letter with the description of a strange and extraordinary ceremony performed by Missouris who came here as ambassadors when the Chevalier de Boisbriant was commander. This tragic story will serve as a lesson to those officers who, through noble ambition, aspire to become commanders one day. They must have theoretical and practical knowledge of geography and must make an effort to know the terrain of the country in which they may be fighting in order to avoid any surprise attacks by the enemy and to safeguard the lives of the men under their command. What I am going to tell you should convince them of this. Spain was not happy to see us establish settlements along the Mississippi during the Regency. The English did not hesitate to use deceit and intrigue to wipe out this newly founded colony, tactics which serve them even today on the banks of the Ohio, to which they lay claim; they also say that the Mississippi is theirs.

In 1720, the Spaniards had the idea of settling among the Missouris, near the Illinois, in order to keep us toward the west. This territory is very far from New Mexico, which is the northernmost Spanish province. To safeguard their colony, they thought it necessary to destroy the Missouris entirely. Since their forces were not strong enough, the Spaniards decided to make allies of the Osages, neighbors and mortal enemies of the Missouris. With this idea in mind, the Spaniards formed a caravan at Santa Fe composed of both men and women civilians and soldiers, with a Jacobin chaplain and a captain of the engineers as chief and guide. They had with them enough horses and livestock for the needs of a permanent settlement.

The expedition took the wrong direction and, instead of coming to Osage territory, wound up among the Missouris. The head of the expedition, thinking that he was dealing with the chief of the Osages, had his interpreter tell the Missouri chief that they had come to form an alliance to destroy their common enemy, the Missouris.

The great chief of the Missouri nation, hiding his true feelings, pretended to be very happy and promised to help the Spaniards carry out this pleasant project. He invited them to rest for several days after their hard journey, while he assembled the warriors and held counsel with the elders. The decision of this war council was that the Missouris were to treat their guests well and pretend sincerest friendship. They planned with the Spaniards to leave on their joint expedition in three days. The captain distributed to the Indians 1,500 rifles and as

88

many pistols, sabers, and hatchets. The very night of this decision, the Missouris came upon the Spanish camp and massacred everyone with the exception of the Jacobin priest. Because of his clothes, they knew that he was not a warrior. They gave him the name Magpie, and amused themselves by making him ride a Spanish horse at all their assemblies.

Although the Jacobin was treated and fed well, he was always worried that these games would end with his being sacrificed to the Manitou. That is why he took advantage of the Indians' trust in him one day and fled. The Missouris themselves told of all these happenings when they came here wearing the chapel ornaments. The chief wore a beautiful chasuble, and hanging from his neck was a paten, pierced with a nail and serving as a breastplate. Crowned with a feather headdress and a pair of horns, he walked gravely in front of the others. Those who followed him wore chasubles; after them were those dressed in stoles, and then came Indians with maniples around their necks. There came next two or three young men in albs and others in surplices. The acolytes, out of usual order, came at the end of this new-style procession, since they were not dressed up enough. They carried a cross or a candelabrum. These people, knowing nothing of the respect due the sacred vessels, hung a chalice around a horse's neck as though it were a bell.

You can imagine the ridiculous spectacle afforded by this peculiar procession as, displaying the large peace pipe, it marched in cadence to the home of Monsieur de Boisbriant, the King's lieutenant. The first Frenchman to see the arrival of these masqueraders ran to tell Monsieur de Boisbriant about it. This officer, who was as pious as he was brave, was greatly pained when he saw the Indians and did not know what to think. He was afraid that they might have destroyed a French settlement, but when he saw them close by, his sadness left him, and he could hardly keep from laughing like the others.

The Missouris told him how the Spaniards had tried to destroy them. They were bringing him everything that he saw since they could not use these things. If he wanted to, he could give them in exchange things which suited them better. He did this and then sent the ornaments to Monsieur de Bienville, at that time commanding general of the province of Louisiana.

Since they were well supplied with horses from the Spanish expedition, the Missouri chief presented the most beautiful of these to Monsieur de Boisbriant. They had also brought the map which had misdirected the Spaniards and led them to deliver themselves stupidly to their enemy.

I am going to New Orleans during the leave of absence which I have just been granted. If I find our general and a letter from you. I shall be doubly satisfied. I remain, sir, . . .

Illinois territory
May 15, 1753

LETTER VIII

To the Marquis de l'Estrade.

The author leaves the Illinois country for New Orleans; the arrival of Monsieur de Kerlérec; the departure of the Marquis de Vaudreuil; the author's second voyage among the Illinois; the story of a heroic father who sacrifices himself for his son.

SIR:

In June, I arrived at the capital of Louisiana where I found your letter waiting for me. I was happy to hear that you are in good health. That makes up in a way for my sadness in learning that our dear governor had left for France. Even a greater misfortune is Monsieur Michel de la Rouvillière's death, brought on by a stroke. He had written me that he had learned of the sad loss of my boat and that he would gladly do all he could to help me, although one was not usually reimbursed by the King for such losses. I would have to make out an exact report of my losses, certified by Monsieur Macarty, commander of the convoy. He said that this report would be absolutely necessary to justify the expenditure and that as soon as he had received these papers, he would see to it that I was reimbursed. Before he left, the Marquis de Vaudreuil advised me to see his successor, Monsieur de Kerlérec, who has paid absolutely no attention to the Marquis' recommendation. His character is exactly the opposite of his predecessor's. The new governor says that he has not come all this way just for a change of air. He kept me in New Orleans and did not allow me to rejoin my garrison before 1754, when I left with the convoy headed by Monsieur de Faverot. The King's boats were so loaded down with packs of trinkets that there was no room for the provisions I had to take along for the trip. I complained to Monsieur de Kerlérec, who was rather disagreeable about it. He asked me what I was taking along to trade with the Indians, and I answered that I understood nothing about commerce since I was a military man, that the King had sent me to Louisiana to serve him, and that it was my duty to do so. Finally, Monsieur de Kerlérec permitted me to join my garrison.

I left New Orleans on August 17, but the boats, as I have already said, were so loaded down with merchandise that we were caught by cold weather and ice and could not go on to the Illinois territory. We had to spend the winter en route and did not arrive at our destination until January, 1755. All of this caused a great deal of damage and added immensely to the King's expenses. The hardship of such a long voyage so impaired my health that I could hardly go on. I had the Indians guide me on foot, and when I was tired, they carried me in an oxhide litter strung from a pole, hammock fashion. They took turns carrying me, and in this way I arrived for the second time at old Fort de Chartres. I stayed in a cabin as I waited to be put up in the new fort, which has almost been finished. It is built of stone, flanked with four bastions, and can hold a garrison of three hundred men. I asked Monsieur Macarty to permit me a change of air among the Cahokias, who are only one day's journey by water or land from Fort de Chartres. At this post there is a little fort on the left bank of the Mississippi. This center of the important fur trade in New France is on the main route taken by the Illinois when they go to Canada.

The priests of the order of St. Sulpice, who are the masters of the island and the city of Montreal, have established a mission here called the Holy Family of Jesus. Of the three priests stationed there, I knew particularly well Abbé Mercier, the Canadian grand vicar of the Illinois country. He was a very righteous man whose friendship was valuable because of his great knowledge of the ways of the Indians.

He set them a good example by his virtue and his unselfishness. Because of the fluency with which he spoke the language of the country, the Indians thought a great deal of him and frequently consulted him. He spent forty-five years cultivating the Lord's vineyard in this far-off country, and the Indian tribes of the region always respected him. Because of the good a man of this type does for the Indians, his life always seems to be too short regardless of how long he lives. This worthy Louisiana apostle had a sudden decline in health during Lent and died as a Christian hero at eleven-thirty one Friday night. I greatly regretted the death of this admirably intelligent man. The French and the Indians were inconsolable. In accordance with their custom, the Indians sent delegates to mourn at his tomb. They came in groups, and as soon as they approached the home of the deceased, they lamented with cries and groans. The consternation and the grief of these poor people could be seen on their faces. The Indians, whom we call savages, recognize true virtue in a man. The Abbé had worked for their salvation almost all his life, and they called him their father or the "prayer chief."

What a difference there was between this missionary and his predecessor, who falsely claimed that he had discovered Louisiana. I am speaking of Father Hennepin, a Recollect friar. In 1683, he published an inaccurate report. The country that he and Sieur Decan discovered when they went up the Mississippi from the Illinois River to Sault Saint Antoine is not in Louisiana, but in Canada. The account of a second trip made by Father Hennepin, in the *Recueil des voyages du nord,* bears an equally false title, *Voyage in a Country Larger Than Europe, Between the Glacial Sea and New Mexico.* Even if one goes as far up the Mississippi as possible, the glacial sea is still far off. When the author published this second report, he was angry with Monsieur de la Salle. It even appears that he was forbidden to return to America, and in anger he retired to Holland, where he published a third work entitled: *A New Description of a Very Large Country, Situated in America Between New Mexico and the Glacial Sea, With Reflections on Monsieur de la Salle's Enterprises, and Other Things Concerning the Description and the History of North America.*[1]

In this work, the author vents his anger not only on La Salle but also on France, a country which he thinks has mistreated him. He believes he can save his honor by declaring that he was born a subject of the Catholic King,[2] but he ought to remember that it was France who paid the expenses for his trip to America and that it was in the name of the very Christian King that he and Sieur Decan took possession of the lands which they discovered. He even dared claim that it was with the consent of the Catholic King, his first sovereign, that he dedicated his report to the king of England, William III, asking him to send missionaries to teach Catholicism to the Indians. This claim made the Catholics laugh and even scandalized the Protestants, who were amazed that a Catholic missionary would ask a Protestant king to found a Roman church in the New World. In addition, all his works are written in a declamatory and turgid style. The liberties taken by the author and his indecent invective when dealing with fundamentals shock the reader. Father Hennepin thought that he could take advantage of the privilege of explorers to tell less than the truth. He has been strongly criticized for this by those who traveled with him. It is easy to see that his undertakings were motivated more by vanity than by a zealous desire to make converts in the New World.

While I was among the Cahokias, some members of the Osage tribe arrived. Their Manitou was an enormous dried snake, which, according to these Indians, had swallowed an entire wildcat and had done a great deal of damage in their territory. As a result, they set out to kill it and tracked it down. Neither their bullets nor their arrows could penetrate its body, which was covered with very hard scales similar to those of an alligator. They succeeded in killing it,

---

[1] *Nouvelle description d'un très grand pays, situé dans l'Amérique entre le Nouveau Méxique et la mer glaciale, avec des reflexions sur les entreprises de Monsieur de la Salle, et autres choses concernant la description et l'histoire de l'Amérique Septentrionale.*—Ed.

[2] Father Hennepin came from Douay.

94

however, by firing bullets and arrows into its eyes. The man who killed it bore a tattooed image of the snake on his body. The tattoo was done in much the same way as the deer design which the Arkansas drew on my thigh. Here is how they go about it. First they draw on the body with blackening or gunpowder the object or the animal they wish to represent. After that, they prick the skin with one or several needles until they draw blood; they then rub the drawing lightly with a fine sponge dipped in a solution of rock salt. This mixes the blood with the gunpowder and draws up the skin, making the tattoo indelible. This is not entirely painless, but since it confers a type of knighthood on only those who have done extraordinary deeds, they endure it with pleasure in order to be considered valiant men. The more brave deeds a warrior does, the more such marks of distinction he bears on his body.

If anyone should take it into his head to have himself tattooed without having distinguished himself in battle, he would be disgraced and considered a coward, unworthy of the honor due only those who risk their lives to defend their tribe. Even the sons of chiefs are not held in special consideration unless they are as brave and virtuous as their fathers and their ancestors.

I knew an Indian who, although he had never done anything outstanding in defense of his tribe, decided to have himself tattooed with one of these marks of distinction in order to impress those who judge others by outward appearances. This show-off wanted to pass himself off as a valiant man so that he could marry one of the prettiest girls of the tribe, who was ambitious even though she was a savage. Just as the match was about to be concluded with the girl's relatives, the warriors, who were indignant upon seeing a coward display a symbol of military merit, called an assembly of war chiefs to deal with this bit of audacity. The council decided, in order to prevent such abuses which would remove the distinction between courageous men and cowards, that this false hero who unjustly decorated himself with the tattoo of a tomahawk, without ever having struck a blow in battle,

95

would have the design torn off him, skin and all, and that the same would be done to all others like him.

Since there was no hope for a pardon from a verdict decreed by this Indian senate, which jealously protected the honor of the tribe, I offered through pity to make French medicine. I assured the Indians that I could remove the skin and the tattoo without hurting the patient and that the operation would turn his blood into water. The Indians, not knowing my secret, thought that I was making fun of them. Imitating their medicine men, I gave the false hero a calabash bowl full of maple syrup, into which I had put some opium. While the man was asleep, I applied some cantharides to the tattoo on his chest and then added plantain leaves, which formed blisters or tumors. The skin and the tattoo came off and a serous fluid was secreted. This type of operation amazed the medicine men, who knew nothing of the properties of cantharides, although they are very common in North America. They give off a light at night by which you can read even the smallest letters if you hold them close and follow the line of print.

Although European customs seem to differ greatly from those of the Indians, they are often quite similar. The following story proves my point.

In 1749, an officer of the Île de France regiment fell in love with a girl in Paris. The young lady's mother said that she would approve the marriage only if the officer were decorated with the Croix de Saint Louis. He was spurred on by love and a desire to be married as quickly as possible to award himself this honor, which only the King can grant. He was practically the lady's son-in-law, when another officer with longer service in the regiment ran into the false chevalier quite by chance. The senior officer, who did not yet have such an award, was rather surprised to find that the young man had been decorated before him. The new chevalier told the older officer that with influence anything could be had. Not knowing the truth of the matter, the latter went immediately to Monsieur d'Argenson and complained of the fact that his junior had received the Croix de Saint

Louis. The Minister, denying this, sent for the last promotion list and, naturally, did not find the name of the false chevalier, who was thereupon arrested and brought before the Tribunal of the Marshals of France. Marshal de Belle-Isle presided at the court-martial held in the hospital of the Invalides. The accused was found guilty and was sentenced to have the cross taken from him, to be degraded, and to be imprisoned in a fortress for twenty years.

Indian women have themselves tattooed everywhere on their bodies without serious consequences. I have seen several of them with designs on such delicate and sensitive parts of the body as the breasts. They bear the pain with the same courage as the men in order to please them and to appear more beautiful to them.

To get back to the Osage Manitou, I would like to have had that supposed relic in my possession so that you could decorate your natural history study with it. I tried to trade European merchandise for it with the priest who was in charge of it. I argued that it was wrong to worship this animal and that he should recognize the Great Spirit or the Author of Nature, just as we do. This cunning minister of the devil, admitting that his ignorant and superstitious fellow tribesmen worshipped anything unusual, told me that he intended to profit a great deal from the Manitou. Since he was a witch doctor and a magician, he made the other Indians believe that this god and the Evil Spirit ate together at night. Therefore, food for the meal and fine skins in which to dress the Manitou had to be brought to the priest's cabin. In this way, through deceitful speeches, the impostor encouraged the errors and prejudices of these ignorant people. These religious men make the people believe that they can talk to the spirit of the shadows, who is greatly feared because of his evil deeds. The priests say they have nothing to fear from the Great Spirit, since he is good and will not harm them.

I shall finish this letter by telling you of the tragic death of an Acolapissa Indian, who sacrificed himself for his son. I have admired this as a heroic act and one which epitomizes human generosity. One day an indignant Acolapissa shot and killed a Choctaw who had called the Acolapissas the dogs of the French, whom he had also maligned. The Choctaw nation, which is the largest and the most warlike on the continent, armed itself immediately and sent delegates to the governor in New Orleans. They asked for the head of the murderer, who had placed himself under the protection of the French. The Choctaws were offered gifts to pacify them. The terrible nation refused them and threatened to wipe out the Acolapissa village. In order to avoid unnecessary bloodshed, we had to surrender the unfortunate Indian to them. Sieur Ferrand, the commander of the German post on the right bank of the Mississippi, was entrusted with this mission. A meeting was arranged between the Acolapissa village and the German post. The sacrifice was made in the following manner.

The Indian victim was named *Tichou Mingo,* which means "Servant of the Chief." As is customary among these people, he stood up to deliver a speech. "I am a true man. I do not fear death, but I pity my wife, my young children, and my old father and mother, whom I leave behind and who depend on my hunting.[3] I leave them in the care of the French, since I am going to be sacrificed for having taken their part."

He had hardly finished this short and pathetic speech when his good and kind father, moved by this filial devotion, arose immediately and spoke in these terms, "My son is dying valiantly.[4] But since he is young and vigorous, he is more capable than I to feed his mother, his wife, and his four small children. He must live in order to take care of them. I am at the end of my life. I have lived enough. I wish that my son may live to be as old as I am so that he can raise my grandchildren properly. I am no longer good for anything. A few years more or less make no difference. I have lived like a man; I want to die the same way. That is why I am going to take my son's place."[5]

---

[3] He was the best hunter in the entire nation.

[4] This term, in their language, means anything which is strong or extraordinary.

[5] These people follow the law of retaliation, a life for a life. Any member of the

Upon hearing these words, which expressed paternal love in so strong and moving a manner, his wife, his son, his daughter-in-law, and his grandchildren began to weep around this kind and courageous old man. He embraced them for the last time, asking them to remain faithful to the French and to die rather than to betray them by any act of cowardice unworthy of his blood. He said, at the end, that his death was a sacrifice which he was happy and proud to make to the nation. When he had finished these last words, he offered his life to the murdered man's relatives, who accepted it. Then he stretched out on a log, and his head was cut off with an ax.

Everything was settled by this death. The young man was obliged to give his father's head to the Choctaws.[6] As he picked it up, he said these words, "Forgive me for your death and remember me in the land of the spirits." All the French who were present at this tragedy were moved to the point of tears. The virtue of this admirably and heroically loyal old man can be compared with that of the famous Roman orator who was hidden by his son in the days of the Triumvirate. He was tortured for having hidden his father, and the old man, unable to stand seeing so kind and virtuous a son tormented, gave himself up to the murderers. These soldiers, who were more barbaric than the Indians, killed both of them at the same time and on the very same spot.

Monsieur Ferrand, my traveling companion during our last trip among the Illinois, fell into the Mississippi during the most severe weather while he was drilling some soldiers. At the very moment when the current was carrying him off to a sharp drop in the river, an Arkansas hunter who was crossing in a boat saved him at the edge of the precipice. The officer told the Indian that he intended to reward him generously for this favor. When the Arkansas heard the first few words of this assurance, he replied that it was his brotherly duty to

nation, even though he is not a relative, may be sacrificed. Only slaves are not acceptable.

[6] They put it at the end of a pike and carried it off to their tribe as a trophy.

rescue those who were unfortunate enough to find themselves in a perilous situation. Since the Great Spirit had given him the ability to swim like a fish, he could use it to no better avail than to save his fellow man.

Indians of both sexes learn to swim from earliest youth. I have often seen mothers put their children into a pond of clear water. Watching these little innocents swim as naturally as frogs has always given me the keenest pleasure. Would not such training be better than all the education over which we make such a fuss in Europe? The subject which I treat here is of the utmost importance, especially in a country where almost all traveling is done by water. I shall not spend too much time on boring details; I shall say that, following healthy reason, the first law of nature is self-preservation. It would be desirable for European mothers to imitate American mothers in such things as nursing their children themselves. This act, dictated by nature, would prevent many mix-ups among children who are presumably legitimate. Without referring to the many well-known cases concerning this subject, I have before my eyes a very recent example of the inconveniences which are so often caused by mercenary nurses. A gentleman, who is an officer in my detachment, was lost for a long time as a child when he was given away to be nursed. As soon as he was born in Paris, he was sent off to the backwoods of Normandy. Through some quirk of fate, he was not recognized by his parents until he was twenty-two years old and had undergone all kinds of hardship and danger.

I remember that in 1749, while I was on my way from Paris to Arpajon, I witnessed an accident that happened to one of these little victims sent off by parents who do not want to be annoyed by the crying of their children. The nurse in charge of the child put it in her apron. When she tried to get into the large carriage used on these trips, her apron strings came loose and the child fell dead on the pavement.

I should like to say in passing that there is a great deal of difference in the way European women and Indian women think.

> *At least your honesty, fierce and coarse,*
> *Has the laws of nature as its source.*
> THOMAS, *Jumonville*

Indian women would consider themselves disgraced if they abandoned their children to the care of a far-off nurse. Unlike European women, they are not afraid of losing their husbands' affection for having carried within themselves the proof of their love for each other. On the contrary, their love grows. The pleasure of perpetuating the race and of seeing themselves live once again, day by day, in this little creature to which they have given life more than makes up for any hardship they may have to bear.

The white women, who are called Creoles, follow European custom in America and do not nurse their children. As soon as a child is born, they give it to a black, colored, or Indian slave, without thinking that the child's blood may be contaminated. Several competent doctors have demonstrated that the milk drunk by the child influences his character. I have often seen in America innocent children become the victims of the disorderly life led by their nurses. This is disastrous to the propagation of the human race. I leave this subject to the faculty of the medical school. They will do a better job of it than I.

I end this letter, sir, by assuring you that I am, . . .

Among the Illinois
July 21, 1756

P.S. An Indian messenger, who has just arrived, brings us the agreeable news of the capture of Oswego and all the territory depending upon it on famous Lake Ontario.

The 1,500 regular troops of the garrison have become prisoners of war. They have accepted the terms of the surrender which General

Montcalm has offered them. The General immediately sent to Quebec the five regimental flags which were there. Monsieur Rigaud,[7] governor of Trois Rivières, commanded the Canadians and the Indians. He captured an advantageous position from which he could prevent reinforcement of the garrison and retreat of the enemy.

The Colonial, the Canadian, and the Indian land troops all distinguished themselves. We still do not know the number of men the enemy lost. We know only that their general was killed[8] at the beginning of the attack. We lost only three soldiers in that glorious expedition. Monsieur de Bourlamaque, an infantry colonel, and seven or eight Canadians received light wounds; but, unfortunately, Monsieur Decomble, an engineer, was shot and killed by one of our Indians who mistook him for an Englishman because of his uniform, which was different from that of the other French officers.

Marquis de Montcalm is engaged in destroying the fortifications of Oswego and is sending to Frontenac the supplies, the ammunition, and one hundred cannons which were found there.

[7] The Marquis de Vaudreuil's brother, who came back to America with the title of Governor General of Canada and of New France.
[8] Colonel Hugh Mercer.—ED.

LETTER IX

To the Marquis de l'Estrade.
    The author leaves Cahokia territory for Fort de Chartres; his observations on the American people; a description of a migrating herd of elephants which came to the vicinity of the Ohio River.

SIR:

In all likelihood, this will be the last letter that I shall write you from Illinois territory. I am preparing to leave on doctors' orders. They think that I should go back to France to take the baths at Bourbonne because of the serious after effects of a gunshot wound which I received a long time ago during the attack on Château Dauphin.[1]

Yesterday, our commanding officer received a message from Fort du Quêne informing us that the English were feverishly preparing to attack that post again. Monsieur de Macarty has sent a convoy with supplies to the fort. The Chevalier de Villiers has taken command of the convoy in my place, since bad health will not permit me to undertake such a trip. This expedition would have given me the opportunity to examine the place where an Indian found some elephant teeth. He gave me a molar which weighed about six and one-half pounds.

---

[1] A fortress in Piedmont on top of one of the Alps. It was captured July 19, 1744, by troops under the command of the Prince de Conty.
    The Poitou Brigade, commanded by the brave Monsieur de Chevert, distinguished itself in this battle by its extraordinary valor, acclaimed by all Europe. See the journals of the period.

In 1735, the Canadians, who had come to fight the Chickasaws, discovered the skeletons of seven elephants in the vicinity of the Belle, or Ohio, River. This leads me to assume that Louisiana is joined to India and that the elephants came here from Asia through the west, which we do not yet know. A herd of these animals must have wandered off on dry land and through the forests to this new continent. Since the Indians did not have firearms at that time, they could not have destroyed them all. Seven of them could have come all the way to the place that I have mentioned and which has been marked with a cross on the map of Louisiana. These elephants evidently came to a swamp into which they sank up to their bellies because of their enormous weight and from which they were unable to extricate themselves.

In 1752, the Indians gave the commander of the French fort in Missouri territory, Baron de Porneuf, the fur of an American animal which we still do not know. The officer sent it as a gift to the Marquise de Vaudreuil, who has had it made into a muff. This animal could have been twice as big as a European fox, with fur as fine and soft as velvet, spotted with black and pearly white.

Several writers claim that it was possible to cross on the ice through Novaya Zemlya, situated north of Europe, to Greenland. They think that this was the route taken by those who first came to live in America. The strait that separates all of this from the mainland has tall mountains of ice to the east of it. All those who have tried to find a passage to the Indies through the north have been eaten by polar bears or have died in the snow and ice.

Here are my thoughts on this subject. If the first inhabitants had taken that route to come to America, they probably would have preferred Canada, New England, and Louisiana, whose northern territories resemble the countries they came from. Yet we know that when the French and the English discovered North America, they found very few inhabitants. The Spaniards, on the other hand, when they conquered Mexico and Peru, found kings and emperors, who had great armies and who sacrificed twenty thousand captives a year to their false gods. There is reason to believe, therefore, that the Indians came to America from the west, from Mexico and Louisiana.[2] The elephants which crossed over are still another argument to support my theories. In addition, when I questioned the nomadic Sioux, they told me that they had heard from other Indians that to the west of their country there were people who wore clothing and sailed their canoes on a large salt-water lake.[3] These people lived in large villages built of white stone and were ruled by a despotic chief who commanded formidable armies.

Moreover, the Mexicans worship idols like the people of India. The Natchez have a temple and a cult. Chinese terms have been found in their language. Some of the Indians cut or pluck out their hair, leaving a tuft like a monk's crown, to which they fasten feathers of different colors. They never bite their nails. In China it is a sign of nobility to let the nails of the right hand grow very long.

If we suppose that men had crossed over from our own continent, the white race would have perpetuated itself in America. We know that since the discovery of America by Christopher Columbus two and one-half centuries ago, the Europeans who have settled here have remained as white as their ancestors. The animals that were found here were different from ours, and neither Pliny nor other naturalists mention them. It should satisfy us to admire the Creator's work with respect, without trying to discover its secrets.

I should like to add in passing that when the Spaniards discovered the islands of Santo Domingo and Cuba, they found a great number of Indians there whom they massacred, presumably for religious reasons but really for their gold. This is why an island chief, having escaped from the Spaniards, informed his people that gold

[2] Louisiana is bordered on the north by Canada, on the east by Florida and the English colonies, and on the west by New Mexico. The northwestern boundaries are not determined.

[3] The Indians call the sea "the great lake," and ships are "big canoes."

was the god of their enemies, who had come so far and had undergone such great hardship to get it. He advised the Indians to abandon everything in order to live in peace. Another chief, condemned to be burned by the Inquisition, was asked by a Jesuit to become a Christian so that he might go to heaven. The Indian protested vociferously that he did not want to go to heaven if there were Spaniards there. These unfortunate Indians hated the Spaniards so much that they refused to be with their wives so as not to have children, who would in turn be slaves to these European masters. When they ate the Spaniards, it was through vengeance rather than taste. They said quite frankly that Spanish flesh was worthless.

I forgot to tell you in my last letter that I was invited to the war feast given by the great chief of the Illinois in order to recruit warriors to march with Villiers. This chevalier had received permission from the commanding officer to form a party of Frenchmen and Indians to avenge the death of his brother, Monsieur de Jumonville, who was killed by the English before the war.

> *The fierce, childlike people of this clime*
> *Heard in the wilderness of the terrible crime.*
> *They came to seek vengeance over pathways*
> *   and tracks,*
> *And added to the French firearm the Indian axe.*
> Thomas, *Jumonville*

The great chief of the Illinois, Papapé-changouhias, was related to several distinguished Frenchmen who had settled among these people. This chief succeeded Prince Tamaroas, nicknamed "Chikagou," who died in 1754. The present chief was decorated with the medal belonging to his predecessor, after having proved to the French that he had earned it by his loyalty to our nation. When the Chevalier de Villier's[4] detachment was ready to leave, Papapé-changouhias and his warriors wanted to serve as guides. They left Fort de Chartres

---

[4] Monsieur de Villiers, called "the Great Villiers," who went out to avenge

April 1, 1756, and toward the end of May arrived at the Virginia border, where the English had a fortress enclosed by large stakes. The Indians approached under the cover of night, each one carrying a bundle of combustible wood with which to burn the stockade. While fighting the fire, the English commander was shot by an Indian who took aim by the light of the flames. This same Indian shouted in the enemy's language, "Surrender English dogs or you will be burned or eaten." The leaderless soldiers were intimidated by these cries and surrendered the next morning at their own discretion. The Indians took them captive and tied them two by two, except for a sergeant who was recognized by one of the Indians as the man who had beaten him with a stick in time of peace. This unfortunate sergeant was the victim of the Indians' resentment and was burned without pity. I have said that the Indians never forgive and that they consider them-selves free and independent. That is why it is important never to strike them; sooner or later they even the score.

The forty English prisoners taken in the fort were divided be-tween the French and the Indians, who stripped them, according to their custom, and plucked out their hair and their beards. At the request of the French, they were merely made slaves. But the French officers and inhabitants of the Illinois territory took up a collection and, through pity, ransomed the English. The Indians, wanting to gain our favor, treated the English like dogs merely because they were our enemies.

From the village of the Cahokias, we came through a beautiful, large prairie twenty-five leagues long to the Peorias, allies of the Illi-nois. The Indians who accompanied me used sticks to kill little birds, which they called strawberry bills. These birds, whose plumage is of many colors, are as good as the warblers of Provence. The Indians said that these migrant birds assemble in flocks each year like spar-

Jumonville immediately after his death in 1753, should not be confused with the Chevalier de Villiers, the commander of this detachment.

See the poem that the famous Monsieur Thomas has written on this subject.

rows and come to eat the strawberries which turn the entire prairie red. The Peoria village is on the edge of a little river and is fortified by a stockade, as is the custom in America.

When we arrived, I asked for the dwelling of the chief and was shown to a large cabin where the entire tribe was assembled because of the defeat of a party of their warriors at the hands of the Foxes, their mortal enemies. The chief and his most important warriors gave me a warm welcome and came one after the other to shake my hand as a sign of friendship. They said, "How! How!," which means "welcome." A young Indian, who may have been a slave, immediately lit the peace pipe, and the chief followed their usual custom by handing it to me.

After the first formalities, they brought me a calabash full of maple sap. The Indians draw the sap in January by using a gimlet to drill a hole at the bottom of the tree. They then place a tube in the hole. At the first thaw, about one barrel of juice flows out. This is boiled until it is reduced to a syrup; it is then boiled again and becomes a reddish-colored sugar similar to Calabrian manna. The apothecaries rightly prefer it to cane sugar. The French who have settled among the Illinois have learned to prepare this syrup as a cure for colds and tuberculosis.

At the end of the session, I was brought persimmon bread, bear paws, and beaver tails. I also ate dog, not through preference, but in order not to offend my hosts. I have made it a point to conform to the customs of the people with whom I have to live and to assume their habits in order to gain their friendship. For a side course, I was given corn meal and maple syrup, a rather good and refreshing Indian dish. At the end of the meal, there was a dessert consisting of dried blueberries, a fruit which is very common in the Illinois territory and is as good as currants.

The next day I noticed many people scattered throughout the countryside. They had come together for a religious dance honoring a new Manitou. The priests were dressed in a very striking manner.

Their bodies were covered with clay in which they had made peculiar drawings, and their faces were painted red, blue, white, yellow, green, and black. The high priest wore a feather bonnet like a crown, and as adornment, a pair of horns of a wild goat.[5] I assure you that I had a wild desire to laugh at this prelate's getup. Since these ceremonies are serious, one must be very careful not to burst out laughing. The Indians would consider this indecent and sacrilegious. It should be said, too, that the Indians never interrupt the Catholics when they are engaged in the divine service of the true God. What a sight I saw! A living monster made into a god! I was at the door of the false god's temple. The ceremonial leader asked me to enter.[6] Since I was not yet used to the ways of these people, I hesitated. One of the Indians who accompanied me, noticing my embarrassment, said that I would insult them if I refused their invitation. This determined me to enter. Here is the description of the Manitou. Its goatlike head grew out of its stomach; its ears looked like those of a lynx, and it had similar hair; its feet, hands, thighs, and legs were of human skin and form. This false god must have been about six months old. The Indians had found it in the woods at the foot of the Santa Barbara mountain chain, which runs as far as the rich mines of Santa Fé in Mexico. The purpose of this gathering was to seek the Manitou's protection against enemies.

I told these poor ignorant people that their Manitou was an evil spirit. The proof of this was that he had permitted the Fox nation, their cruelest enemies, to win a victory over their fellow tribesmen. They ought to abandon that evil spirit and punish it. They answered, *"Teekalabay, houay nee gai."* That means "We believe you. You are right." They put it to a vote and decided to burn the Manitou alive. The high priest and sacrificer pronounced the sentence in these terms,

[5] These animals are found in Missouri territory. Their horns are black and are bent backwards.

[6] The priest chosen to guard the temple, before making his offerings, bathes his body with resin. Then he smears swan's down or beaver hairs on this melted gum. In this ridiculous costume, he dances in honor of the false god.

according to the interpreter: "Monster, engendered in the excrement of the Evil Spirit in order to bring misfortune to our people, who mistakenly thought you a Manitou, you took no recognition of our offerings. You permitted a party of our tribe to be beaten and enslaved by our enemies, whom you openly protect. Our elders have voted unanimously, and the chief of the white warriors has advised us to burn you alive so that you may atone for your ingratitude toward us." At the end of this verdict condemning the false living god to death, the spectators shouted, "Hoo! Hoo! Hoo! Hoo! Hoo!"

This is what I did to try to gain possession of this monster, since I had not been able to obtain the one I mentioned to you earlier. I approached the priest and gave him a small present. Then I told him through my interpreter to inform the other Indians that, if they burned this spirit of bad omen, another monster that would be harmful to them could be born from its ashes. I also said that I was going to cross the large lake just to save them from this. He approved of my reasoning, and with the aid of the gift which strengthened my argument, the sentence was changed from death by burning to death by clubbing. Since I did not want the false god mutilated, I told the priest to turn it over to my men who would strangle it. If a member of the tribe killed it, misfortune would befall him. The Indians agreed with what I said and found that my arguments were just. Finally, they turned it over to me with the condition that I remove it far from their lands. I had it strangled, but, having neither spirits of wine nor brandy in which to preserve it, I had to have it dissected so that I could take it to France with me in order to satisfy your curiosity about natural history.[7]

I am going to finish this letter with another account of the superstition of these people and of their worship of frightful animals. In 1756, a delegation of Missouri Indians[8] came to Fort de Chartres.

[7] The skeleton of this false god and monster is at present in the natural history collection of Monsieur de Fayolles, a clerk in the French Colonial Office of America.

[8] A people who live west of Louisiana, on the river which bears their name and which empties into the Mississippi.

Among them was an old woman who was supposed to be a magician. She wore around her naked body a live rattlesnake, whose bite is fatal if the victim is not treated immediately. This priestess of Satan spoke to the snake, which seemed to understand what she said. "I see," she said to it, "that you are bored here. Go home and I shall meet you there when I return." The snake took off immediately through the woods and headed toward Missouri territory. If I had wanted to believe in superstition or in false miracles, I would have told you that I had seen the devil appear to these people in the form of a snake. A number of missionaries have persuaded us in their edifying reports and letters that the devil appeared to these people so that they would worship him. But it is easy to see that there is nothing supernatural about all this; it is a case of pure charlatanry.

You know, of course, that all animals, even the fiercest, can be tamed by man. I cannot tell you if this so-called sorceress' snake really went home. All that I can assure you of is that I have always had a great antipathy toward these animals and that it pleases me no end to crush their heads whenever I encounter them.

I remember that in the village of the Piankashaws, a tribe related to the Illinois, one of our soldiers had a narrow escape. He entered a cabin and found a snake there, which he killed with his ax. He did not know that this was the cabin owner's Manitou. The Indian arrived just at that moment and shook with anger when he found that his god was dead. He swore that it was the soul of his father, who had fallen ill and had died a year ago, shortly after having shot two snakes which were mating on a rock. In his feverish delirium, the old man thought that he saw two snakes and that they blamed him for their death. As he lay dying, he warned his son not to harm these animals or they would cause his death too.[9] Since I knew the ways of these people, I advised the soldier, who was accused of deicide, to pretend

---

[9] I have seen a peasant in France kill an owl on his neighbor's roof because the peasant's father had died shortly before, and the bird was considered a bad omen and the cause of the death.

III

that he was drunk or mad and that he wanted to kill me and his comrades. The Indians, who did not know that this was put on, were the first to say that the white warrior[10] had lost his mind. I pretended to be very angry with him and asked the Indians for ropes with which to tie him. The chiefs and the warriors asked me to pardon him, since he had drunk too much and was not responsible. They said that this happened to red men too. To make my anger seem even more authentic, I waited until the chief's wife came to me, and I pretended finally to give in to her entreaties through deference to her sex, since I greatly respected women.

I gave the owner of the snake a bottle of brandy with which to drown his sorrow. The Indians have an excessive liking for this liquor, and they become completely mad when they have drunk too much of it. When they have become sober again, they say that they are not to blame for what they said or did; they attribute all their madness to the brandy and believe themselves to be perfectly innocent when they admit that they were out of their minds. If an intoxicated Indian kills another, the death goes unavenged. They take the precaution of not all drinking at the same time. Those who remain sober restrain the others, and the women hide all the arms. We can count brandy as one of the plagues that has decreased the population of the North American Indians. This liquor reduces man to the level of animals and often brings him to his grave. I have frequently seen drunken Indians kill each other with clubs and axes.

I am just about ready to leave Illinois territory. I hope to be in New Orleans in January, 1757. This letter is leaving in a canoe which Monsieur de Macarty is sending off with messages for the Governor.

I am, sir, . . .

Illinois territory
November 10, 1756

[10] This is what they call our soldiers.

LETTER X

To the Marquis de l'Estrade.
The author leaves the Illinois; his trip down the Mississippi;
he camps on an island in the river; his soldiers make him governor of the island.

SIR:

You ask me if the Indians have captains and a king who gov-
erns them. Thanks to the time I have spent among them, I can satisfy
your curiosity. You know that they are divided into tribes or nations,
each of which is governed by a chief or a minor king, who is given
his power by the Great Spirit or the Supreme Being. Although these
chiefs are despotic rulers, their authority is not resented because they
know how to gain love and respect. They have the great satisfaction
of knowing that their subjects consider them demigods, born to make
them happy in this world. The chiefs consider themselves the fathers
of their people and are prouder of this than is the ostentatious Great
Mogul of his pompous titles. As a matter of fact, such great emperors
of Asia are often subject to revolution in their vast states. They are not
even sure of their lives; we have seen their subject kings rise up and
kill them and their families.

The crime of high treason is unknown among the Indians. The
chiefs go everywhere without fear. If anyone were rash enough to try

to kill a chief, the parricide would be punished as a horrible monster, and his entire family would be exterminated without pity.

As for captains or war chiefs who command armies against enemy tribes, they are chosen only after they have given definite proof of their courage in several battles. These captains go naked, like the other warriors, and the scars on their bodies distinguish them from their men and take the place of military commissions.

The old men, who can no longer go off to war, are, nevertheless, still useful to the tribe. They harangue the people, who consider them oracles and heed them. Their advice is taken for everything, and the young people say that since their elders have lived longer, they should have more experience and knowledge. When I admired the happiness enjoyed by the old men, they explained that since they could no longer fight for the tribe, the least they could do was teach others to defend it. Upon returning from their military expeditions, the warriors never fail to throw part of the booty into the cabins of these elderly orators, who by their exhortations excite the younger men to deeds of courage. The prisoners of war are given as slaves to the oldest members of the tribe. The old warriors, who can no longer go to war, harangue the fighters. An orator begins by hitting a post with his club and then mentions all the great deeds he has done in battle and tells of the number of scalps he has taken from the various tribes. The audience replies with shouts of, "How! How!" which means, "True! True!" The Indians hate lies; they say that anyone who lies is a braggart and is not a real man.

The old orator speaks: "If I were younger and more vigorous, you would see me lead you on the tips of my toes against the enemy, as I used to in days gone by. Leave like brave men, my comrades, be lionhearted,[1] keep your ears open, sleep like hares, be as speedy as the deer, do not fear the cold, take to the water like a duck; if you are followed, hide your tracks well. Above all, do not fear the arrows of the enemy. Show that you are true warriors and men. When you have

1 This figure of speech is obviously the author's invention.—Ed.

the chance, use all your arrows against the enemy, then use your tomahawks; strike, kill until they are all dead. It is better to die fighting than to be taken and burned at the stake."

When the harangue is finished, the old warrior hands the peace pipe to the *Tacha-Mingo,* the general or war chief, and to all the officers, who smoke in turn according to rank. All those who are going to battle for the first time enlist by coming up to smoke. They do a war dance and then pass around dog meat, which is, as I have already said, the principal food of the warriors.

Monsieur du Tissenet told me what happened to his father, one of the first officers to come to Louisiana with Monsieur de Bienville. While Monsieur du Tissenet was visiting an Indian tribe with some traders,[2] the natives wanted to scalp them. In his travels, Tissenet had learned the language of these Indians and, therefore, understood their discussion. He pulled off his wig, threw it on the ground, and said to the Indians, "Do you want my scalp? Pick it up if you dare." The astonishment of these people is indescribable. They were even more petrified because his head had been shaved the evening before. Monsieur du Tissenet then told them that they were wrong in wanting to hurt him, that he had come to be their friend, and that if they insisted on acting in this way, he would burn the water of the lakes and the rivers so that they could not sail on them and would set fire to the forest. He poured some brandy out of a little barrel into a dish and lit it with a match. The Indians, who were not yet familiar with brandy, were amazed. He then took a magnifying glass from his pocket and with the aid of the sun set fire to a rotten tree. These people actually believed that the officer had the power to burn the rivers and the forests. They caressed him, showered him with presents, and sent him off with an escort to protect him from harm. From that time on, Monsieur de Bienville used Monsieur du Tissenet as his agent in making treaties with the Indians.

Monsieur du Tissenet's adventure brings to mind the one ex-

[2] Those who trade European merchandise for furs.

perienced by an Italian in Fort Louis, in Illinois territory, when it was commanded by Monsieur Tonty. The Italian left the post and traveled overland to join La Salle, to whom he could have been very useful, if he had arrived on time, in pointing out the route to take to get to the Mississippi. The Italian, too, saved his life by using a rather peculiar trick. When some Indians wanted to kill him, he told them that they were wrong to want to do this to a man who carried them all in his heart. This statement astonished the Indians. He assured them that he would prove what he had said, if they would give him until the next day. If he lied to them, they could do whatever they wished with him. He obtained this day of grace without any difficulty. Then he put a little mirror on his chest and went back to the Indians, who were very surprised to see themselves, as they thought, in the heart of this man. They spared his life.

When the expedition which Monsieur Aubri had brought up-river was ready to return to the capital, I took command of it. Monsieur de Macarty put me in charge of delivering to New Orleans the English prisoners taken by the Chevalier de Villiers and Papapé-changouhia. I hurried to get to the capital before the onrush of ice, which breaks loose from the northern rivers and flows south with the current. I would have run the risk of being stopped by the ice if I had not made everyone row as hard as possible. I used the English prisoners to relieve my soldiers. Since on such occasions everyone has an equal right to life, the officers too lent a hand to encourage the crew.

There are no rocks in the Mississippi past those at Prud'homme,[3] so that when there are several boats, they are tied together and can drift with the current day and night. There is just one man at the rudder and another forward in each boat to watch out for drift wood. It is a pleasure to go down this beautiful river. The distance covered

---

[3] These rocks form the banks of the Mississippi and are as steep as a wall five hundred feet high. Fort Prud'homme used to be on this site. It was named after one of La Salle's traveling companions who had died there.

in three and one-half months going upriver is done in ten or twelve days going in the other direction when the water is high.

I should remember to tell you that it is the custom on these trips, at daybreak of January 1, for the soldiers to wish the commander and the other officers a happy New Year. The men receive some brandy in return. On New Year's Day we were camped on an island about two leagues in circumference, located in a branch of the Mississippi, down which we were sailing. This island was covered with very tall trees. A Gascon soldier, who was as facetious as are all the people of his nation, insinuated to his comrades that they might get an increased New Year's gift if they would perform the ceremony of receiving me as governor of the island. The sergeant approved this amusing idea and gave the necessary orders for carrying it out. He began by carving my name in the bark of a tree and having the troops charge the swivel guns with powder. They then took up their arms. The drum rolled, and the sergeant, as master of ceremonies, removed his hat and proclaimed, "In the name of the King, all you cats, bears, wolves, buffalo, deer, and other animals of this island shall recognize our commander as your governor, and you shall obey and serve him as he commands you." Then a soldier fired the boats' swivel guns, which were accompanied by a general musket salvo. The sudden noise of the artillery alarmed the buffalo, who jumped into the river and swam to the mainland. The soldiers followed in canoes and killed four of them as well as two deer which were quite close to the opposite bank. They presented these to me as my lordly right. We had to stay there for a while so that we could dry the meat, which we were to use on the rest of the trip. To get into the spirit of the fun of the soldiers, whom I was careful to reward, I began to explore the interior of the island I governed. I had hardly gone half a league when I ran into a bear which was peacefully eating acorns under a large oak. I fired at him, but the bullet entered only as far as the fatty layer of this very large animal. As soon as he felt that he was wounded, he tried to rush at me, but he was much too fat to be able to run. I pre-

117

tended that I was trying to escape from him and drew him toward the huts built by my soldiers. He was soon surrounded and treated as a traitor and a rebel. They held a court-martial at which the sergeant presided. The opinion of the corporal, who acted as king's attorney, was that they crush the bear's head in order not to spoil the fur of this subject who had revolted against his lord. This sentence was carried out immediately. After that he was skinned, and I shall keep the black fur just as Hercules kept the skin of the Nemean lion which he killed.

The soldiers rendered the fat, from which they got more than 120 pots of grease.[4] You know, sir, that the bear leaves its lair just as soon as the fruit begins to ripen. He does not go back until it is all gone and stays there until there is a new crop of fruit. During this interval he does not eat or drink. His fat is the only thing he eats, which he does by sucking his paws. It is dangerous to meet a bear when he is thin and one is traveling alone. The Indians consider bear skins valuable for trading purposes and find its paws and tongue delicious when smoked. They have often served these to me, and I have found them quite good.

I am sending this letter to Monsieur d'Arragory, the French naval agent at Campeche, who will forward it to Cádiz. It will reach you more surely from there than if I sent it by one of our ships, since Spain is not at war with England. I am not sending a duplicate of this letter. Besides, I hope to leave for Europe next April. I am, sir, . . .

New Orleans
February 25, 1757

[4] Bear grease is very good to eat. In Louisiana, it is used in the preparation of salads, fried foods, and sauces. It is considered even better than lard!

Letter XI

To the Marquis de l'Estrade.
   The author leaves for Europe; he fights an English privateer;
he embarks at Cap François on one of a fleet of twenty-six merchant ships, almost all of which he saw captured by privateers;
the capture of a small enemy ship; his arrival at Brest.

Sir:
   Since I could not find a ship going to France, I had to take the
brigantine *Union*, fitted out for war. It was commanded by Captain
Gaujean, famous for having captured five English ships since the beginning of the war on his way from France to Louisiana.
   On April 1, 1757, we set sail from Balize for Cap François. On
May 20,[1] within sight of Turks Island,[2] we saw what we supposed
was an enemy ship. It chased us during the night, and since it was a
good sailing ship, it caught up with us in three hours. The English
privateer greeted us with a cannon shot and, at the same time, shouted
out for us to surrender to the King of England. We answered him
with a broadside and a volley of musket fire. Then I shouted to him
through a megaphone to strike his colors for the King of France or
we would sink him. The English privateer, realizing that he was

---

   [1] This date is obviously incorrect, since it would not have taken one month and
twenty days to get from New Orleans to Haiti. The author probably meant April 20.
—Ed.
   [2] A small island in the Bahamas, north of Haiti.—Ed.

dealing with an armed ship, took off among the reefs and rocks near Turks Island hoping we would draw near and run aground. But our prudent captain, who was a good sailor, saw through the scheme and, instead of following the privateer, headed for his destination. We arrived at the port of Cap François on May 1. There we found Monsieur de Beaufremont's squadron, which was to go to Canada's aid. It had brought Monsieur de Bart, the King's governor and lieutenant general of Santo Domingo. The first thing I did upon landing was to pay him my respects. Always ready to help unfortunate officers, he arranged for me to sail four days later. This saved me the expense of having to stay on the island. He obtained passage for me at the King's expense on one of a fleet of twenty-six merchant ships which left for France. Monsieur de Beaufremont escorted them up to the Caicos Islands,[3] where he left them to go on to his destination as ordered by the Court.

I should tell you, sir, that I carefully chose a ship from Bordeaux, commanded by Captain Odouoir and called the *Soleil* (imitating the Indians who worship the sun as though it were a god). Events proved that I had chosen well, since the twenty-six ships which made up this fleet were almost all captured before my very eyes. The *Soleil* was the first of only four ships to get to France. It made the crossing to Brest in forty-four days, after having captured an English ship at the banks of Newfoundland. I landed at Brest June 15, 1757, and went immediately to pay my respects to Count du Guai, the port's naval commander. I then went to see Monsieur Hocquart, state counselor and the department's naval intendant. I informed him of the death of Monsieur d'Auberville, who had temporarily replaced Monsieur Michel de Rouvillière as commissioner general of the navy and procurer of supplies for Louisiana. Monsieur Hocquart was known for his integrity when he was intendant of New France. It is a fact that he came back forty thousand pounds in debt. The King, pleased with Hocquart's service, has given him this sum as a present. This is an

[3] In the Bahamas, north of Haiti.—Ed.

excellent example for his successor, Monsieur Bigot. If Hocquart did not bring back a fortune, he at least had the satisfaction of knowing that he was considered one of the most gallant men of his rank. All the Canadians and even the Indians, who, as I have said, respect virtue, were sorry to see him go.

When I admitted to this intendant that I did not have enough money to get to the Court, he was kind enough to have Monsieur Gaucher, clerk of the colonial treasurer general, give me some. In addition, he has invited me to take my meals at his home during my stay in this city. I intend to leave the twenty-second of this month.

You will perhaps be surprised to learn, sir, that in eight months time I have seen two winters, two summers, and two springs. Here is the explanation. I informed you that I had left Illinois territory at the end of December, 1756, when the Mississippi began to freeze. After my trip down the river, I arrived in New Orleans in January, 1757, and found a climate similar to that of Hyères, where our regiment was stationed in 1744. It was gardening time. I left Louisiana April 1, 1757, for Cap François, where I arrived May 1. It was like summer there. On the fourth, I left for Europe and found spring once again in the Bahama channels. Arriving at the great banks of Newfoundland, we saw, at sunrise of the twenty-second, a mountain of floating ice, which we took for a sail at first, but we knew from the coldness of the air that it was a block of ice which had broken loose from the Arctic Sea. On June 15, 1757, we arrived at Brest, where we found summer once again. This is rather extraordinary. I am, sir, . . .

Brest
June 18, 1757

Letter XII

To the Marquis de l'Estrade.
The author arrives at the Court, receives a gift from the King, and is ordered to go to Rochefort; he sets sail for Louisiana.

Sir:

Here I am at Rochefort again, the city from which I sailed to Louisiana eight years ago. I have just come back from the Court, where I presented to Monsieur de Moras, controller general and naval minister, the letter from the Governor explaining the reasons for my trip. He was kind enough to speak to me in his office in the presence of Monsieur de la Porte, chief of the Colonial Bureau. He questioned me about the present condition of Louisiana. I assured the Minister that I had left all the nations that I had visited on that vast continent kindly disposed toward us and that the Cherokees had come to make peace with the French. He also asked me if I thought the colony was vulnerable to attack. I answered that it did not appear that the English were thinking of attacking because of the difficulty of getting past Fort Balize and into the interior. Finally, I told him that the country needed no fortifications other than those provided by nature.

Monsieur de Moras had the King grant me a sum of one thousand pounds so that I could take the waters that I needed to regain my health. After that, His Majesty ordered me to return to Louisiana and resume my duties there. I came here immediately, and we intend to set sail as soon as the Cape Breton convoy is ready.

Monsieur Druis Imbuto, naval intendant, has succeeded Monsieur le Normant de Mési. The King could not have chosen a better man for this position insofar as ability and integrity as well as zeal for the King's interests are concerned. The Intendant has advanced me the same sum as did his predecessor seven years ago.

I am, sir, . . .

Rochefort
September 12, 1757

Letter XIII

To the Marquis de l'Estrade.

The author leaves Rochefort; Monsieur de Place captures three English merchant ships; he burns one and sinks another; he stops at the island of Grenada; sailing off Jamaica.

Sir:

I wrote you from Rochefort that we intended to leave December, 1757; but because part of the convoy sent to the aid of Cape Breton was taken by the English fleet, another had to be rigged. We were delayed until May because a fleet of ten large English ships was causing a great deal of alarm along the Aunis coast. We set sail on May 10, after the enemy ships had disappeared.

I was aboard the King's store ship *Fortune* with Monsieur de Rochemore, commissioner general of the navy and financial director of the province of Louisiana. Captain de Place was in command of our convoy ship, the *Eopalme,* a frigate carrying cannon. On our way, we came across three English ships and took them with only three cannon shots. Monsieur de Place burned one and sank another after having removed the men and the cargo. The third came from the Guinea coast, was richly laden, and carried aboard 440 Negroes, part of whom were sold in Grenada. The Baron de Bonvoust, the newly appointed governor, overwhelmed us with his kindness and generosity during our stay on the island, where we remained until July

22. We then set sail for Louisiana, staying close to Jamaica to avoid large enemy ships, which never take that route. We went that way in order to fool the *Spy*, and on August 20, we arrived safely at the mouth of the Mississippi.

Monsieur de Rochemore,[1] the extremely honest and zealous financial director for the King, will have a great deal of difficulty in correcting the abuses which have multiplied in this colony since the war. During our crossing, I warned him of the administrative trouble he would have. Everything that I predicted happened, and the very ships that brought us to Louisiana carried, on their return, a request that the Court remove him from office.

I had hardly arrived at New Orleans when the Governor notified me that I was to prepare to go with a detachment to the Alabama Indians, a tribe which lived about 250 leagues from the capital. I am taking advantage of the fact that some royal ships are leaving at the end of the year to send you this letter, which I am writing in duplicate. If one ship is taken, the other may arrive. As soon as I learn about the way of life of the people I am going to visit east of New Orleans, I shall describe them and their country, which is said to be very fine and beautiful.

New Orleans
November 10, 1758

[1] The brother of Commodore de Rochemore.

Letter XIV

To the Marquis de l'Estrade.
The author leaves New Orleans for the Alabama territory; sailing on Lake Pontchartrain; a short description of Mobile.

Sir:

On December 14, I left New Orleans for Alabama country, by Monsieur de Kerlérec's order. I sailed from Bayou St. Jean, a little port on Lake Pontchartrain. There is a portage of about a quarter of a league from New Orleans to this bayou,[1] which is about two leagues long. The winds were favorable, and on December 20, I arrived at the bay and the port of Mobile, fifty leagues from the capital.

Mobile was formerly the most important settlement in Louisiana. It was the home of the governor, the financial director, and the general staff, and the meeting place of the upper council.

There is a rather good fort, which can resist an army of Indians, but would not be able to hold out very long against Europeans. This fort is situated on a bay which rises and falls with the tides and is between two rivers. The smaller one is called the Choctaw; the other, wider than the Seine at Rouen, is the Mobile, whose source is in the Appalachian Mountains. This river is the meeting place of all the eastern Indians. They come here each year to receive the presents

[1] A small estuary.

126

which the governor gives them on behalf of the King. Although the soil in the Mobile region is composed of thick sand, cattle thrive and the herds are growing larger. The industrious inhabitants trade with the Spaniards, who come from the presidio of Pensacola nearby to get salt beef, fowl, corn, rice, and other staples. The inhabitants of Mobile are also in the tar business. As for the fur trade, it is entirely in the hands of the officers, contrary to the King's wishes.

At this post, there are white laurels and red ones, wild cherry trees, and both white and red cedars. The latter are made into beautiful inlaid work, keep insects away with their odor, and do not rot. In the forests there are several kinds of trees which are unknown in Europe and others which contain a gum similar to turpentine. There are cypress trees of such large dimensions that out of a single trunk the Indians can make a canoe holding sixty men.

Here is how the Indians built their boats before the arrival of the French in Louisiana. The great number of rivers in this vast region move so rapidly that they uproot the trees on their banks. The Indians measured these trees until they found the one which was the right size for their purpose. They set it afire, and as the tree burned, they would scrape away the embers with a flint or an arrow. When the tree was sufficiently hollowed, they would set it afloat. The Indians handle these small boats with a great deal of skill on the lakes and the rivers. They use them in war and for transporting the furs and the smoked meat they bring back from the hunt.

Their tools and their weapons were made in the following manner. They cut a slit in a sapling with a razor-sharp flint or pebble; into this incision, they fitted a stone cut into the shape of an ax. As the tree grew, the stone became so firmly fixed it could not be removed from the young tree. The sapling was then cut down when they needed it. Their lances and darts were made in the same way. They had clubs of very hard wood.

For agricultural instruments, they used animal bones or spades made of hardwood. The soil is extremely fertile everywhere in America. When the tall, thick grass is dried by the frost in the winter, the Indians burn it. Then they dig up the ground with their spades and sow it. Three months later they harvest their crop, which consists of corn, millet, beans and other vegetables, potatoes, pistachios, and watermelons. Pumpkins, which the French inhabitants call *giromonds,* are very common too.

The kitchen utensils were earthenware plates and pots and wooden dishes. Cups were made of calabashes, and spoons, called *micouenes,* were fashioned from buffalo horns, split in two and shaped over a fire.

As soon as we shall have gathered up enough supplies for our trip and for the garrison at the Alabama fort, Monsieur Aubert and I shall leave in a boat manned by soldiers and Mobile Indians, whom we have hired to do the rowing. Although Monsieur Aubert is assistant adjutant at Mobile, Monsieur de Kerlérec has appointed him commander of Fort Toulouse in Alabama territory. This is against the King's order forbidding adjutants and assistant adjutants to serve any place but at their assigned stations.

If a ship arrives from Europe, perhaps I shall receive some letters from you. Monsieur de Velle, who is in command here, will be kind enough to send them on to me with the first convoy. I am, sir, . . .

Mobile
January 6, 1759

Letter XV

To the Marquis de l'Estrade.
The author leaves Mobile for the land of the Alabamas; detailed description of the customs of these people; the punishing of adultery.

Sir:

I have arrived at Fort Toulouse in Alabama territory. The journey took me fifty days because I set out during the rainy season. There were times when I saw the Alabama River rise twelve to fifteen feet above normal. This sudden flood was caused by storms, which are frequent in this country, and the high mountains on the sides of the river. Because we had to fight against the rapid current, there were days when we traveled only one league. Sails are useless because of the woods, the mountains, and the winding of the river. We had to land frequently and travel close to the river's edge. One day my boat was snagged by a submerged tree;[1] night came and we had to wait until morning. Since the river rises and falls suddenly, depending upon the storms, I found myself and my boat stuck on the tree, high and dry in the air. I should tell you that we were only twenty-five leagues from the mouth of the river, and I was assured by the Indians

---

[1] There are cypress trees along the river which are so big that ten men can hardly put their arms around them. This is evidence that the soil is among the most fertile in the world.

from Mobile who were with me that there was nothing to worry about. All we had to do was wait for the tide to rise. That is exactly what happened. The river, which empties into the Bay of Mobile, rose with the tide and set the boat afloat. You can see, sir, by this story that there is a great deal of difference between American and European rivers.

Monsieur Aubert became ill during the trip, and I persuaded him to stay at Mobile to regain his health. He came here later on horseback through very sparse pine forests. According to the Governor's orders, Monsieur de Montberaut[2] is to instruct Aubert in three months of all there is to know about the country. After that period of time, Aubert is to take over command of the post. Monsieur de Montberaut is greatly respected by the Indians of this region and is called a man of valor, or a hero. He is well known for the clever speeches he has made to the Indians in their own style. Because of trouble with the Jesuits, this officer asked to be recalled. His successor is Monsieur Aubert, the brother of the Jesuit missionary to Louisiana, Father Aubert. Monsieur de Montberaut is the avowed enemy of these missionaries. When Father LeRoi was in the Alabama territory, he wrote a letter to the Governor condemning Montberaut, but the military messenger delivered it to the Commanding Officer instead. Monsieur de Montberaut later saw the Jesuit, who was extremely obsequious. These good fathers find this procedure to be quite politic. The Commanding Officer asked the missionary if he had not written a letter condemning him. The Jesuit, not knowing that Monsieur de Montberaut had intercepted the letter, swore on all that is holy that he had not. Then Father LeRoi was called a sneak and a liar by Montberaut, who showed him the letter and posted it on the gate of the fort, where a guard watched over it. Since then, as long as Monsieur de Montberaut has been here, there has not been a Jesuit missionary among the Alabama Indians.

I am now going to speak once more of the Louisiana Indians,

[2] He is the brother of Count de Montaut, a member of the Dauphin's entourage.

this time of the Alabamas, Outachepas, Tonikas, Cowetas, Abihkas, Talapoosas, Conshacs, and Pakanas, all of whom have very much the same customs and live along the rivers. Together, these tribes of tall men have about four thousand warriors. These Indians and their beautiful wives are very friendly. Upon landing among them, you are greeted with a handshake and the peace pipe. After you have smoked, they ask you the reason for your trip, the length of time you have been traveling, if you intend to stay for a long time, and whether you have a wife and children.[3] They also ask about the war in Canada and inquire about their father, the King. They then bring mush made of pounded corn, often boiled with venison, bread made of the same flour and baked in hot ashes, roasted turkeys, grilled venison, and dough fried in nut oil. They also serve chestnuts in season, cooked in bear grease, deer tongue, and both hen and turtle eggs.

The soil of lower Louisiana is similar to that of Egypt after the flooding of the Nile. This soil is excellent, especially in the territory occupied by the Indians about whom I have been telling you. Everything that is planted here comes up abundantly. The melons are extraordinarily large, succulent, and plentiful. The watermelons are so delicious that they are given to the sick to quench the thirst brought on by fever, and the pumpkins are more delicate in flavor than ours. There are large quantities of potatoes, a type of earth apple greatly appreciated by Europeans, which taste very much like chestnuts cooked in hot ashes.

These Indians generally have just one wife, of whom they are very jealous. When an unmarried brave passes through a village, he hires a girl for a night or two, as he pleases, and her parents find nothing wrong with this. They are not at all worried about their

---

[3] It is customary among the Indians to offer you their girls. In the morning, the chiefs address the village in these terms: "Young men, warriors, be wise, love the Master of Life, go hunting for the French, who bring us what we need. You girls, do not be hard or ungrateful. Offer your bodies to the white warriors so that we can have children of their blood. Through such an alliance, we shall have their intelligence, and we shall be feared by our enemies."

daughter and explain that her body is hers to do with as she wishes. The Indian girls do not abuse their freedom, since they find it to their interest to appear modest if they want to be sought in marriage. The married women, however, say that they sell their freedom when they become wives and must be faithful to their husbands. The men reserve the right to have several women and are free to leave their wives, although that happens rarely. If a woman is found guilty of adultery, the least that can happen to her is that she will be repudiated. Her husband leaves the cabin; if there are children, he takes the sons with him, leaving the daughters with his wife. The woman must remain unmarried for one year, but the man can take another wife immediately. The husband may take the same wife again; that is the reason she must wait one year before remarrying.

Marriage among the Indians, as I have already said, is completely natural and takes no form other than the mutual agreement of the parties involved. The future groom gives gifts of furs and food to his bride's family. After the presents have been accepted, there is a feast to which the entire village is invited. When the meal is over, the guests dance and sing of the battle exploits of the groom's ancestors. The next day, the oldest man in the village presents the bride to her husband's parents. That is the entire marriage ceremony. All the Indians trace their ancestry from their mother's family, since they are sure that they are her children but cannot be certain of their male parent. The good hunters and warriors choose the prettiest girls; the others take the rejected and the ugly ones. The girls, knowing that they will not be free in matters of the heart once they are married, try to make the best match possible. Once they have husbands, there are no more love affairs. The woman's job in the household is to prepare meals, dress skins, make shoes, spin buffalo wool, and weave little baskets, a job at which Indian women are quite skillful.

This is how a wife's infidelity is punished. First of all, the husband must witness with his own eyes his wife's misbehavior. Then both her husband's relatives and her own spy upon her. Even if her husband should want to keep her, he cannot, since the Indians believe that a real man would consider it beneath his dignity to live with a woman who has betrayed him. When a woman is guilty of adultery, her husband presents his case to the chief, who orders some of his people to go out secretly and cut switches. Everyone—men, women, boys, and girls—is then forced to attend a dance. Those who fail to come are fined, but as a rule no one is absent. At the height of the dance, the adulteress is thrown to the ground and she is mercilessly beaten on her back and her stomach. Her seducer is given the same treatment.

When the two unfortunates have been sufficiently whipped, a relative of each places a stick between the guilty couple and those punishing them. The whipping stops immediately, but the woman's punishment is not yet finished. Her husband then shaves off her hair[4] and reproaches her for her conduct before the entire assembly. He tells her that she was wrong to act as she did, since he had always given her everything she needed, but now that things have turned out this way, she can go off with her lover. His braids are cut off too. These Indians usually wear their hair parted in the middle, with braids hanging on each side of their forehead. Then the lover is told, as the adulteress is pointed to, "There is your wife." He is free to marry her immediately, but they must leave the village.

When a woman seduces someone else's husband, the women gather, carrying sticks as long as their arms. They find the guilty woman and beat her mercilessly, much to the amusement of the young men, who finally snatch the sticks away from the women to keep them from killing the poor wretch.

The only arts that interest the Indians are medicine, war, hunting, and fishing. Their children, who are raised with great severity, are forced to go swimming at dawn in the wintertime. Then they present themselves to the war chief, who tells them that they must never be afraid of the water and that if they are pursued by the enemy

[4] Indian women wear their hair in big braids, German fashion.

133

and captured, they may be burned alive at the stake. They must then prove that they are true men by not crying out.[5]

When the chief is finished speaking, he cuts scars on their thighs, chests, and backs to inure them to pain. He then whips them with leather straps.[6] After this initiation, they take their places among the warriors. When they have done something outstanding in battle, they are tattooed, as I have already explained in the article on the Illinois.

Nursing children are bathed in cold water in the winter. When they grow up, they sleep on the ground. The Indians accustom their children to hardship early in life, because they love them. They say that habit becomes second nature. It is true that their naked bodies are no more sensitive to the cold than are their hands and faces.

The old men, who cannot follow the tribe in case of retreat, ask to be beaten to death with clubs in order to be spared the hardship of senility. They also fear falling into the hands of the enemy and being burned alive or eaten. In their wars, the Indians massacre men, women, and even children still at their mothers' breasts. This and smallpox, an epidemic disease among the Indians, are two of the causes of the decrease in population in America.

In passing, I should point out to you, sir, that when a son takes the life of his father, it is really an act of humanity, for reasons which I have already explained. The Indians have a great deal of esteem for their elders, whom they treat with great care, and act only with their advice and consent. I have often noticed that when the Indians return from hunting, the chiefs carefully set aside the old men's share, which is used also for widows and orphans whose fathers have been killed in battle defending the tribe. The Indians are very hospitable toward strangers with whom they are at peace and are kind to their allies and friends, but they are cruel and unmerciful to their enemies. They are

---

[5] Indians must bear pain heroically so that their bravery will set an example for posterity.

[6] They are three fingers wide. The Indians carry their bundles with these straps when they are traveling.

surprised and even scandalized to see Englishmen, who have come to New Orleans presumably to negotiate the exchange of prisoners,[7] carrying on business affairs and wandering about in our settlements. Shortly after his return from New Orleans, a native chief told me that he was tempted to bash in the heads of these English dogs to avenge the Frenchmen they had killed up north during the siege of Quebec. He added that the Indians spoke to their enemies only with the tomahawk and the murderous ax. This means that once war is declared, you speak to the enemy only by beating him on the head. There is no communication with him, either direct or indirect, for any reason whatsoever. Anyone who disregards this is considered a traitor and is treated accordingly.

When peace is made, they bury the ax, or the war club, as a sign to their enemies that all hatred is buried, that all the horror and the destruction of war are finished, and that friendship and harmony between them and their neighbors will flourish again like the flowers of the tree of peace, the white laurel. This tree will spread its branches over the white land, which is what the Indians call a land that is at peace.

The chief of whom I spoke, Tamathlemingo, is very devoted to the French. I know that when the English tried to shower presents on him, he refused to accept them and even threatened to break their heads for proposing such a thing. He told the English representatives that he did not want anything from the dogs, who were the enemies of his father, the King of France. It would be fine for us if all the chiefs thought like this noble Indian. He has been awarded a silver medal, which he wears on a leather strap around his neck. He has

---

[7] There are ships which bring prisoners of war to be exchanged. When there are no prisoners, these ships are seized for carrying spies, whose mission it is to gather information about our forces. This is exactly what happened in the case of the English captain, Bouls, who caused so much trouble during his two visits to this colony.

This trade can only be to our disadvantage and to the enemy's advantage. To get furs, we employ Indians, who could be put to better use. These furs are publicly loaded into English ships, which, contrary to law, are certainly used to gain information about our positions.

told me several times that he would like to be buried with this image of his father, the King, which he wears on his heart. Since he has always been faithful to the King, he would like to shake his hand in the spirit land, where he hopes to meet him one day. After the worthy chief had expressed these noble, heartfelt sentiments, I gave him a bottle of brandy to drink the King's health and mine. Some times a small act of generosity has a great effect on these people. When I have wanted to express my friendship, for example, I have removed my shirt and given it to them in the name of their father, who felt sorry for them upon learning from the "talking paper" that his children were naked. This type of gesture touches them deeply.

These people generally have no idea of the political system prevalent among European powers. According to the Indians, the friends of a European nation must take its side in war and must have no dealings with its enemy. I had a long and serious conference with an *allekxi mingo*, a magician and district chief, who claims to have been abused by Spanish soldiers from the presidio of Pensacola. This chief told me quite frankly that he had formed a plan to avenge himself. He and his warriors wanted to invade Florida up to the gates of Fort Pensacola. He thought that he would gain my approval of the plan by assuring me that he was doing this in part because the Spaniards "lie on their mats" (they are at peace with the English) and receive the English in Spanish ports.

I answered this Alabama chief in the strongest terms possible to discourage him from carrying out his plan to shed the blood of the Spaniards, our allies and neighbors. I spoke to the Chief in the manner of his nation.

"*Allekxi Mingo*, prepare your heart, open your ears so that you may hear the strength of my words. They will help you get back the sense which you have lost today.

"I tell you that the great sovereign chief of the Spaniards, who lives beyond the great salt lake, in the old world where there are many men, is the brother[8] of the red men's father, the King of France. I must, therefore, say that I strongly disapprove of your daring plan.

"I declare loudly that if you still insist on carrying it out, you must begin by breaking my head."

The Chief replied, "Your blood is as dear to me as mine. Besides, the French have never harmed me. I am even ready to sacrifice myself for them. You can assure my father of this. I wish I had 'talking paper' like you so I could send him my words. No, I wish rather that my heart had one hundred mouths so that he could hear me."[9]

After this declaration of friendship, the Chief gave me his peace pipe. I took a puff, returned the pipe to him, and thus made peace between him and the Spaniards, who had presumably offended him. To put the final seal on the transaction, I said to him, "Here is a bottle of firewater. Purify your mouth with it so that it will utter no more evil words against our Spanish allies." To strengthen the effect of my words, I added a roll of tobacco which the warriors were to smoke in the calumet. When I had finished my speech, all the young men came one after the other to shake my hand in the traditional sign of friendship.

I still wanted to satisfy completely this regional chief, who had claimed to be angry with the Spaniards for being at peace with the English and for receiving at Pensacola ships which came to spy on our coastal positions. It is true that such suspicion should be taken seriously; where there is smoke there is fire.

To appease this Indian, I told him that the Governor was expecting the arrival of a big canoe any day. Speaking in the manner of the Indians, I added that this ship would bring a "talking paper" from the great chief of the Spaniards, ordering them to dig up the war

[8] The Indians call their allies "brothers."

[9] Some time after my departure, the Indians of this region killed several Englishmen who had ventured within two leagues of Fort Toulouse, commanded at that time by Monsieur de Grand-Maison, who is now a major in New Orleans.

hatchet and to club the blond men to death. The Indians call the English "blond men" to distinguish them from the French and Spanish.

The Chief seemed satisfied with what I had said. Since he had drunk a little brandy and was in a talkative mood, I questioned him about his hatred of the Spaniards in Florida. He told me that tradition had it that the first fire warriors[10] to come through these lands had been guilty of hostile acts and had disregarded the rights of the natives. From that time on, it had been recommended from father to son that vengeance be sought for this uncalled for shedding of blood. My answer to this chief medicine man was that the Master of Life had avenged them through the death of Ferdinand de Soto and almost all his warriors.

I added that the Indians should not be bitter against modern Spaniards and that Philip II, their great chief who was ruler at that time, had denounced all the evil committed by his captains, against his will, in these far-off lands. I told this American prince a story about Don Francisco de Toledo, the viceroy of Peru, who hanged publicly the heir to the Inca throne and had all the royal princes massacred. He did not even spare the Spaniards who, through their mothers, were descended from Atahualpa. After his expedition, Don Francisco de Toledo expected to receive the greatest honors upon his return to Spain, but he was very badly received by the great chief of the nation, who ordered him in an angry tone to get out of his sight. The King said to him, "I did not appoint you executioner of kings. You were to serve me by helping the unfortunate." These words left the Viceroy thunderstruck, and he died of a heart attack several days later. The same king caused the death of a minister who had taken advantage of him, with the single word *houlabe*, which in the Indian language means "You lie."

---

[10] In 1544, Ferdinand de Soto came through this territory. The Indians, who had never before seen Europeans, called the Spaniards "fire warriors" because they were armed with rifles and pistols. The natives said that the cannon was thunder that caused the earth to tremble and killed men from a great distance.

The Chief answered gravely, "But if this great chief of the men of fire was as angry as you claim with the viceroy because of his cruel actions, which were contrary to orders, why did not the chief have him burned at the stake?[11] Why was not his head cut off and sent to Peru? This example of severity and justice would have, to a certain extent, satisfied the people whom the viceroy had so greatly mistreated when he hanged, like a thief, the heir to a great empire. The Inca prince was responsible only to the Master of Life, the Supreme Being. This is how we red men, called savages and barbarians by the Europeans, treat evil murderers who deserve no more consideration than the wild animals of our forests."

I answered the Chief again. "You must know that the great chiefs of the white men, who live in the old country, are absolute and that they chase from their presence captains who have mistreated their children and subjects. This affront is a thousand times more cruel for these proud captains, hated by God for their misdeeds, than being burned at the stake or having red men beat them on the head one hundred times with clubs."

I finally appeased the hatred of these people for the Spaniards, and I assume that everything is calm now. My explanations satisfied the Chief.

I think I have already mentioned to you, sir, that the Indians are very sensitive and are easily insulted. It is when they are drunk that they usually remember those who have insulted them. I have often acted as mediator between two Indians. I have told them that they should live like brothers, forget the past, and use their courage only in defense of our common country. I have assured them that if they did not listen to me, the Great Spirit would be angry with them and would ruin their corn crop.

When the men were ready to come to blows, the women would come quickly and ask me to arbitrate. I did all that I could to reconcile the two parties and made sure that no one's honor was at stake.

[11] A punishment meted out to prisoners of war who are guilty of cruelty.

This pleased these pretty women, who are not at all wild despite their reputation. In the New World, as in the Old, the fair sex is made to bear children and not to destroy.

There is so much to be said about the customs of these people that I shall have to save for another letter a description of their mourning habits and the manner in which they bury the dead.

I am, sir, . . .

Alabama territory
April 28, 1759

LETTER XVI

To the Marquis de l'Estrade.

Mourning and burial customs among the Alabamas; the Chevalier d'Erneville demands justice for a soldier killed by a young Indian; the religion of the Alabamas; the tricks used to catch deer and turkeys.

Sir:

A letter received the day before yesterday informs me that you are in good health and that you have not forgotten me. In my last letter to you I spoke of marriage among the Indians. Now I am going to tell you of their mourning customs. When a great chief of the nation dies, the people show their grief by remaining unkempt and unbathed and by giving up all entertainment. The men smear their bodies with a mixture of soot and bear grease. When a woman loses her husband, she dons mourning clothes for one year and wears no ornaments.

The Alabama Indians drink cassina;[1] this is made of the small serrated leaves of a very dense bush. The Indians roast them just as we roast coffee and drink the brew with a great deal of ceremony. When this diuretic drink is ready, the young men serve it in calabash cups to chiefs and warriors, according to rank. The same order of rank is observed in smoking the calumet. While you drink, the young men

[1] This was also called the "black drink" and was made from the yaubon plant. —Ed.

141

set up a loud howl, which they diminish gradually. When you stop drinking, they take time to catch their breath, but they begin to howl again just as soon as you start drinking. This type of orgy sometimes lasts from six in the morning until two in the afternoon. These Indians are in no way incapacitated by this drink, to which they attribute many virtues. They vomit it up without any effort or embarrassment.

The women never drink this beverage, which is prepared only for the warriors.

At the assemblies, where cassina is drunk and to which women are never admitted, the Indians announce the latest news and discuss matters of war and peace. The Chevalier d'Erneville, however, reports that the wife of a great chief used to attend these assemblies as a warrior because of her quick and penetrating mind. Sometimes it was her opinion which prevailed in treaty making.

The Alabamas are very fond of the French. There is even an agreement stating that a Frenchman who kills an Indian will be put to death, and an Indian who kills a Frenchman will suffer the same fate. Here is an incident which occurred while the Chevalier d'Erneville was commander among the Alabamas. A young native shot a soldier of the garrison and then escaped. The Commander, not knowing where the murderer was to be found, spoke to the chiefs of the Indian nation and told them that justice had to be done. They answered that the young man had taken refuge with another nation. The Chevalier, not satisfied with this excuse, said that the dead man cried out for vengeance. As the Indians say, blood must be avenged with blood. The murderer's mother had to die in his place. They answered that it was not she who had committed the crime. He replied that he was speaking like the red men, who, when one of their people is killed and justice is not done, seek vengeance on a member of the guilty man's nation. He then reminded them that if good relations between the whites and the red men were to be maintained, criminals must be punished. The chiefs offered him many furs and even horses loaded with booty. The Commander, known for his zeal and his altruism, preferring the King's welfare to his own and the nation's honor to fortune, refused all the presents. He added that he could not rest because his murdered warrior cried out every night, "Avenge my death!" Seeing that they could not move him, these poor people held a council and sent out eight men led by a young war chief. He immediately led his detachment to the murderer's mother and told her that she would have to pay for the Frenchman's death since her son could not be found. The amazed and tearful woman was led away, followed by her sad relatives. When the family saw that there was no hope for a pardon, one of them said to the leader of the troop, "My mother-in-law is dying courageously since she did not commit the crime." He suggested that they wait while he went to find the murderer. He brought the criminal to the assembly where the Chevalier d'Erneville was waiting and said, "Here is the guilty man; do what you wish with him." The Commander replied that it was up to them to see that justice was done. The Indians bashed in his head immediately.[2]

After justice was done, the chiefs made speeches to the young people and advised them to be the friends of the French. They added that any time one of them was mad enough to kill one of our people, he would suffer the same fate.

The Chevalier d'Erneville then spoke to the assembly and gave the tribe a gift sent him by the Governor. The Indians then offered him the peace pipe, which all the French soldiers and settlers smoked as a sign of amnesty. Then they drank cassina, which is the drink of the "white word" or oblivion.

Since that time the tribe has never failed us. In 1714, Alabama Indians offered to build, in their territory and at their own expense,

[2] That is how justice is done among the Indians. It is not necessary to prepare trials. All legal formality is unknown. A murderer must be killed, unless his crime is an accident due to drunkenness, a fit, or participation in games.

Fort Toulouse and asked the French to occupy it. Monsieur de Bienville, who was then governor, took possession of their country in the name of the King.[3]

They have never permitted the English to do so, and laugh at the King of England's threats. Each village chief considers himself a sovereign responsible only to the Master of Life, or the Great Spirit.

The Alabamas call their country the white land, or the land of peace, and they rest on their mats, which means that they attack no one. This is an allegorical way of announcing to all of the earth's nations that the war hatchet is buried and that trade can be carried on safely in Alabama territory.

Here is a speech that I heard delivered to the Alabama chiefs: "Young men and warriors, do not mock the Master of Life; the sky is blue, the sun is spotless, the weather is balmy, the earth is white, and everything on its face is peaceful. Human blood must not be spilled on it. We must ask the Spirit of Peace to prevail in purity and spotlessness among the nations which surround us. We should wage war only against wildcats, bears, wolves, and deer, and we need to support our women and children."

The Americans are generally illiterate. The art of writing is unknown to them, and they are surprised to see that we can speak to each other at great distances with "talking paper." They greatly admire the letters we send. When they are entrusted with letters, they deliver them to the exact address. Despite rainy weather and rivers that have to be crossed, the letters are never wet. The Alabamas trade with the French, the English, and the Spanish, whom they do not like very much. They would rather fight the Spaniards than any other nation because of their cruelty to the Mexican Indians. They

[3] This governor is so well thought of by the Indians that they always mention him in their speeches. His name is so deeply rooted in the hearts of these good people that his memory will always be dear to them. As soon as they saw me, they asked me about him, and I told them that he was well and was living in the great village, Paris. They were very happy when they heard this.

have remarkable memories and never forget the harm that has been done them.

The Indians that I have been talking about worship a Supreme Being that they call "Soulbieche." When I asked them what they thought of the hereafter, they replied that, if they had not taken someone else's wife, stolen, or killed during their lives, after death they would go to a very fertile land where there would be plenty of women and hunting grounds and where everything would be easy for them. If, on the other hand, they had acted foolishly and had disrespected the Great Spirit, they would go to a barren land full of thorns and briars where there would be no hunting and no women. This is all that I have been able to learn about their belief in the hereafter.

The Alabamas bury their dead in a sitting position. In order to justify this custom, they say that man is upright and has his head turned toward heaven, his eventual home, and for this reason they bury their dead in that position. The dead man is given a pipe and tobacco so that he can make peace with the people in the other world. If he was a warrior, he is buried with his arms, consisting of a rifle, powder, bullets, a quiver full of arrows, a bow, a club or a hatchet, a mirror,[4] and some vermilion with which to paint himself in the spirit world.

If a man kills himself either in despair or because of illness, he is considered a coward and is deprived of a grave and thrown into the river.

I have said that Indians are supposed to bear their misfortunes with unflinching heroism. When one of these fanatic people is made a prisoner in battle, he expects to be burned at the stake, and he composes his own death song. "I fear neither death nor fire. Make me suffer. My death will be avenged by my people." This makes the

[4] The young Indians never go out without having a little hatchet or a mirror tied around their wrists.

enemy cut short his agony. Occasionally, he may be adopted by the enemy tribe because of his bravery.

When there is a disturber of public peace among them, the elders speak to him in this way: "You may leave, but remember that if you are killed, you will be disowned by the tribe; we will not mourn you, and we will not avenge your death." These people, like all others, scorn those who lead a dissolute life.[5]

The Indians usually go hunting at the end of October. The Alabamas travel sixty, eighty, and even one hundred leagues from their village, and they take their families with them in their canoes. They come back during the planting season in March. They bring back many furs and a great deal of smoked meat. When they return to the villages, they have feasts for their friends and give presents to the old men, who could not go with them and remained to guard the huts.

These people use some strange tricks to kill deer. They take with them into the woods a dried head of the male of the species. They cover their backs with a deer skin and put an arm through the neck of the dried head, into which they have put little wooden hoops for their hands to grip. Then they get down on their knees, while holding the head in view, and imitate the deer's cry. The animals, fooled by this trick, come quite close to the hunters, who kill them easily.

There are Indians who have used this ruse to kill up to four hundred deer in a single winter. They use almost the same technique to catch turkeys in the woods. Several of them put the skins of these birds on their shoulders and place on top of their heads a piece of scarlet cloth which flutters in the wind. The disguised Indians attract the turkeys while others shoot them with their arrows rather than with rifles, which would scare off the birds. As long as there are any perched in the trees, the hunters shoot at them with a great deal of

[5] Sometimes young Indians run through the villages and carry off women. These kidnappings often cause wars among the tribes. They do not fight over land since they have more than they can cultivate. It is a capital crime among the Indians to carry off another man's wife. If the woman is a chief's wife, the entire nation must seek revenge for the affront to their leader.

skill. The turkeys stay there waiting for those that have been killed to come back. I have often feasted on turkey among the Indians. This bird is excellent in the autumn.

The Indians are also skillful fishermen, although they use neither hooks nor nets. They gather reeds, which are very plentiful on the river banks, dry them over a fire or in the sun, sharpen one end like a dart, and tie to the other end a cord made of bark. They go out into the lake in their canoes and spear the fish in the water. Others hunt them with bows and arrows. The wounded fish come to the surface of the water.

Before finishing the article on the Alabama Indians, I must not forget to tell you that they have a big feast at harvest time in July. On that solemn day they fast, kindle a new fire to make medicine, purge themselves, and offer their Manitou the first fruits of the harvest. At the end of the day they do a religious dance.

These Indians also have medicine men. I shall tell you about a rather amusing little adventure that I had with one of them. At a time when we were rowing up the Alabama River, a medicine man, accompanied by several men and women, came to see me. I gave him a bottle of brandy, which he had asked for, and he and his friends drank it. He asked me for more and would not believe me when I told him that that was the last of it. Realizing that he was getting no place, he thought he would intimidate me by declaring proudly that he was a magician and that if I did not give him any more brandy, he would make bad medicine against me. He would cast a spell over me and would keep my boat from moving on. I replied that I was not afraid of him since I was a medicine man myself. This information surprised my adversary.

This would-be sorcerer asked me to show him what my medicine could do. I answered that it was up to him to begin, but his reply was that I was to go first since I was a stranger. After a long argument, I began to make ridiculous gestures and movements while looking into a book which was absolutely incomprehensible to the medicine man.

He obeyed me when I told him to go off and leave me alone, because this is customary among medicine men who do not want the other Indians to learn their tricks. I had the skin of a striped wildcat, whose flesh and bones had been removed through an incision below the neck. I gave the skin to the medicine man, telling him to restore its sight and to make it walk. When he told me that he could not, I answered that he was still a beginner in the art of magic and that I would do it.

I should tell you, sir, that I had brought back from France with me on my last trip some enamel eyes which look remarkably like real ones. This is something that these people had never seen. I stuck enamel eyes in the eyeholes with pine gum; then I put a live squirrel into the cat skin with its head protruding through the hole in the neck. A soldier whom I had instructed stood ready with a club. I then opened the door to the ship's cabin. The Indians, with the medicine man in the lead, drew close. I held the cat skin in my arms as the squirrel jumped around inside it. The amazed sorcerer cried out that I was a true medicine man since I could restore life, sight, and movement to dead cats. When the other Indians had taken a good look at what I held in my arms, I stuck the squirrel with a pin and let him go. He ran, cat skin and all, towards the spectators who thought he was going to devour them. They drew back, and the women, as is natural to their sex, fled in terror from my boat and swore that I was a sorcerer. I then pretended to leap angrily upon the wildcat. I skillfully removed the squirrel and the enamel eyes. Then, pressing the teeth of the cat's head against my stomach, I cried out as though the animal had bitten me. I threw it on the ground immediately, and the soldier beat the skin with his club as though he were killing the resuscitated animal for having revolted against its master and having tried to attack our redskin allies and friends.

After this comical scene, I gave the medicine man the skin and told him to bring the animal back to life as I had done. He told me that one medicine man was powerless against another and that I was a master in this art while he was just an ignorant man.[6] All the Indians who were hunting along the river that winter came out of their huts and brought me their provisions of deer and turkeys so that I could make medicine again. Fearing that I would be found out and wanting to save face, I told them that I could not do it because of the possibility that one of the Indians might be devoured. To convince them of this, I showed them the marks of the cat's teeth on my stomach. They then approved very much of what I had said and thanked me for the interest I had taken in them when I had so generously exposed myself to the fury of the revived wildcat, who had wanted to kill their wives and children. I had done well to send it back into oblivion where it would serve as an example to other evil spirits. These poor people think that the French have supernatural powers.

Sometimes it is dangerous to be a medicine man. When someone dies, the Indians attribute the death to the medicine and not to the patient's condition. That is why I would advise that no one take advantage of the gullibility of these people. I therefore told them that since I had been bitten, I no longer believed in the magicians' religion and recognized only that of the Master of Life. I recommended that they pray to Him, since He is the Father of the red men and their older brothers, the white men.

Because of the pretended resurrection of the cat, I gained a great reputation among the medicine men of this area and even among those of Spanish Florida, who came to see me out of that curiosity which is so natural to the Indians. They joined with the Alabamas in

---

[6] The Indians have a great deal of confidence in their medicine man, whose hut is covered with skins which he uses for clothing and blankets. He enters the hut completely naked and utters words, understood by no one, in order to invoke the spirit. After that, apparently in a complete trance, he gets up, shouts, and moves about as the sweat pours from every part of his body.

The hut shakes, and the spectators think that this is evidence of the presence of the spirit. The language that the medicine man speaks in his invocations has nothing in common with everyday speech. It is nothing but the product of an overexcited imagination that these charlatans pass off as a divine language. Throughout history, those with a certain amount of ingenuity have been able to fool others.

asking me to make the same medicine—to use their terminology—
that I had made during the voyage. I told them that I was very sorry
to have to disappoint them but that I had "struck the post." In order
not to send them off dissatisfied, however, I told them that I was very
happy that they had come and that the great chief of the French, the
father of the Indians, was pleased with their nation, especially with
the medicine men. Since they were more enlightened than the others
in the art of curing diseases, as well as in the zeal with which they
inspired the tribesmen with friendship and loyalty to the French, I
had come purposely to present them with gifts from their father,
which Monsieur Audibert was ordered to divide among them.

Adding that I was very happy to meet them and confer with
them, I asked them to give me their names. Since these people are
neither baptized nor circumcized, they generally take animals' names,
such as Bear, Wildcat (Tiger), Wolf, Fox, etc. Because of the serious-
ness which I affected to give me more stature among these Indian
doctors, they asked me if I was going to put their names on "talking
paper" and send them to their father. I said that I intended to do so.
I sometimes used their names to mystify them. I would close myself
up in a hut after informing a soldier of the number of letters in each
name. He would put his hand on the shoulder of one of the medicine
men and would tap with a stick as many times as there were letters
in the man's name. I would then guess which person the soldier was
touching. They could not understand how I was able to do this and
admitted that it was completely beyond them.

Monsieur Godeau, chief surgeon and quartermaster at the Alabama fort, made medicine for these Indians before I did. He showed
them a phial of mercury, which they had never seen before. After
having looked at it attentively, they asked him for it. He answered
that he would be very happy to oblige them but that he needed the
phial. Pouring the quicksilver on the floor, he told them to pick it up.
They could not possibly succeed, as the mercury kept rolling off in
every direction. The astonished Indians said that this was a spirit that

divided itself into several parts, becoming one again when they were put back together. Their amazement grew even greater when Monsieur Godeau gathered up the mercury with a card and placed it back in the phial. The surgeon thus did what not a single one of them had been capable of doing. He then caused the mercury to dissolve and disappear by pouring nitric acid on it. From that time on, he has been considered a great medicine man among these people.

Monsieur de Montberaut has just turned over command of Fort Alabama to Monsieur Aubert, the assistant adjutant of Mobile. I am taking the liberty of writing to the Governor to inform him respectfully that since I have seniority over Monsieur Aubert, I cannot stay here under his orders; that the King's instructions state explicitly that the assistant adjutant is to have no duty outside his specific functions;[7] that since our profession is based on honor, I would be cheapening the honor which I have earned in His Majesty's service if I were to fail to make these observations as a soldier whose zeal for the military is well known; and that it is quite natural for me to think, for this reason, that he would consider himself obliged to grant me the benefits due my rank or to recall me to New Orleans, where I could seize the first opportunity to return to Europe. There I shall have the pleasure of assuring you that I am, sir, . . .

Alabama territory
May 2, 1759

P.S. I forgot to tell you, sir, of the visit paid us by the Coweta Emperor some time after Monsieur de Montberaut's departure. As we had been informed by a courier of His Indian Majesty's arrival, I went out to meet him at some distance from the fort. I had posted soldiers who were to shoot off their rifles as a signal for the cannoneers to fire a salute as soon as the Prince put his hand in mine.[8] He had a

---

[7] I am, however, obliged to do Monsieur Aubert justice. He has been given command of Fort Alabama to my detriment, but I must praise the consideration he has shown in offering to share authority with me so that we could live together as friends.

[8] There are no compliments or ceremonies of greeting among the Indians. They

Spanish mount with an English saddle, and his trappings consisted of the skin of a wildcat.

The Emperor walked very gravely at the head of his retinue. I could hardly keep from laughing when I saw these tall, well-built, naked men, painted in various colors, walk in single file according to rank like Capuchin friars.

The Prince seemed very pleased with the honor we paid him; he had never before seen cannons and called them "big rifles." He had feathers on his head and wore a scarlet coat with gold braid and English cuffs. He had no vest or breeches, and his loin cloth, which was made of a small piece of red material, was drawn up between his thighs and held fast with a belt. He had on under his coat a white cloth shirt. His footgear consisted of a type of ankle-boot made of deer skin dyed yellow. Since he was still a young man about eighteen or nineteen years old, his nation had appointed a noble and wise elder to serve as regent. It was he who spoke in his sovereign's name and handed Monsieur Aubert the peace pipe. After mutual compliments were paid, our commander told him to rest. It is customary among the Indians to wait until the next day before discussing political matters so that they may have time to think.

Monsieur Laubène, the King's interpreter, translated the speech of the Regent, who acts also as the Emperor's chancellor. He did not fail to mention the services rendered the French by the boy's father, the deceased king. The son had always wanted to come see the French and strengthen the friendship which had never ceased to exist between his nation and ours. He wanted us all to smoke the peace pipe together. It is true that the boy's father had always been unwaveringly loyal to Monsieur de Bienville, who, as a sign of recognition, had granted this chief the title of Emperor. The Governor had wanted all the Alabama tribes to recognize this emperor as their great chief. They refused to do this, claiming that one chief over each village was

laugh at our greeting each other with bent body and one foot placed forward or backward.

enough. In brief, they were unwilling to make any changes at all in their form of government.

The Emperor, his regent, his war chief, his medicine man, and his servant came to see our commanding officer at ten o'clock the next morning. We were all assembled in uniform and made up a small court for him. On this occasion, the Emperor was not more magnificently dressed than were the lords of his court. They were all dressed in the clothing of Adam in the Garden of Eden.[9]

This young, handsome, and well-built prince was of noble and intelligent appearance. During his stay among us, he was treated at the King's expense. Since the Prince was my size, the Commander asked me to give him a blue coat, a waistcoat with gold braid, a plumed hat, and a white shirt with embroidered cuffs.

Monsieur Aubert also gave some trifles, at the King's expense, to the American prince and his officers. They went home quite happy with these gifts. Their country is situated east of Mobile, between Carolina and eastern Florida. Although these people have never been conquered by the Spaniards, they are their sworn enemies.

Our commander always had the Emperor and his regent eat at his table. By not granting this privilege to the others, the French officers hoped to gain greater respect from the Indians. I should add here, sir, that the son of the noble Coweta, whom the French honored with the pompous title of Emperor, was very embarrassed the first time that he ate with us. Since he had never before used a fork, he watched closely so that he could imitate us. The Regent, who was more impatient, tore at the turkey carcass with his fingers and excused himself by saying that the Master of Life had created them before he had made forks and knives.

Toward the end of the meal a little joke was played on the Emperor's servant, who was stationed behind his master. Having noticed

---

[9] The coat that the Emperor wore when he arrived at the fort had been given him by an English captain. The Emperor thought it politic to take it off, hoping that the French would give him another one.

that we had mustard with our boiled meat, the native asked Monsieur Boudin what this food was that we seemed to like so much. This officer, who has lived among these people for forty years, speaks their language. He told the servant that he could try some if he wanted to; the French are not stingy with their possessions. The Indian immediately put into his mouth a spoonful of this very strong mustard, which made him go through all kinds of ridiculous contortions. His master laughed, but the servant, thinking that he was poisoned, did not think that this was funny. Monsieur Aubert called for a bottle of brandy, made the "poison victim" swallow a mouthful of it, and assured him that he would be cured instantaneously.

The Cowetas are very reserved about their religion in the presence of strangers. They never express themselves in public without first having thought deeply about what they are going to say.

They have an annual general assembly in the principal village of the nation. They build a large cabin for this occasion, and each one takes his place in it according to rank. Each one speaks in turn,[10] depending upon his age, his ability, his wisdom, and the services he has rendered the nation. The great chief of the tribe opens the meeting with a speech on the history and the traditions of their land. He tells of the military exploits of his ancestors, who distinguished themselves defending the nation, and urges his subjects to imitate the virtues of these men by bearing hardship and misery without muttering against the Great Spirit, who is the master of all living beings. He advises them to face adversity courageously and to sacrifice everything for the love of nation and liberty. It is a thousand times more glorious to die as a true man than to live as a vile slave.

After the chief's speech, the oldest of the nobles, naked to the waist, gets up, greets his sovereign, and begins his harangue. Sweat pours from all parts of his body because of the heat and the gestures he uses. The ideas in the talk are expressed in metaphors. The orator

[10] The Indians disapprove of the Europeans' habit of all speaking at once during meetings.

154

persuades the listeners with the force and eloquence of his speech. Nothing is more edifying than these assemblies. You hear no chattering, no indecent remarks, no untimely applause, and no immoderate laughter. The young men, convinced that it is for their own good, listen attentively and respectfully to the words of their elders.

Letter XVII

To the Marquis de l'Estrade.
The author leaves Alabama territory; sailing on the Tombigbee River; how he escapes the jaws of an alligator; he meets a group of rebellious Choctaws and persuades them to return to their duty; his return to Mobile.

Sir:

The only answer to my letter to the Governor arrived while I was among the Alabamas. It ordered me to return to Mobile where I would serve under Monsieur de Velle, the King's lieutenant. Instead of obtaining permission to return to France, I was ordered to lead a convoy taking supplies and ammunition to the fort situated on the Tombigbee River, ten leagues from the Choctaw nation. I followed instructions to the letter to the entire satisfaction of my superiors. I have letters and certificates which attest to this.

On August 22, 1759, I left Mobile with three boats manned by soldiers and Mobile Indians, who volunteered to help this Frenchman on his trip in exchange for a few trinkets. We took off from Mobile and, after having gone fifteen leagues, arrived at the juncture of the Alabama and the Tombigbee rivers. On August 27, we started up the Tombigbee to reach the fort. Since the weather was good, I chose a campsite on the edge of the river. Out of their abundant catch, the Indians gave me a catfish, a species which can attain a length of four feet and which the natives usually dry. Because of the fine weather, I did not bother to pitch my tent but simply chose an isolated spot on a grass-covered height overlooking the river. Finding this a good place to rest, I spread out the bearskin I had taken on the island we had pretended was mine. I wrapped myself in my tent and covered my face against the evening dampness, which is dangerous in this season. This little precaution almost cost me my life, as you will see.

I carefully placed the fish near my feet so no one could steal it, but something worse happened. I had already been sleeping deeply and peacefully for an hour, with no fear of the local Indians, who are our friends and allies, when I suddenly felt something of extraordinary strength dragging me off. I awoke with a start, thinking that someone was playing a trick on me. I had never before been so frightened, and I think that I had good cause to be this time. I thought the Devil was dragging me off. I shouted for help. My men answered that I was having a nightmare. You can imagine my amazement when, fully awake, I saw a twenty-foot-long alligator![1] Attracted by the catfish in the bottom of my tent canvas, the alligator had come out of the river in the dead of night. These amphibians are extremely voracious. This one threw himself hungrily on my fish, and, carrying its prey into the river, dragged me off, too, by a corner of the tent in which I was wrapped. I had just the time to untangle myself on the very edge of the precipice and was fortunate enough to get off with only a good scare. I was able to save the bearskin, which never leaves me. As simple as this event seems, it is considered a miracle by those who believe in the supernatural.

The Acolapissas and the Washas, small tribes which live north of New Orleans, wrestle alligators in the water. This is how they do it. Armed with a piece of hardwood or an iron bar pointed at both ends, which he holds in the center, an Indian swims out with his weapon in front of him. The alligator approaches with his jaws wide

---

[1] I was frightened by his size as well as by the disgusting smell of musk exuded by these animals.

open to snap off and eat the swimmer's arm. The Indian jams the piece of wood into the mouth of the alligator, who, in biting down, pierces both his jaws and so locks them that he can neither open nor close his mouth. The Indian then drags the animal out of the water. These people engage in the sport quite often, as do the Negroes of Guinea and Senegal.

After traveling sixty leagues between the forests and the mountains which border the river, we came to water which was so shallow that we had to unload the boats and hide all our cargo in the woods, with the exception of the ammunition and the food. I was particularly careful with these supplies. I have never been in a worse situation; we had to drag the boats fifteen leagues. Placing myself at the head of the soldiers and the Indians, I helped pull on the rope in order to set a good example. You can imagine the predicament I was in when you consider that, during this operation, we could easily have been attacked, defeated, and robbed of our supplies.

I met a rebellious party of Choctaws, who were on their way to the English after having crossed the river at a point which they call *Tuscalousa*. This means "white mountain"[2] in their language. Their chief, Mingo-Houmas, was insolent enough to try to make me give him some brandy. He even had the audacity to raise his ax over my head. At this point, I told him that I was a real man, that I was not afraid to die, and that I had given up my body.[3] I added that I was perfectly satisfied to die, since I was sure that if he killed me and my small group of warriors, the great chief of the French across the big lake would seek revenge by sending against their nation as many warriors as there were leaves on the trees. Surprised at my resolution, these people decided that I was a "man of valor" and that I had restored to them the sanity which they had lost when they devised the plan to abandon their father. They hoped that since I was kind, I would forget the past. At the end of the speech, they handed me a

[2] This is a type of marl or chalk that would be very valuable in Europe.
[3] This means that I was ready to die for my country.

158

peace pipe, which I accepted on the condition that it be lighted with a new fire. This would mean that the past was forgotten and that our alliance would be renewed with the Choctaws, the children of the great chief of the French. To convince them that the past was really going to be forgotten, I said that the fire would light itself. I had with me a small phial of phosphorus that I had brought back from France during my last trip. I put some of this powder in the pipe, looked up at the sky, and uttered a few words to the Great Spirit. During this time, the powder, which had been exposed to the air, lit the tobacco. This surprised not only the Indians but also my French companions, who had never before seen an experiment performed with this powder.

After this mysterious ceremony, I gave some European trinkets to the people and a bottle of brandy to the Chief. Giving gifts to seal a bargain is customary among the Indians. Then they all shook my hand in friendship and started back to their village. They had given me proof that they were ashamed of their mad plan, and we parted the best of friends.

Shortly afterwards, the heavy rains caused the river to swell greatly. I had an Indian go on to Fort Tombigbee. Monsieur de Chabert, the fort's commander, sent out a detachment headed by Monsieur de Cabaret, a very intelligent officer who was of great help to me on this occasion. He brought us food supplies at a time when we had completely run out of provisions.

Our European dandies, who carry with them mirrors, toiletries, dressing gowns, etc., would be considered women and not war chiefs by the Indians. They would not distinguish themselves in this type of campaign, where they would have to endure excessive summer heat and the rigors of winter, sleep on the ground, and expose themselves to the weather in order to keep the Indians from taking them by surprise. Braddock, the commanding general of New England, learned this much to his sorrow in 1755, when he took Fort Duquêne. He and all his army were massacred at some distance from this post by a small number of Frenchmen and Indians, our faithful allies, led by brave Canadian and European officers, who accomplished great feats of heroism in this engagement.

I was very happy to arrive, at last, at Fort Tombigbee on September 25, after having gone about one hundred leagues by boat without coming to a single inhabited area. We had to camp in the woods along the river every night. The mosquitoes are most annoying during this season; they are absolutely unbearable throughout Louisiana. To protect ourselves from them, we stuck big reeds into the ground and bent them to form arches. We covered these with a cloth and put a bearskin, which served as a mattress, under them. Everyone in the colony travels by water in this same manner.

Upon landing to establish a camp for the night, the commanding officer must be careful to post guards in the woods to prevent surprise attacks. Great care should be taken in choosing a well-located campsite on an island or a cape. If Monsieur D—— had taken these precautions in 1735 when he was delivering a boat full of powder sent by Monsieur de Bienville to the Illinois, a band of enemy Chickasaws would not have taken him by surprise. It is certain that this officer's negligence was just as disastrous as the Natchez commander's cowardice, ignorance, and greed. The Chickasaws, using the captured powder to wage war against us for more than thirty years, killed a great number of good people and cost the King a fortune.

This, in short, is how Monsieur D—— was surprised by an attack and taken prisoner. One day, when there was a north wind, he had to make the boat fast to the shore and set up camp while waiting for the winds to shift. After everyone had landed, he and his soldiers went off hunting. The Chickasaws, who had been following them and spying upon them for a long time, captured the boat and the powder and took the soldiers as slaves. When Monsieur D—— got back from his hunting, he was surrounded and captured like the others. Because the Indians were happy to have taken such a group of prisoners without any losses, they spared the Frenchmen's lives. Some

160

time later, Monsieur D—— had the good fortune to escape and make his way back to New Orleans.

When traveling, one should always have an Indian along to scout ahead in search of enemies and game. During my trip up the Tombigbee, I ran out of provisions, but Providence supplied me amply. The Indians, who are real ferrets in the woods, came to inform me that they had discovered the nest of a golden eagle, which is a large species. They came for axes to chop down the tall tree in which the nest was found. They were well rewarded for their trouble. In the nest there was a great deal of game of all sorts, such as fauns, rabbits, turkeys, grouse, partridges, and wood pigeons. There were also four young eagles almost full-grown, which the Indians kept for themselves, much to the consternation of the parent birds, who were so furious that they would have torn the eyes from the heads of the Indians had they not been armed with rifles. These winged creatures have certainly earned the title "King of Birds" because of their fearlessness. Bullets, however, did not spare their feathered majesties, who fell victim to paternal love. The Indians told me that it was the Great Spirit who had sent us food. This was, indeed, manna from heaven sent to us in the desert.

I have just received news from the capital. A friend of mine notifies me that New Orleans is in an uproar because of an English ship from Jamaica which came to Louisiana to engage in smuggling. The ship is called the *Texel*, and her captain is Dias Arias, an English Jew. The finance officer, finding that there were grounds for confiscating the ship in accordance with naval directives, seized it in the name of the King. Major de Belle-Isle, the temporary commanding officer, was asked to lend military assistance for that purpose. Monsieur de Kerlérec, however, returned from Mobile and prevented Monsieur de Belle-Isle from performing his duty. The Governor then sent a detachment of soldiers to arrest Monsieur de Rochemore's secretary at three o'clock in the morning. After having broken in his doors and windows, they dragged him from his bed and placed him aboard a ship whose destination is unknown. Because of this action, Monsieur de Rochemore has sent Monsieur de Fontenette, a member of the Upper Council, to see the minister.

Just as soon as I am better informed about all that has happened, I shall send the news on to you. I am writing the Governor to ask to be recalled to New Orleans. I remain, sir, . . .

Tombigbee
September 19, 1759

LETTER XVIII

To the Marquis de l'Estrade.
   A description of the country of the Choctaws; their wars; their
method of treating illness; their superstitions; their trade; their
games and exercises; the country of the Chickasaws, our enemies.

SIR:

I intended to leave here in two days, but my desire to become
acquainted with the largest and most warlike nation in Louisiana
made me change my mind. I am taking advantage of some leisure
time to write you what I have learned about these Indians and what
I have seen. They gave proof of their loyalty to the French under
Governor Perrier when he used them to punish the Natchez for having massacred our people who had settled among them. The Court
gives them presents every year to keep them on our side. This nation
can muster four thousand warriors who would be happy to fight. If
we went about it in the right way, it would be a simple matter to get
them to sing their war chants and to stir them up to attack the English, who have opened hostilities in our Canadian possessions. These
Indians could be of great service to us in raiding British territory,
especially Georgia and Carolina which have been left unprotected
since their national militia has left for the siege of Quebec. Several of
our brave Louisiana officers, such as Rouville, Tissenet, and others
who speak the language of our Indian allies, are burning with the

desire to lead them into enemy territory where they would destroy the harvest, pillage, burn settlements, and spread panic to the very port of Charleston. This could divert the English from Canada.

The Choctaws like war and are good strategists. They never stand firm and fight; they move about and courageously harass their enemy. When they engage in hand-to-hand fighting, they remain quite cool. Some of the women love their husbands so much that they follow them into battle. They remain at their sides, carry quivers full of arrows, and encourage their husbands by crying to them not to fear the enemy and to die like real men.

The Choctaws are very superstitious. When they go off to battle, they consult their Manitou, which is carried by the chief. They always place it in the direction in which they intend to march against the enemy and post guards around it. They revere it to such an extent that they will not eat until the chief has offered it the first share of food.

As long as they are at war, the chief is obeyed without question, but once they have returned, his prestige depends on how liberal he is with his possessions. It is customary among them for the chief of a war party to distribute the booty among his warriors and among the relatives of those who were killed in battle, "to dry their tears," as they say. The chief keeps nothing for himself except the honor of being the defender of the nation.

> *Under their reed roofs, strong and brave they*
> *grow,*
> *Their only possession a quiver and a bow.*
> THOMAS, *Jumonville*

The selfishness which causes so much crime in the Old World is unknown among the people of the New. The Cuban Indians had every right to say that the true god of the Spaniards was gold and that it was best to give it to them in order to have peace. You never see in America, among these people we call savages, anyone barbaric enough to kill his brothers in cold blood or to bear false witness against them in order to gain their possessions. Intrigue for the purpose of becoming rich through inhumane means is unknown. There are no women who poison their husbands, as in Europe, so that they can marry again. There are no women so lascivious and brazen that they would call their husbands impotent in public, as do European women. A chief's wife would not act like that Italian princess who had her husbands strangled because they could not satisfy her brutal passion. There are no girls here who destroy their children in order to make their husbands think they are chaste. The Indian girls are horrified by Christian women who do such things. They point out that even the wildest beasts in the woods care for their young.

If the chief of a band of Choctaws does not succeed in a battle he has undertaken, he loses prestige, no one has any further confidence in his leadership, and he is reduced in rank to a mere warrior. We may, however, admire the diversity of opinions among the different nations. It is not considered shameful if a member of these warlike people does not stand his ground in battle. Such desertion is attributed to a bad dream. If the chief of a big war party tells his people that he has dreamed that the losses will be heavy, they turn around and go back to their village. After making medicine, as they do on all occasions, they set out again. If they meet the enemy and kill five or six of their number, they go back home as happy as though they had conquered a great empire.

A chief who won a victory involving a great loss of men would be very badly received by his people. They consider absolutely worthless a victory bought with the blood of their friends and their relatives. Therefore, the chiefs are very careful to spare their warriors and to attack the enemy only when assured of victory either because of superior numbers or advantageous battle positions. Since the adversary uses the same strategy and knows just as well as anyone else how to avoid the traps set for him, the shrewder of the two contenders will win. Because of this, the Indians hide in the woods during the day and travel only at night. If they are not discovered, they attack at daybreak. Since they usually stay in covered terrain, the warrior in the lead sometimes holds a thick bush in front of him as camouflage. They walk in single file, and the last man covers their tracks by arranging the leaves and the earth on which they have stepped so that no telltale trace is left behind.

The things which betray them most often to their enemies are the smoke of their fires, which can be smelled a long way off, and their tracks. Indians can read these with almost unbelievable skill. One day an Indian showed me, in a place where I had noticed nothing, the foot steps of Frenchmen, Indians, and Negroes; he even told me how long ago they had gone by. I must admit that this knowledge seemed almost miraculous. It can be safely said that when Indians apply themselves to a single thing, they excel in it.

The art of war among them, as you see, consists of vigilance and the ability to avoid surprise attacks and to catch the enemy off balance, in addition to the patience and the stamina required to withstand hunger, thirst, the elements, and the inescapable hardship of battle.

A warrior wears as a trophy the scalp of an enemy killed in battle. He commemorates the event by having a mark tattooed on his body and then goes into a month's mourning for his victim. During that time he is not permitted to comb his hair, and if his head itches, he scratches himself with a little stick which is tied to his wrist for that purpose.

The Choctaws are very dirty, since they live for the most part quite far from rivers. They have no religion. They take things as they come, with no concern for the future; yet they believe that the soul is immortal. They revere their dead, which they do not bury. When a Choctaw dies, his body is exposed on a bier made of cypress bark and placed on four forked posts about fifteen feet high. After the worms have consumed the body, the entire family gathers. One of them dismembers the skeleton and removes whatever muscles, nerves, and tendons still remain. These are buried, and after the skull has been painted red, the bones are placed in a box. The relatives weep during this entire ceremony. Then a meal is served to the friends who have come to pay their respects. After this, the remains are carried to the common cemetery where the bones of the dead man's ancestors are buried. During all of these lugubrious ceremonies a mournful silence is maintained. There is no singing or dancing, and everyone goes off weeping.

In the early part of November they have an important holiday called the feast of the dead or the feast of souls. Each family gathers at the cemetery and weeps as it visits the boxes containing the bones of its ancestors. After leaving the cemetery, the Indians indulge in a great feast.

It is to the Americans' credit that the love they show their relatives, so rare among Europeans, is worthy of imitation. The examples of this feeling which I have mentioned surpass those of antiquity. This love which the Indians have for each other makes them humane enough to help the sick and the ailing. This sincere love can be seen in the care they give their dying relatives and friends and in the tears that are shed when their dear ones have departed.

The Indians generally revere their medicine men or seers, true charlatans who take advantage of the stupid people and live comfortably at their expense. These medicine men, who have a great deal of authority, are asked for advice and are consulted on every occasion, like oracles. When a Choctaw is sick, he gives all that he owns to be cured. If, however, the patient dies, his relatives blame it on the medicine and not on the sick man's condition. They can kill the medicine man if they want to,[1] but this rarely happens since he usually has a good excuse ready. The medicine men are familiar with several plants

---

[1] I have known many people in France who blamed the doctor for the death of their relatives. They think exactly the way the Indians do in this matter.

which are excellent for curing the common diseases of this country. They have a sure cure for the bite of the rattlesnake and of other venomous animals.

When an Indian is wounded with a bullet or an arrow, the medicine man first sucks the wound and then spits out the blood. In France this is called "curing through secretion." In their dressings, they do not use lint or compresses. Instead, to make the wound suppurate, they blow into it powder made of a root. Another root powder is used to dry and heal the wound, and still other roots are used in a solution with which the wound is bathed to help prevent gangrene.

When the Indians return tired and worn out from battle or from hunting, they take sweat baths in steam cabinets[2] in which are boiled all sorts of medicinal and sweet-smelling herbs. The vapor filled with the essence and salts of these herbs enters the patient's body through his pores and his nose and restores his strength. This remedy also eases pain and causes it to disappear. Gout, kidney stones, and other diseases to which we are subject in Europe are unknown among the Indians. This may in part be due to frequent exercise. There are no paunches, as in Holland, or goiters, as in Piedmont.

The Choctaws believe in the existence of sorcerers and witches. When they think that they have discovered one, they bash in his head without any kind of trial.[3]

I knew a member of this tribe who had been baptized a short time before. Because he and his comrades had had a poor hunting season, he thought he was bewitched. This new Christian went immediately to see Father Lefèvre,[4] the Jesuit who had converted him,

---

[2] These cabinets are round and shaped like a stove. A public medicine man, called an *Alexi*, is in charge of these steam baths, which are found in the center of the village.

[3] In 1752, when I was in Mobile, I saw an Indian killed with an ax because he said he was a sorcerer. The Indians blamed him for the tribe's bad luck.

[4] The Indians call the Jesuits "men in black dresses." They say that they are not like other men and laugh at them as though they were women.

and told him that his medicine was worthless. Since he had received it, he had not caught any deer or roebucks. He asked the priest if he would be kind enough to remove his medicine. In order to avoid the Indian's resentment, the Jesuit pretended to "debaptize" him. Some time afterward the "debaptized" Indian, through skill or luck, killed a roebuck and was happily convinced that he was no longer bewitched.

The people of this nation are generally of a brutal and coarse nature. You can talk to them as much as you want about the mysteries of our religion; they always reply that all of that is beyond their comprehension. They are morally quite perverted, and most of them are addicted to sodomy. These corrupt men, who have long hair and wear short skirts like women, are held in great contempt.

The Choctaws are very fresh and alert. They play a game similar to our tennis and are very good at it. They invite the men of the neighboring villages to play and tease them by shouting insulting remarks at them. The men and the women gather dressed in their best clothing and spend the day dancing and singing. They even dance all night to the sound of drums and rattles.[5] A game takes place on the day after a village lights its own special fire in the middle of a large field. The players agree upon a goal which is sixty steps away and which is marked by two large posts. The aim is to get the ball between these posts. The game is finished as soon as one side has sixteen points. There are forty players on a team, and each one has a racket two and one-half feet long, made of walnut or chestnut wood and covered with deerskin. These rackets are shaped almost like ours.

An old man, standing in the middle of the field, throws up a deerskin ball. The players then run to try to catch the ball in their rackets. It is fun to watch them play naked, painted with all kinds of colors, and with a wildcat's tail tied behind them. The feathers at-

[5] *Chichikois* in the text. *Chusoquah* means "the rattling of a chain." See Ben Watkins, *Complete Choctaw Definer* (Van Buren, Ark., J. W. Baldwin, 1892), 56.— ED.

tached to their arms and heads look odd as they wave back and forth in the wind. The players push and throw each other down. Anyone who is skillful enough to get the ball passes it on to a teammate, and his opponents try to get it away from him. Both teams play with such ardor that shoulders are often dislocated in the fray. The players never become angry, and the old men, who act as referees, remind them that they are playing for sport and not for blood. There is a great deal of gambling; even the women bet among themselves.

When the men's game is finished, the women get together to play to avenge their husbands' losses. Their rackets are different from those that the men use in that they are bent. The women, who are very good at this game, run swiftly and push each other around just as the men do. They are dressed exactly like the men, but with a little more modesty. They put red paint on their cheeks only and apply vermilion instead of powder to their hair.

After having played hard all day long, everyone goes home in glory or in shame. There is no bitterness as each one promises to play another day when the best man will win. This is how the Indians practice running. They are so swift that I have seen some of them run as fast as deer.

The children shoot arrows for prizes. The winner of the first prize is praised by an old man and is given the title of "apprentice warrior." Children are reasoned with and are not beaten. They are very handy with the blowpipe, a weapon made of a reed about seven feet long into which is placed a little arrow feathered with thistle down. When aimed right and blown into, this weapon can often kill small birds.

Almost all Choctaw assemblies take place at night. Even though they are barbarians and savages, the Choctaws lose all confidence in anyone who does not keep his word. If you break your promise to them, you will be treated scornfully and called a liar, a name which the Indians have given to the present governor, whom they call *Oula-bay-Mingo,* "Chief Liar."

When their wives are pregnant, the husbands refrain from eating salt or pork in the false belief that these foods will harm their children. The women never give birth in the cabins. They go off into the woods alone and bear their children without any assistance. Once the children are born, the mothers wash them and place a lump of earth on their foreheads to flatten their heads. As the child grows stronger, the weight on the head is increased. A flat head is a mark of beauty among these people. They never swaddle or bind their children. Children are never weaned until they themselves no longer want to take the breast. I have seen children big enough to say to their mothers, "Sit down; I want to suckle." The mothers sit down immediately. Mothers place their children in reed cradles, with their heads two or three inches lower than their bodies. This is why there are no humpbacked people among the Indians.

The women are considered valorous when they leave their cabins during their menstrual period. At this time, they prepare their own food and drink and do not come back among the men until they have purified themselves. The men think that if they approach a menstruating woman they will become ill and will have bad luck in battle.

Even though the Indians trace their ancestry through their mothers, women do not have the right to correct boys; they have authority only over girls. If a mother took it into her head to strike a boy, she would be severely reprimanded and would be struck too. If her little son disobeys her, she takes him to an old man who scolds him and pours cold water on him.

If a woman is unfaithful to her husband, she must "pass through the field." That means that all the young men, and sometimes even the old men, take turns subjecting her to their brutality. After her infamous conduct, the guilty woman is sometimes clever enough to find a coward who is willing to marry her. The suitor explains that the woman must be thoroughly disgusted with the crime that caused her such punishment and will, therefore, behave herself in the future. She is, nevertheless, always considered a depraved and immoral woman.

171

Before finishing my letter, sir, I should say a few words about the Chickasaws. They are not as numerous as the Choctaws, but are much more formidable because of their fearlessness. All the northern and the southern tribes, as well as the French, have waged war against them without being able to drive them from their lands, which are the most beautiful and the most fertile on the continent. These tall, well-built people are of unequaled bravery. In 1752 and 1753 they attacked Monsieur Benoist and Monsieur de Reggio, who were in command of the Illinois convoys on their way down the Mississippi. The Chickasaws always attack from some advantageous site, their favorite spot being Prudhomme Rock where the river is narrow and their bullets can reach these boats which have no decks.

It is believed that the Chickasaws killed Bousselet and La Morlière, two brave officers who fell into an ambush because of their lack of experience. They did not know the terrain of the country they were in any more than General Braddock did. An officer must always be familiar with the country in order to avoid surprise attacks, or else he must be constantly on the defensive.

The English have always maintained an alliance with these valiant Indian warriors, have kept up trade with them, and have taken care of all their needs. The men, excellent riders, leave plowing and planting to their women, who are beautiful and very clean. When a Chickasaw kills a deer, he tells his wife where he has left it. She goes for it, dresses it, and serves it to her husband. The women do not eat with their husbands, who seem to treat them with indifference. Yet the men of this tribe love their wives more than do those of any other nation.

When adultery is committed, the Chickasaws whip the guilty couple as they run naked through the village. After that the wronged husband repudiates his wife.

Because the Chickasaws had given refuge to the Natchez, after their massacre of the French, our people armed themselves in 1736 and unsuccessfully attacked them with all the strength the colony could muster. Major d'Artaguette, the King's commanding officer in the Illinois territory, joined forces with Bienville, the governor of Louisiana. He brought troops from his area and from the Canadian border, but they were taken by surprise and defeated because of the defection of our Indian allies. Monsieur d'Artaguette, seven other officers, and twenty-six soldiers and settlers were captured and burned alive. Among these men was Father Senat, D'Artaguette's Jesuit chaplain. This tragedy was revealed by Louis Gamot, a sergeant who witnessed the sad fate of his unfortunate companions. He was supposed to be burned last, but he escaped this ordeal through a rather peculiar trick. Since he was familiar with their language, he shouted insults at the executioners. He untied himself and threw at them everything he could reach. "You are dogs! You have burned my chiefs, and I want to be burned too. I am not afraid of death or fire. I am a real man. I demand that you torture me." When the Indians saw his firmness of purpose and his resolution, they decided that he was an extraordinary man and granted him his life. Some time afterward, he was ransomed by an Englishman from Carolina. At present, Gamot is in Charleston, the capital of the English colony.

Another expedition against the Chickasaws was led by Bienville on May 26 of that same year and was no more successful than the first. Several brave officers were killed, the adjutant was fatally wounded, and the major general of the army was severely injured. I learned from the Chevalier de Lucer, who is of Swiss origin, that his father, a captain in our army, had been a member of that unfortunate expedition. Lucer also told me the story of the Chevalier de Grondel, at present the commander of the Swiss troops in the Halwill Regiment stationed in Mobile and attached to the navy. He was formerly commander of a detachment of grenadiers in the Karrer Regiment and served under Bienville against the Chickasaws.

To make a long story short, I shall tell you only that this officer, who was impetuous, young, loyal, and as brave as are all the members of his nation, was shot five times by the enemy in this attack. Having remained behind on the battlefield after the retreat, he would have fallen victim to the fury and the vengeance of the savages if several soldiers of his troop had not generously risked their lives to save him in the face of a shower of bullets and arrows coming from the Chickasaw fort. Five of these brave men were killed one after the other. A sixth one however, disregarding the danger, ran forward and returned to the troop, carrying his officer on his shoulders. The chief army surgeon used all his skill to save him. The General, who appreciates military merit, told this story at the Court, and Monsieur de Maurepas, in gratitude for Grondel's wounds and service, granted him a bonus and recommended him for the Croix de Saint Louis. The soldier[6] who risked his life to save Grondel was promoted to sergeant by the commander of his troop. In this short account, you can see, sir, how admirably discipline is maintained in the Swiss corps, which is absolutely loyal to our august monarch, and how beneficial this discipline is to those who impose it. The names of the soldiers who took part in this heroic action should be transmitted to posterity.

In 1754, Baron de Porneuf told me about his plan to explore the western part of Louisiana, by going up the Mississippi and the Missouri, whose sources are unknown to us. This Canadian officer has the necessary qualifications for such an enterprise, but the war which has broken out between England and France over their territorial boundaries on this continent has prevented him from carrying out his plan.

I can assure you that I would have been very happy to accompany him for the glory of the King as well as for my own satisfaction. Despite the hardship and the danger I have undergone in my travels, I have not at all become tired of this life. An explorer constantly sees new things to instruct and amuse him. He cultivates his mind in an agreeable manner, and he learns to read in the great book of the universe what cannot be found in a library, where there are as many systems, opinions, and contradictions as authors. If you were in my place, sir, you would have many things to philosophize about.

[6] His name is Régnisse.

"Striking the Post"

From a water color by Seth Eastman

An Indian Stockade

From Joseph-François Lafitau, *De Zeden der Wilden van Amerika* (1731)

Tombigbee
September 30, 1759

P.S. Since I may not have the honor of writing to you for a long time, sir, because of the war, I am enclosing an account of the differences which have arisen between us and the Choctaws. Some time after the Chickasaw war, the French had some trouble with the followers of Red Shoe, an insolent Choctaw prince who had committed several hostile acts. When Monsieur de Vaudreuil, who was then governor of Louisiana, found out what was behind this difficulty, he ordered the French not to visit that tribe or to sell it arms and ammunition, so that their frenzy would cool off without bloodshed. After having taken these precautions, the Marquis de Vaudreuil sent a message to the chief of the entire nation to find out if he too, like Red Shoe, was angry with the French. The sovereign answered, through the interpreter, that his general, Red Shoe, had lost his mind.

After this reply, we sent the chief a gift, but he was very surprised to find that among his gifts there were no arms, powder or shot at a time when his people were our friends, as they always have been. This event, coupled with the fact that they knew there was a prohibition against giving them arms, increased their astonishment and led them to ask the Governor for an explanation. He answered that it would be impossible to sell them arms and ammunition as long as Red Shoe was out of his mind. If they were given powder, since they were all brothers, they would have to give a large part of it to Red Shoe's warriors. This answer forced the Choctaws to warn the offending tribes that if they did not go to the French in peace, the other tribes of the nation would wage war against them as rebels. This threat made Red Shoe's people sue for peace and offer reparations to the French, who were in no position to fight a war against so large a nation.

That is how Monsieur de Vaudreuil's wise policy ended this war without any expense to the State and without exposing a single man to danger. The French general put Monsieur de Grand-Pré in charge of this important negotiation. The Marquis de Vaudreuil could not have made a better choice. Monsieur de Grand-Pré is a Canadian who serves the King zealously, bravely, and selflessly. I was about to go off to serve under his command at Fort Tombigbee, among the Choctaws, when I came here in 1751.

LETTER XIX

To the Marquis de l'Estrade.

The author returns to Mobile; the remarkable events which took place on Cat Island; the tragic death of Monsieur Duroux, the island's commander.

SIR:

I have returned from my trip on the Tombigbee River. I have carried out my important and difficult mission to the satisfaction of my superiors. While waiting to be ordered back to New Orleans, I was led through curiosity to visit the small islands off the coast of Louisiana.

The first French settlement was on Massacre Island, so named because of the number of skeletons found there of either Spanish or Indian origin. The name has since been changed to Dauphin Island.[1]

---

[1] This island [situated just south of Mobile, at the entrance to the bay—ED.] is not to be confused with the one discussed in the West India Company's account of the first trip to Madagascar, which was too hastily named Isle Dauphine (Dauphin Island). A member of this expedition wrote this account in 1665, stating that the English and the Dutch, who had already settled in India, were the models that Monsieur de Colbert wanted imitated and surpassed, but all of this worthy minister's plans failed because of the imprudence and vanity peculiar to our nation as well as the inefficiency of those in charge.

The same author adds that he found the officers to have been poorly selected, violent, and incapable of doing the work assigned to them. They should have been men who were above the more vulgar passions and who were interested only in the

The population grew little by little, and storehouses, a fort, and barracks were built.

In 1717, a hurricane which swept up a great amount of sand blocked the port, flooded the island, and drowned many of the cattle. Since it was necessary to find another port, Surgere Island, now called Ship Island,[2] was chosen for its rather good harbor. In 1722, Monsieur de Bienville had everyone moved to New Orleans, which became the capital of Louisiana.

Six leagues from Ship Island, there is Cat Island, so named because the first people to land there found a large number of wildcats. This island is notorious for the number of murders and robberies which were committed there during the administration of the two officers sent by Monsieur de Kerlérec, the governor of Louisiana. In 1757, he appointed Monsieur Duroux commander-in-chief of the island and gave him a detachment composed of marines and members of the Halwill Regiment from Switzerland. As soon as Monsieur Duroux arrived on the island, he began to act like a sovereign. He had the soldiers of his garrison make him a garden, as though it were his right to do so, and he used them to make lime out of sea shells and charcoal, without paying them. Those who refused to submit to these indignities were tied naked to trees and exposed to the unbearable stings of the mosquitoes. The type of punishment meted out by this officer to the soldiers of his garrison is beneath the dignity of savages.

Monsieur Duroux had his men eat food made with flour salvaged from a Spanish ship, wrecked on the coast, while he sold at a profit to himself the flour supplied by the King for the men's bread. Because

good of their country. This should be the sole guide for those who wish to do a good job.

It seems to me that this useful lesson should be taken to heart by all those who are sent to the colonies in positions of authority.

I have told this story because it is singularly significant today in view of what goes on in our colonies. There are, however, good governors and finance officers who must not be confused with those who have made quick fortunes by odious means, through public misery, and by the blood of many unfortunate victims.

[2] This island is directly south of Biloxi, Mississippi.—Ed.

of the bad treatment at the hands of their commanding officer, several soldiers decided to go to New Orleans to present their grievances to the Governor and to show him the bad bread that they were eating. Monsieur de Kerlérec, who had no interest in their justified complaints, sent them back to be dealt with at the discretion of their commanding officer. Fearing his resentment, these poor men met and plotted to make an example of their officer.

The group of rebels decided to carry out their plot to kill Monsieur Duroux one day when he was out hunting on a little island near his post. Such a strange decision could have been inspired only by the despair brought about by the Governor's refusal to grant them justice. All that the Governor had to do to avoid this tragedy was to place a superior officer over Monsieur Duroux, who would then have been only second in command. As Duroux was returning from his hunting trip, a sentinel spotted his boat and raised the French flag. At this signal, the garrison took up arms and beat the general salute. Led by a corporal, the rebels advanced to the shore and shouted through a speaking trumpet, as is customary at sea, "Ahoy! Ahoy!" Monsieur Duroux answered, "Commander." He drew close to the shore, and as he set foot on land, the corporal gave the signal. The soldiers fired, and the Commander fell pierced with bullets. They then stripped him and threw his body into the sea. This was the grave and this the punishment for the indignities committed by a petty tyrant, who was mourned by no one and whose only recommendation was that he happened to be the protégé of Monsieur Thiton, first secretary to the Governor. Having taken over the island, the soldiers freed a settler called Beaudrot, whom the late commanding officer had unjustly kept in chains for a long time. Monsieur Duroux had assumed the privileges of an admiral of France, claiming a share of all that his soldiers and the settlers could salvage from ships wrecked off the coast of Cat Island. All who refused to pay him this tribute were punished as severely as though they had committed a great crime. This was Beaudrot's case. He had been put into chains simply for having refused to share with the Commander the things he had salvaged from the debris of the Spanish ship, *Situart,* which had been wrecked on the coast of the island in 1758.

The soldiers who had killed Monsieur Duroux pillaged all of the King's goods on Cat Island and then forced the settler, whose chains they had broken, to show them the way to the English colony of Carolina. When they arrived in the lands of the great Indian chief, whom the Europeans call the Emperor of the Cowetas, they sent Beaudrot back with a letter certifying that he had been forced to act as their guide. One group of these soldiers left for English territory, while those who remained among the Indians were soon arrested by order of Monsieur de Montberaut, who was then commanding officer in Alabama country. Among these was a corporal of the Halwill Regiment who, in order to avoid the customary Swiss execution, being sawed in two, stabbed himself with a knife which he wore around his neck Indian fashion.

An officer of the garrison, Monsieur Beaudin, was put in charge of a detachment which was to deliver the prisoners to Mobile. Meanwhile, Beaudrot's two sons came to Mobile from New Orleans. Without knowing it, they carried the order for their father's arrest, which was sent by the Governor to Monsieur de Velle, the commanding officer of Mobile. Beaudrot was at that time under heavy guard on his plantation. He went to prison willingly, not being aware of the arrest of the deserters whom he had guided. Monsieur de Velle had all the prisoners transferred to New Orleans where they were tried by court-martial. Beaudrot, found guilty of having acted as guide for the murderers of the Commander of Cat Island, was broken on the wheel, and his body was thrown into the river. One of the soldiers suffered the same fate, and a Swiss was sawed in two.

When serious thought is given to poor Beaudrot's fate, it is evident that his irregular trial was carried out by military men who were ignorant of both civil and criminal law. He could not have deserved the cruel punishment which he received. If law demands that crime must not go unpunished in the interest of public safety, then justice demands, in the name of humanity, that a judge's sentence be too lenient rather than too severe. According to the proverb, it is better to let one hundred guilty men go free than to punish one innocent man.

If the law wanted this settler to serve as an example, his sentence might have been lightened out of consideration for his wife and four children who were left desolate. Among these four children was a pretty daughter whom the entire colony admired for her virtue even more than for her beauty. This charming Creole, as well as the rest of her family, has retired to a remote plantation where she mourns her unfortunate father.

This poor man had been successfully employed in carrying on important negotiations with the Indians, who had a great deal of respect for him. He spoke their language and had as much practical knowledge of the terrain of the country as they had. In addition, he was extremely strong. Because of all these qualities, the Choctaws admired him so much that they made him a member of their nation. The Indians would have revolted in an effort to save him if it were not for the wise precautions taken by Monsieur de Velle,[3] who kept Beaudrot's imprisonment and execution a secret from them.

After Monsieur Duroux's tragic death, Monsieur de Kerlérec appointed Monsieur de C—— commander of Cat Island. This officer left New Orleans in 1758 with a garrison composed of soldiers and New Orleans settlers, vagrants sent out by the important people of the colony as their own replacements to do duty at the post. This was done with the Governor's consent. These vagrants remained on Cat Island just so long as they were paid by the citizens who should have been serving. It is easy to understand that troops of this kind, who are not relieved from their post from time to time, as they should be

---

[3] He knew the Choctaws well, since he had been commanding officer at Tombigbee for several years. The Indians respected him because of his valor and his honesty.

according to military regulation, take every opportunity to desert. We have seen this happen at several other posts in this colony.

A three-masted ship bought in Havana by a merchant called Saint-Criq came within sight of the island in March, 1759. Its cargo consisted of sugar, coffee, tafia, cables, and some war supplies. The crew consisted entirely of Spanish sailors, who abandoned Captain Saint-Criq on the coast near Balize. Because of the desertion of his crew, the Captain was forced to set out in his launch with the few men who remained loyal to him. When he arrived at New Orleans, he went to Major de Belle-Isle, the acting commanding officer. He asked the officer to give him enough men to help him look for his ship, which must have drifted somewhere off the coast of Cat Island.

Monsieur de Belle-Isle assigned to Monsieur Saint-Criq an intelligent sergeant and ten soldiers to sail the ship. At the same time, he wrote to Monsieur de C—— that if the ship had drifted to a point near his post, he was to station guards on it immediately and punish by death anyone who removed merchandise without the consent of the owner, Monsieur Saint-Criq. Lastly, he was to conform to the rules of the King's navy, especially the one headed "Shipwrecks, etc."

Unfortunately for Monsieur Saint-Criq, Monsieur de Belle-Isle's instructions came too late. Monsieur de C—— had already gone to the trouble of having the soldiers and residents of the garrison remove the cargo and bury it nearby in the sand. They had taken the necessary precautions to cover up this bit of work. Monsieur Saint-Criq arrived on Cat Island, delivered the Major's letter to the Commanding Officer, then he and his men climbed aboard to inspect the ship. Noticing, however, that he had forgotten the billfold in which he kept his bill of lading, he got off the ship again. What providential luck! He had hardly stepped onto the shore, when a raging fire broke out suddenly aboard ship. Three men died in the hold; the others saved themselves by jumping into the sea and swimming to shore.[4]

---

[4] At the very time Monsieur Saint-Criq had asked Monsieur de Belle-Isle's help in finding the ship and had received the letter instructing Monsieur de C—— to pro-

Monsieur Saint-Criq complained to Monsieur de Kerlérec. After a long delay, the Governor forced the Captain to settle his differences with Monsieur de C—— for fifteen hundred pounds. After the commander of Cat Island was called back to New Orleans, he went on such a spree that he scandalized the entire colony. When he had spent all that he had earned so dishonestly, he left on a Dutch ship from Curaçao, one of Holland's colonies. Opinions are divided on the reason for his secret departure from Louisiana. Some think that he left to escape the punishment he so richly deserved; others believe that the Governor entrusted him with documents for the Court. Time will tell.

His restitution of fifteen hundred pounds to Captain Saint-Criq as well as his admission to Monsieur La Perlière, his successor as commander of Cat Island, are sufficient proof that he had stolen the ship's cargo, for which he received sixty thousand pounds. Yet, he escaped death, the penalty for piracy, as the regulation cited above states: "All those who endanger the lives and the property of shipwrecked persons shall be punished by death." This is such an enormous crime that even if we were not Christians, natural religion would lead us to help the unfortunate in time of danger.[5] The Governor of Louisiana put his trust in this type of officer.

We have just learned that a war party of Cherokees, commanded by Wolf, has captured Fort Loudon, belonging to Great Britain, and that the commanding officer, Mr. Demerè, was killed by the Indians. They stuffed earth in his mouth and said, "Dog, since you are so hun-

tect the cargo, the Commander of Cat Island wrote the Major that on a certain day a three-masted ship had drifted within sight of his post. After having signaled it without receiving an answer, he had assumed that it was an enemy ship and that the crew was hiding in the hold. He had armed the post boat and set out in it with all his men. When he had hailed the ship once more and still received no answer, he had boarded it and had not found a living soul. He had found the cargo removed and all that had remained on the deck was a cut cable. He discovered, too, that the ship had had holes bored for twenty-six cannons.

[5] Monsieur de C—— hoped to enjoy his ill-gotten fortune in France, but he died, by decree of Providence, as he lived—in debauchery.

gry for land, eat your fill." They treated several others the same way.[6]

If I do not leave for France, I shall write you from New Orleans about the two chiefs of the colony, Governor de Kerlérec and Rochemore, the finance officer.

I am, sir, . . .

Fort Mobile

January 10, 1760

[6] Bossu speaks of "Fort London" and "Monsieur Dameri." This is obviously Fort Loudon commanded by an officer named Demerè. The fort was built at the junction of the Tellico and the Little Tennessee rivers in what is now Tennessee. There is a serious discrepancy in the dates, however. According to the *Dictionary of American History*, edited by James Truslow Adams and R. V. Coleman (New York, Charles Scribner's Sons, second ed., 1942), III, 304, Fort Loudon was taken by the Cherokees on August 7, 1760. The date of Bossu's letter containing the news of the fort's capture is January 10, 1760, about six months prior to the actual event.—Ed.

Letter XX

To the Marquis de l'Estrade.
The author leaves for New Orleans; the cause of the disturbances in the city; the sad story of Monsieur de Belle-Isle's captivity among the Attacapas; curious animals and medicinal herbs found in Louisiana.

Sir:

I have so much news to tell you that I do not know where to begin. I wrote you from Tombigbee that the situation in the capital is explosive. Everyone here is talking about quarrels, difficulties, and dissension. Greed and self-interest are the cause of all the trouble. Since I neither have nor want to have any part in all these quarrels and since I cannot serve the King with any degree of zeal in this colony where everything is in turmoil, I keep asking to be sent back to France. The most loyal subjects who want to do their duty are rewarded only with frustration, disgrace, and cruel persecution for their zeal. Without going into detail about the hardships visited upon many of the good officers and honorable people, most of whom are still living, I shall tell you only of the suffering to which Monsieur de Belle-Isle was exposed. This respectable officer, whose honesty and irreproachable conduct have earned him the friendship and the esteem of all good people, including especially generals Périer, Bienville, and Vaudreuil, deserves to have his story told. I heard it in great detail from him.

I shall tell you everything that has happened to him during the forty-five years he has served the King in this colony. Everything that I shall tell you will be the absolute truth, although some of the events will seem unbelievable. Monsieur de Bienville, who is still alive in Paris, can verify all of my statements since he is the one who ransomed Monsieur de Belle-Isle from the Indians who rescued him.

I know that you have a kind heart, sir, and will be touched by this unfortunate officer's ordeal.[1] Great souls are not ashamed of being moved by the misfortunes of others. The Indians themselves say that he who does not feel the sufferings of his brothers is unworthy of being called a man; he is a monster that mankind should flee like the plague.

In 1719, the administration of Louisiana was transferred from Monsieur de Crozat to the West India Company, which sent one thousand settlers to the colony. Monsieur de Belle-Isle was among the officers and volunteers who set sail from Lorient to Louisiana. The ship was carried by currents and contrary winds to St. Bernard's Bay on the Gulf of Mexico. When the captain sent his launch to shore in search of water, Monsieur de Belle-Isle and four of his friends received permission to go along. These gentlemen stayed on shore to hunt while the launch made a trip back to the ship. The launch came back to land once more, took on drinking water and rejoined the ship without waiting for the young officers, who had not yet come back from hunting. The impatient captain weighed anchor and sailed off to his destination, abandoning his five passengers on shore. You can imagine their consternation when they came back to the beach and found the launch and the ship gone. Abandoned in an unknown country, they wandered about for a long time on the uninhabited

---

[1] The story of Monsieur de Belle-Isle, Knight of the Royal and Military Order of Saint Louis, major of New Orleans and major general of the naval troops of Louisiana, was told in a report on Louisiana printed in Paris in 1758. The author, who had left the colony in 1733, had forgotten many of the most interesting events, and the happenings which he did report were denied by Monsieur de Belle-Isle himself. My account is the abstract of a manuscript written in Belle-Isle's own hand.

coast where they saw nothing on one side but the sea and on the other a land peopled by the cannibalistic Caribs. The Frenchmen did not dare leave the swampy coast lands, and, finding no solution to their problems, they gave way to despair. Needless to say, they nearly went out of their minds. Nothing worried these young Europeans more than the fear of falling into the hands of cannibals. Praying and bemoaning their sad fate, they followed the shore in the vain hope that the ship had gone westward. They lived on insects and herbs without knowing whether or not they were harmful. The mosquitoes, against which they had no protection, were especially annoying and numerous in that region. The men spent several days in that predicament. Monsieur de Belle-Isle had taken with him from the ship a young hunting dog which was very fond of him. His starving companions were tempted on several occasions to make a good meal of it. Monsieur de Belle-Isle sacrificed the animal to them, but he refused to kill it himself. One of the officers seized the dog but was so weak that when he tried to stab it, he let go his hold. The dog took off for the woods and could not be found. Monsieur de Belle-Isle saw the men die one after the other. To keep the bodies from being eaten by wild animals, he tried his best to dig graves with his bare hands in the sandy soil. He paid them this last tribute as he sighed over the suffering of mankind. He survived his companions only because of the strength of his constitution. In order to keep alive he courageously ate worms which he found in rotting wood. Several days after the death of his friends, he saw his dog far off holding something in its mouth. He called it, and the dog came to him with a great show of joy and dropped an opossum at his feet. The dog licked him and howled as though he were trying to say, "I am bringing you something which will save your life." These opossums, which are about the size of suckling pigs, are quite edible. Monsieur de Belle-Isle, with his dog as his only companion, wandered about looking for food. In the evening, he built himself a little entrenchment at the foot of a tree to protect himself against wild animals. One night, a wildcat approached the place where he was sleeping. His dog, watching at his side, saw the ferocious animal and ran at it howling fiercely. Monsieur de Belle-Isle awoke and ran to help his dog. The wildcat let go of the dog but not before he had wounded it. His master, fearing the dog would go mad, killed it and ate it. Then, alone in the wilderness, he fell to his knees, raised his arms to heaven, and thanked the Almighty for having spared him until then. Resigning himself to the will of Providence, he headed inland to see if he could find other people. He soon saw the footprints of men, which led him to a river bank. There he found a canoe, crossed the river, and saw on the other bank Indians who were drying human flesh and fish. They were Attacapas.[2] They approached Monsieur de Belle-Isle, whom they took for a ghost because he was so thin. He pointed to his mouth indicating that he was hungry. The Indians did not want to kill him and eat him because he was so emaciated. They offered him human flesh, but he chose fish which he ate greedily. The Indians then stripped him naked and divided his clothes among themselves. Then they took him to their village to fatten him up. There he had the good fortune to become the "dog"[3] of an old widow. Little by little, he began to regain his strength, but he was extremely downcast, since he was in constant fear that his hosts would sacrifice him to their false gods and then eat him. His imagination was always troubled by the horrible spectacle of these barbarians feasting on their fattest prisoners of war. I cannot describe this to you without shuddering. He expected that he would be clubbed to death at any moment if he got fat. These people held an assembly and decided that it would be cowardly of them to kill a man who did not come to do them harm but to ask for hospitality. Consequently, the widow kept him as her slave. Although the first days of his captivity were not hard, they were

[2] Among the peoples of America this name means "eaters of men." When they take a prisoner of war, they feast on his flesh. They usually live on fish and drink cassina. They can speak sign language and hold long conversations in pantomime.

[3] This is what they call a slave.

disagreeable because he had to take care of the little children of these cannibals. He was obliged to carry them around on his shoulders, which was very annoying since he was as naked as they were, except for the bit of clothing which kept him from being completely indecent. He received better treatment after the Indian woman took him under her protection.

Since Monsieur de Belle-Isle was young and strong, he did his work well as a slave and even managed to get into the good graces of his mistress, who adopted him. He was then freed and made a member of the tribe. He soon learned to speak sign language and use a bow and arrow like the Indians. They took him into battle with them, and he showed them his skill by shooting an arrow completely through one of the enemy. He was then recognized as a true warrior. The man he killed and a deer, shot by one of the Indians, were smoked and dried together to be eaten during the trip. One day, while they were on the march, Monsieur de Belle-Isle asked for something to eat. An Indian gave him some human flesh and told him that it was deer meat. After the officer had eaten it, the Indian said, "You were very finicky before, but now you eat human flesh just as we do." Monsieur de Belle-Isle threw up everything he had eaten.

After about two years of his captivity, envoys of another nation came bearing a peace pipe to the Attacapas. What a providential stroke of luck! These people lived in New Mexico and were the neighbors of the Natchitoches, whose territory was commanded by Monsieur de Hucheros de Saint-Denis, who was loved and respected by the envoys even though they themselves lived in Spanish lands. After they had studied Monsieur de Belle-Isle very closely, they told the Attacapas that there were white men like him in their own country. The Attacapas replied that they had found this "dog" near the big lake after his companions had died of hunger, they had brought him to their village where he had become the slave of one of the women, and they had taken him to war against an enemy tribe, whom they had defeated. He had distinguished himself in battle by skillfully killing one of the foe with an arrow. Because of this deed, he had been adopted by the tribe and made a warrior.

Belle-Isle pretended not to hear the conversation, but he was determined to get back to his native land. He took one of the envoys aside and questioned him thoroughly on the white men he had seen. Monsieur de Belle-Isle had fortunately kept a box containing his commission as an officer. He wrote the following message on it with ink made of soot and a pen fashioned from a crow's feather: "To the chief of the white men: I am so-and-so who was abandoned at Saint Bernard's Bay. My companions died of hunger and misery before my eyes. I am a prisoner of the Attacapas."[4] The poor man gave his commission to the Indian, assuring him that it was "talking bark" or paper. If the Indian gave it to the chief of the Frenchmen in his country, he would be well received. The native thought that the letter was a sacred thing since it was going to speak for him among the French. The others wanted to take it away from him, but he escaped by swimming across a river. He held the letter over his head to keep it from getting wet. After having traveled 150 leagues across country, the Indian arrived among the Natchitoches,[5] whose territory was then commanded by Monsieur Hucheros de Saint-Denis, a distinguished officer who was the first to have gone from Louisiana to Mexico by land. He married the Spanish governor's niece in Mexico. The messenger was showered with gifts after he delivered Monsieur de Belle-Isle's letter to the Commander. Then Monsieur de Saint-Denis began to weep like an Indian. When the natives asked him what was wrong, he answered that he was grieving over his brother who had been a prisoner of the Attacapas for two years. Since the tribes of this region thought highly of Monsieur de Saint-Denis, the messenger volunteered to go for Monsieur de Belle-Isle, and other Indians joined him. Monsieur de Saint-Denis gave them some shirts and a hat for

---

[4] The captain who had abandoned Belle-Isle and his companions at St. Bernard's Bay went down with his ship, no trace of which has ever been found.

[5] A post near Mexico. This is an Indian settlement on the Red River.

"Ball Play of the Squaws on the Prairie"

From an oil painting by Seth Eastman

Belle-Isle Leaving the Attacapas

From Jean-Bernard Bossu, *Nouveaux Voyages aux Indes occidentales* (1768)

Monsieur de Belle-Isle. Ten of them, armed with rifles, rode off immediately. They promised Monsieur de Saint-Denis that within two moons they would bring back his brother riding on the extra horse they were taking with them.

The shots this group fired to announce its arrival made the Attacapas think it was thundering. The envoys gave Monsieur de Belle-Isle a letter from Monsieur de Saint-Denis telling him that he had nothing to fear from the bearers of the message and that the writer was looking forward with joy to seeing him. I cannot tell you how happy the officer was to receive this letter. He was afraid, however, that the Attacapas would oppose his leaving. The chief of the envoys made him mount up immediately and they all took off together. The Attacapas, frightened by the envoys' rifle shots, did not dare protest, and the woman who had adopted Monsieur de Belle-Isle broke into tears. In this way, he escaped from a captivity which might have lasted his entire life.

The Indian who managed Belle-Isle's escape was as proud as Hernando Cortez when he conquered Montezuma, the last emperor of Mexico. They rode to the Natchitoches territory but found that Monsieur de Saint-Denis had left for headquarters in Biloxi, which was the capital of Louisiana at that time, since New Orleans had not yet been built.

Monsieur d'Orvilliers, who commanded the territory in Saint-Denis' absence, sent Monsieur de Belle-Isle and his party to see Monsieur de Bienville, who was then governor of Louisiana. Delighted to see Belle-Isle, the General gave him a warm welcome and generously rewarded his liberators. Upon the former captive's arrival, everyone crowded around to congratulate him on his escape from slavery. Monsieur de Bienville then gave him some clothing.

Because of Belle-Isle's knowledge of the Attacapas' way of life, he was very useful to the Governor. The Spaniards of New Mexico had never been able to subjugate these Indians as they had the other tribes in this part of their empire.

Monsieur de Bienville sent a present to the Attacapas and another one to the widow who had adopted and protected Monsieur de Belle-Isle. These people, who were not expecting the Governor's generosity, sent envoys[6] to thank him and to form an alliance with the French. Monsieur de Belle-Isle's patroness was among the group. From that time on these Indians have always treated the French humanely, and the French have persuaded them to give up the barbaric custom of eating human flesh.

> *The cruel inhabitants of these far-off shores,*
> *Led, through our training, to the very doors*
> *Through which art and humanity cast their rays,*
> *Will change and soften their savage ways. . . .*
> *Wild and simple, but no fools,*
> *They respect the Frenchman's laws and rules.*
> *The Frenchman, consoling them in their plight,*
> *Treats each as his child, but with citizen's right.*
>
> THOMAS, *Jumonville*

When the Attacapas came to New Orleans, they were well received by all the French, in recognition of their treatment of Monsieur de Belle-Isle, because if it had not been for them, he would have suffered the same unhappy fate as his companions.

Monsieur de Bienville sometimes amused himself with these cannibals by having their pupil, Monsieur de Belle-Isle, converse with them in sign language. The Attacapas are armed with very big bows and arrows. They cultivate corn as do the other peoples of North

---

[6] The chief of the envoys made this speech, interpreted by Belle-Isle, to Monsieur de Bienville: "My father, the white man you see here, who is of your flesh and blood, was bound to us through adoption. His brothers died of hunger. If they had been found sooner by my people, they would still be alive and would have enjoyed the same privileges."

The hospitality offered Belle-Isle by the Attacapas proves that we should consider their cruelty the result of a lack of education. Nature has made them capable of showing human kindness.

America. This part of the continent is so vast that we still do not know its limits or all the tribes that live in it.

In 1759, Monsieur de Marigny de Mandeville,[7] a distinguished officer, drew up plans, which met with the Governor of Louisiana's approval, to explore the area near Barataria Island, whose coasts we know only imperfectly. It is with this project in mind that he made a general map of the colony. He has explored this unknown territory with untiring zeal at his own expense. This preoccupation with the King's glory and the growth of his empire is what characterizes a worthy citizen.

I have tried, sir, to give you in my preceding communications a short history of this country from the time of its discovery until the present and to describe to you the commerce and the general condition of the colony, as well as all that has seemed instructive or amusing to me. I hope that I have omitted nothing essential. I am going to finish this letter with several observations on the natural history of the colony. The individual accounts which you may have read on this subject cannot have been very instructive. Let me say, first of all, sir, that all the European fruit which has been planted here is doing extremely well. Monsieur Fazende, a member of the Upper Council of Louisiana, brought over from Provence a fig tree whose fruit is excellent. Since saplings can be grown from cuttings, all the plantations have been supplied with fig trees. Among the fruits peculiar to this country, there is one that is called the prickly pear, which looks and tastes like a pickled cucumber. This very refreshing fruit is very common in the Mobile region.

The persimmon, called *ougoufle* by the Indians, is similar to and no bigger than the European medlar. This fruit, yellow and red like the apricot, is an excellent astringent and a superb remedy for dysentery and the bloody flux. The bread the Indians make of it looks like gingerbread and is dried for use on long trips.[8]

[7] See this officer's report, printed by Guillaume Desprès, Rue St. Jacques, 1765.
[8] The persimmon has still another virtue. Take some of its seeds, grind them

The papaw has the shape and the color of a lemon, is odoriferous, and tastes like the banana. Its seeds, which resemble beans, are poisonous for hogs.

There are many orange trees and peach trees. Oranges and peaches are so plentiful that the colonists let them rot on the trees. There are apple trees, plum trees, and whole forests of nut trees. There are black nuts, or hickory nuts, and walnuts. Just as in Europe, there are fair-sized ones which are good to eat and others, as big as a fist, which are bitter and have a very thick, hard shell. The pecan trees bear nuts which are long, like almonds, but more delicate in flavor. The Indians make oil of them which they use in their corn meal mush.

The Creator's generosity is admirable. He has sown this great variety of fruit trees in the New World. There are also a thousand species of curious, unknown animals, about whose existence the ancients never even dreamed.

There are some magnolia trees with red flowers and some with white ones. The latter, which bear a white tulip-like flower and have many branches, would be decorative in the royal gardens of Europe. The Indians call them "peace trees."

Along the rivers there are many grapevines that climb so high on the trees that when those in the Illinois country are cut down, a single stem yields a whole barrel of wine. These vines grow wild, and the wine made from their grapes is tart. In the forests there are many blackberry bushes whose fruit is sweet. Jellies are made of some of these berries.

The acacia, a tree with thorns six inches long, is so hard that it dulls and sometimes breaks axes. The Indians use fire to shape this wood into mortars for grinding corn into flour. This tree bears cassia-like pods about one foot long and a gummy, sticky fruit containing

---

into a powder, mix it with fresh water, let it stand for twenty-four hours. Strain the water through a cloth and keep it in a bottle. If you have a kidney stone attack, drink a glass of this water before meals, and continue the treatment until you are completely cured.

seeds that resemble beans. The natives purge themselves with this excellent laxative.

There are trees in the forests which produce resin and tar, and gum similar to turpentine flows from others.

The wax myrtle is a shrub which looks like the olive tree and bears a berry like the juniper. When these berries are melted in water, they form a green, aromatic wax which is used for making candles. Monsieur Alexandre was the first one to do this. Because of his useful discovery, the Academy has granted him a pension. He also has found a way to bleach the product, as we do beeswax in Europe.

Since my arrival in Louisiana, sugar cane plants have been imported from Santo Domingo. Monsieur Dubreuil, the commander of the citizens' militia, was the first colonist to build a sugar mill in New Orleans. Sugar comes from the juice of a reed or cane that can be planted from cuttings. The more fertile the land, the thicker and taller the plant grows. The cane is jointed at intervals. The ripe plant turns yellow and is then cut with a hooked knife above the first joint, where there is no sap. After the leaves growing on each side of the cane are removed, the stalks are tied into bundles and are carried off to the mill, where they are crushed between two steel-covered wooden rollers. A Negro places the cane between the cylinders, pressing out all the juice. This liquid is then collected in a basin from which it flows through a lead pipe to a reservoir. From there it passes into large boilers, similar to those seen at the Hôtel Royal des Invalides, and is heated by furnaces. When the liquid is refined, it is poured into another vat where it is constantly stirred and kept boiling until it becomes quite thick. After the sugar has gone through this first process, it is placed in earthenware forms to be whitened. The opening in the forms is covered over with clay to keep the air from working on the sugar and hardening it before it is completely refined by the removal of the syrup, or molasses.

Tafia is made with the scum of the sugar. This liquor is passed through a still, like brandy in France. The Europeans in America prefer it to brandy for the curing of wounds. It is also used to make rum, which is the essence of the liquor called Barbados water.

In the Illinois territory, there is a little bush about three feet high which bears a fruit the size of a lady apple and tastes like a lemon. Chestnuts and hazelnuts like those in France are found in the forests.

Many plants of medicinal value grow in Louisiana, among them gensing, whose root makes an excellent cough syrup, jalap, rhubarb, smilax, snakeroot, sarsaparilla, and St.-John's-wort, from which an excellent oil for healing wounds is made. Here is how the medicine men make St.-John's-wort oil. They put the flowers of this plant in an earthenware jar and pour bear grease over them. The jar is then stopped up and exposed to the early sun. This sweet-smelling oil, turned red by the heated jar, cleanses and cures all kinds of wounds. There are even plants that act as antidotes to poisons. But recognizing them and knowing how to use them are rare and precious gifts which the Creator has not granted to everyone. The Indians know a thousand medicinal plants good for purifying the blood.

There are entire forests of sassafras trees, used for medicine and dyes. Some trees contain copal, a gummy substance which is a balm as good as that made in Peru. Animals wounded by hunters cure themselves by rubbing against a tree from which this balm flows.

The Indians also have bitter gourds; calabashes, with which they make a syrup for chest ailments; maidenhair, a remedy for the same type of illness; and cassina, an excellent diuretic. A strong dose causes the patient to shiver for a short time. The Alabama Indians call it the "drink of valor." The Americans value their medicinal herbs more than they do all the gold of Mexico and Peru.

Louisiana has all sorts of curious and hitherto unknown animals. The French settlers and the Indians make good use of the buffalo, a very large, strong animal. The meat is salted or smoked, and blankets are made of the hide. The bull is covered with fine wool from which good mattresses are made, the suet is used for candles, and the sinews supply the Indians with strings for their bows. The horns are worked into spoons, with which the natives eat their corn meal mush, or into containers for their powder. The buffalo has a hump on its back like a camel, long hair on its head like a goat, and wool covering its body like a sheep. The Indian women spin this wool into yarn.

All kinds of wild animals are found as one approaches the source of the Missouri. Wild goats and kids are very common in certain seasons. These animals are extremely agile and alert. The females have double-ringed horns and are not as big as ours. The Frenchmen who have tasted them assure me that the young kids are as good as Briançon sheep. Since the Indians of this area rarely use our rifles, they hunt these animals with bows and arrows. Wounded goats, finding it difficult to climb higher into the mountainous regions where they graze, are easily caught by the Indians.

The trappers have also told me that there is a very big bird in this country called the royal eagle. I think that I ought to tell you, sir, of the strange way that the Indians hunt these birds, which the northern tribes greatly prize for their feathers, used to decorate peace pipes. The natives call them "feathers of valor." This kind of hunting is reserved for the old warriors because it does not require much exertion. First of all, the old hunter examines the places usually frequented by these birds. Then he brings with him some meat, snakes, or animal entrails and attaches this bait to a firmly anchored piece of wood. The first eagle that comes along eats the bait, grows accustomed to the place, and attracts others, who fight greedily over the prey. At that same spot, which is on a mountain top, the old man then digs himself a hole, over which he places a sort of chimney covered by a bundle of twigs to which bait is attached. He lets the eagle eat until it has had enough. Then the Indian passes his hands, covered with a skin sack, through the straw, which is under the twigs, and grabs the eagle by its feet. He then wraps his buffalo robe around the bird and kills it. If he is fortunate enough to catch five or six, he is quite happy, for their feathers are traded throughout North America. This kind of hunting is not very difficult. The bait is collected by the hunter's children, who know where he is hidden, and the women send him food.

There are also hares and white bears, whose fur is very fine. The wildcats of Louisiana differ from those of Africa and South America in that they are not spotted. They catch deer the same way that cats pounce on mice. The tiger cat kills buffalo in the same manner. These cats climb trees bordering the narrow paths that the buffalo take when they go to the rivers for water. They pounce upon the necks of the buffalo, bite through their throats, and kill them. The buffalo's strength and his horns are useless against this type of treacherous attack.

The opossum is the size of a European cat; it has a head like a fox's, feet like a monkey's, and a tail like a rat's. This animal is very curious. I once killed a female that had seven young clinging to her teats in a most surprising manner. That is where they develop, and they do not let go until they are able to walk. Then they drop into a membrane pouch. The ones I saw were the size of newborn mice. Nature has provided the female with a pouch located under the belly and covered with hair. When the young are attacked, they enter the pouch, and the mother carries them off to safety. Opossum meat tastes like that of suckling pig. Their hair is whitish, and their fur is like the beaver's. They live in the woods on beechnuts, chestnuts, walnuts, and acorns. I have eaten opossum several times while on trips. An excellent ointment for the cure of hemorrhoids is made of its extremely fine, white fat.

Another animal, called the woodcat, is found here. It is the size of the European fox. This animal is very fond of oysters. It does not look like a cat, except for its tail; it rather resembles the marmot. When trained, it acts like a dog, licking and caressing its master and following him everywhere. It picks things up with its paws like a monkey. I think these must be the "mute dogs" which the Spaniards found in the West Indies.[9]

198

In Louisiana there are four kinds of squirrels: large, black, red, and gray. There are others as small as little rats. These are called flying squirrels because their four feet are connected by a membrane which they spread when they jump from one tree to another.

I have often heard Frenchmen and Indians say that snakes have the ability to fascinate or charm squirrels. I wanted to see this for myself. I must tell you of my observations in this matter. One day I was hunting in Illinois country, where there is a great quantity of hazelnuts. There were also many squirrels, since they are particularly fond of these nuts.

I suddenly heard a squirrel, in a tree under which I was standing, make a pitiful noise, as though it were frightened. I did not know what was wrong with the animal until I saw a snake hanging from a branch of the tree. It held its head raised and waited for its prey. After having jumped from branch to branch, the poor squirrel fell into the snake's mouth and was swallowed.

Without going into great detail, I believe that this is how the squirrel was hypnotized by the snake. The squirrel, which has a natural aversion to the snake, seeing its enemy hanging motionless from a branch, thinks that it is caught in the tree. Not realizing that this is just a trap, the squirrel jumps from branch to branch as though to mock the snake in its trouble. When the animal jumps too close, the snake darts forward, seizes its prey, and swallows it. Some writers believe that the snake has hypnotic power.

The cunning of snakes is amazing. I have seen some stay perfectly still as though they were not there because they knew I was looking at them. They stayed in exactly the same position until I would go off for a stick or a stone with which to crush their heads. When I got back I would find that the snake had slithered off. I have had this same experience several times during my travels in the wilderness where snakes are common.

There are several species, the most remarkable of which is the

[9] This is obviously a raccoon.—ED.

rattler, which has three or four little, round bones under his scales at the end of his tail. When he moves his tail, the bones hit against each other making a noise like a child's rattle. Pregnant Indian women pulverize this rattle and swallow the powder in the belief that this will help them through childbirth without pain. Rattlesnake grease makes an excellent ointment for rheumatic pains. It penetrates the joints up to the bones. It is believed that this snake's age can be told by the number of its rattles. I have seen some of these snakes so large that they could swallow a small doe by sucking it in a little at a time.

There is another type of snake called the whip snake, which is red underneath and has a black back. When this species, which can attain a length of twenty feet, catches someone in the water, it squeezes him until he can no longer breathe and then drowns him.[10]

The snake called the hisser[11] is not quite two feet long. It is very difficult to see because of its small size and is, therefore, even more dangerous than the larger snakes. The Indians and the Negroes often step on them and are bitten. This species has a very large mouth and hisses terribly when it is frightened. Because of this, the Indians call it *ho-houy*, "the hisser." During my trip to Tombigbee, a hisser, hidden under some leaves, bit one of the soldiers who had stepped on its tail with his bare feet. The angry snake grabbed him by the big toe and would not let go. I was very disturbed when I saw the poor soldier, who was my interpreter, at death's door. I asked the help of a medicine man who happened to be passing the vicinity. He took out a little sack of powder and blew some of it through a tube onto the head of the hisser, killing it immediately. He then applied to the

[10] Called the *fouetteur* by Bossu. This is probably the coachwhip snake, a constrictor which grows to a length of about six feet. It is often black with a reddish underside. There is not now, nor was there in the time of Bossu as far as is known, a North American constrictor twenty feet long. The anaconda is capable of killing a man but is a native of the Amazon regions.—Ed.

[11] The hognose snake, also called the puff adder, is about this size and hisses ferociously when in danger. It rarely bites, however, and is only slightly venomous. —Ed.

bite another kind of powder, which prevented the venom from taking effect. He mixed some of the powder with water and gave it to the patient, who suffered no inconvenience at all from the snake bite. I paid the medicine man well. I would very much have liked to know his secret, but he did not think it proper to reveal it to me. This man acted like a charlatan when he said that the Master of Life had revealed this secret to him and to him alone.

There are in the St. Louis, or Mississippi, River extremely big and long alligators. They are so carniverous that when they come across a man sleeping on the ground, they drag him into the water and eat him. As a rule, however, these cowardly animals turn and run when they are approached. They rarely eat a man because it is so easy to get away from them. But they do chase those who run from them, and they are very dangerous in the water. The alligator is the most horrible animal in all nature. I think back with horror of the one which tried to drag me into the Tombigbee River. I thought for a moment that it was the very devil who had come up from hell. I cannot think of a better description of its hideous appearance. Its back is covered with impenetrable scales, almost like oyster shells, which resist rifle bullets. It is very difficult to wound it except through the eye. There are many of them in the Red River. They are torpid in the winter, lie in the mud, and cannot move forward or backward. Fish swim into their open mouths as though they were entering a funnel. During this season the Indians climb on the backs of the alligators and take great pleasure in beating them over the head with axes.

There are also frogs of extraordinary size, whose croaking is louder than the bellows of a bull.

On my way from Mobile to New Orleans, I stopped at Horn Island, where I found a petrified shellfish which the Indians call *naninathelay,* which means "sea spider." Its outer covering was bluer and shinier than Chinese lacquer. Its petrified eyes were as hard as diamonds. This shellfish is about the size and shape of a barber's dish turned upside down. Its tail, about six inches long and very pointed, has a dangerous sting.[12]

There are otters and beavers in the upper part of the colony. The Indians say that these beavers were chased away by their Canadian relatives for being too lazy to help in the joint endeavor of building shelters and dikes to turn the course of the rivers. Beavers are extremely industrious and skillful in this type of construction.

The carrion crow, the size and shape of a turkey, is the most voracious of the carniverous birds. It follows hunters and detachments on their way from one post to another. They wait impatiently, like flocks of crows, for the men to break camp. They avidly eat everything that is left behind and then fly off towards the next encampment. These birds eat human corpses whenever they can find them. The carrion crow has black feathers. The down under its wings is used to stop bleeding.[13]

The flamingo, about the same size as the carrion crow, has black wing tips, a white back, and a fire-red breast.

There are two kinds of red-winged blackbirds,[14] the smaller of which are about the size of European starlings. They are so numerous that one hundred of these edible birds can be killed with a single shot. The settlers have to protect their corn and wheat fields to keep the redwings from eating the entire crop. These birds are jet black with red wing tips. Their beautiful feathers are used to make muffs, pompons, and decorations for ladies' dresses.

Parrots, parakeets, and very beautiful jays are common. In Missouri country there are magpies which are like the European variety, except for their coloring. The feathers of shaded black and white are used by the Indians as hair ornaments.

---

[12] This shellfish is now in the Marquis de Marigny's natural history collection. [Probably the king crab. According to the eighteenth-century translator, these were very common.—ED.]

[13] *Karancro*. The black vulture, sometimes called the carrion crow.—ED.

[14] Bossu mistakenly calls this bird an *étourneau*, or starling. The starling was not introduced into the United States from Europe until 1890.—ED.

Our eyes are charmed by the beauty of nature, unadorned by art, exactly as it was fashioned by the hands of the Creator before the fall of our first ancestor. Travelers are enchanted by the songs of the birds, especially by that of the mocking bird, which enjoys the company of man. It is almost as though these birds were made expressly to help the traveler relax and forget his weariness. At the approach of a traveler, the mocking bird perches on a nearby branch, sings sweetly, and then flies about. Its song is truly unique. As the bird sits in the top of a tree, it imitates the song of all the other birds and even makes fun of cats by meowing. The mocking bird sometimes comes to the towns and settlements. When it hears the music of instruments, it joins in the concert as though it were charmed. It is about the size of a starling and is slate blue in color. It is easily tamed if captured young.

The painted bunting, or nonpareil, has a royal-blue head, a beautiful red breast, and a golden-green back. It has a sweet song and is about the size of a canary.[15]

The cardinal is entirely red with a black throat. It has a crest of feathers on its head. Its beak is red and strong. This bird is a type of sparrow, which likes to live in the proximity of men. It is about the size of a lark and whistles like a merle.

The eastern blue gosbeak[16] is blue with some purple and is about the size of a linnet. The goldfinch is completely yellow with black wing tips. There is also a bird called the harlequin because of its variety of colors, and another, which is red and blue, is called the swiss by the French settlers. These last three species are migrating birds which are found in the Illinois territory in summer.

The hummingbird, no bigger than a may bug, is of many bright, changing colors. Like the bee, it gets its food from flowers. Its nest is

[15] Called the *pape*, or pope, in the original text. From the description, this bird is obviously the painted bunting.—ED.

[16] Called the *évêque* by Bossu. He thus has an entire hierarchy: the pope, the cardinal, and the bishop.—ED.

made of a fine cotton-like substance and hangs from a tree branch. There are many hitherto unknown birds whose description would take up too much time.

Some of the butterflies are very beautiful. Two of them which I collected during my travels were eaten by moths. I have never seen anything so wonderful as these butterflies. It would seem that the Author of Nature took pleasure in painting their wings with the most vivid colors. The finest and purest gold and silver on earth were found mixed with the other colors in admirable symmetry. These butterflies must have been carried into the Arkansas territory by a gust of wind, since in my travels covering more than one thousand leagues, I have never again encountered this species. I asked some Osages who live near the Santa Barbara mines to get me some, but they told me that the country in which these butterflies are found is inhabited by extremely savage people who are human in shape only.

There are several kinds of ducks, the most curious of which are the wood ducks. They perch in trees by means of webbed feet which have claws. They make their nests in tree trunks that lean over rivers and lakes. When the young are hatched, they take to the water immediately. Their feathers have beautiful, shaded colors. The male is crested. These ducks are the best to eat since they feed on acorns and beechnuts in the woods.

Along the river there are egrets, whose extremely white feathers are used to make aigrettes for the ladies. The pelican, called the "big gullet" by the settlers because of the pouch it has under its throat, is as white and as large as a swan. It has a beak about twelve inches long. The grease from this aquatic bird is used in indigo paste, a blue dye made from a plant whose seeds come from the East Indies.

There is also the spoonbill, with a beak like a spatula, a pharmacist's instrument. Another bird is called the lancet-beak. It would take volumes to finish this subject. I leave this work to our learned compatriots, Monsieur Buffon and Monsieur Daubenton, who have already begun this vast undertaking. I hope that you will be satisfied with this short description. I am, sir, . . .

New Orleans
June 1, 1762

P.S. Before finishing my letter, sir, I should like to speak to you of two valuable plants which are found in Louisiana: indigo and cotton. Indigo resembles the broom plant. One type grows wild on the hilltops and near the Louisiana forests, but the indigo plant which is cultivated comes from the islands. It grows two and one-half feet high and is harvested twice a year. When the plant is ripe, it is cut down and brought to a twenty-foot-high shed that has a roof held up by poles instead of walls. In this shed there are three vats placed in such a way that water from one can run into the next. The indigo leaves and a certain amount of water, in which they are permitted to rot, are placed in the highest vat. When the man in charge of the operation decides, after frequent inspection, that the time is right, he opens a spout, and the water runs into the next vat. There is a precise moment when this must be done, for if the indigo remains in the first vat too long, it turns black.

When all the water is in the second vat, it is beaten until the overseer, through his long experience, decides that the process is to stop. The water is then permitted to settle, and the indigo forms a sediment at the bottom of the vat. As the liquid becomes clear, it is run off in gradual stages through a series of spouts placed one beneath the other.

The indigo is then removed from the vat and is placed in cloth sacks through which the remaining liquid is permitted to seep. It is then dried on boards and cut into little squares, which are packed into barrels for shipment to Europe.

Seeds are obtained by permitting the necessary number of plants to grow to maturity. The quality of the plant depends upon the soil, which should be light. In the West Indies there are up to four crops a year, but in Louisiana there are not more than three, and even these are of inferior quality.

Cotton, a shrub about the size of the rosebush, does not grow well in strong, rich earth. Therefore, the cotton grown in the Louisiana lowlands is not as good as that which comes from higher terrain. The cotton of this country is of the type called white siamese. It is not as long or fine as silky cotton, but it is, nevertheless, excellent. Its leaves are bright green and resemble spinach. The flower is pale yellow, and the black oval seed, contained in the capsule, is about the size of a bean. As a rule, it is cultivated in soil that is not yet fit for tobacco or indigo, which require a great deal of care.

The bush is cut close to the ground every two or three years in the belief that this increases its yield. The pistil of the flower develops into a somewhat pointed capsule about the size of a pigeon egg. It turns from green to blackish-brown and becomes dry and brittle. When the cotton is ripe, the heat of the sun swells it, making the pod pop in three or four places with a slight noise. The cotton is then picked quickly to keep it from falling to the ground, where it would spoil. Every ball contains, five, six, or seven flat, rough seeds. Because cotton sticks to everything, it requires a great deal of time and patience to remove the seeds. For this reason, a good number of the settlers have become disgusted with its cultivation.

I have not spoken to you about tobacco. It seems plausible that it is native to this country, since according to Indian tradition passed down by word of mouth, it has always been smoked in the peace pipe. I shall finish with a suggestion that has already been made before and which bears repeating until someone tries to carry it out. Observers have remarked that it would be easy to grow saffron in the Louisiana highlands because of the climate. The colonists would profit by this, especially since they could easily sell it to nearby Mexico.

Letter XXI

To the Marquis de l'Estrade.
Reflections on the American people; the ancients' knowledge of this country; the possibility that the inhabitants entered America over a land bridge connecting it with Asia's Tatary coast; a dissertation on the means of conserving one's health in the New World.

Sir:

I hope to leave for France in the very near future, but I am taking the opportunity of writing you once more. After having given you an idea of the habits, customs, and history of the people among whom I have traveled, I can think of no better way to end my account than to make several comments on the population of this immense continent. The entire subject is so obscure that no one today can clarify it. Several learned writers have tried without success to throw some light on the problem. Modern philosophy has tried to get to the bottom of it with just as little success. The opinions and arguments offered have not been able to convince even the feeblest minds.

When the ancient writers are studied attentively, everything seems to indicate that America was not absolutely unknown to them. Diodorus Siculus seems to have spoken of it in a rather precise way. Father Lafitau[1] cites a passage from the ancient text to which he adds

---

[1] Joseph-François Lafitau, 1681–1746, a Jesuit who went to Canada as a missionary and wrote accounts of his travels. *Mémoire concernant la précieuse plante ging-sang de Tartarie* (1718); *Moeurs des sauvages comparées aux moeurs des pre-*

some enlightening comments. According to the Greek author, the Phoenicians, having grown rich on their Mediterranean colonies, did not venture very far beyond the columns of Hercules. They were frightened by that vast, little-known sea which they discovered on the other side of the Strait of Gibraltar. They very slowly overcame this fear. A few bold sailors dared go out into the ocean but stayed close to the African coast. A violent storm lasting several days carried them far to the west until they reached a large island. Upon their return, they talked eagerly about their discovery, but they embellished their tale with the lies that are so common to travelers of all countries and all times.

When the Tyrrhenians became masters of the seas, they decided to establish a colony on the island. The Carthaginians were opposed to such an undertaking for fear that their compatriots, attracted by the description of the place, would abandon their country to settle on the island. They also considered the new land a refuge in the event that something happened to their empire.

To this passage from Diodorus Siculus, Father Lafitau adds one from Pausanias, who was trying to discover whether there were any satyrs. He was told by a certain Euphemus, born in Caria, that he was carried off during a storm to the very ends of the ocean where there are several islands which the sailors call the Satyrides. The inhabitants of these islands are reddish-colored people with tails. The trembling sailors tried to avoid them, but when a contrary wind forced them to draw close to the shore, the savages surrounded the ship. In order to get rid of them, the crew had to give them a woman.

You will find Father Lafitau's comments quite reasonable. "The description of these islanders fits the Carib Indians perfectly. They were masters of the West Indies until modern times, when they were chased off by the Europeans. The skin of these people is naturally reddish. This is caused less by nature than by the imaginations of the

miers temps (1723); *Histoire des découvertes et des conquêtes des Portugais dans le Nouveau-Monde* (1733).—Ed.

mothers who, thinking that this color is beautiful, transmit it to their children.[2] Daily applications of roucou, which they use instead of vermilion, turn them flame red. Fear caused the sailors to imagine they saw satyrs, and they must have mistaken decorative tails for real ones. Almost all the savage nations of America wear these ornaments, especially when they are at war."

The similarity that is found between the customs of several American peoples and those of some of the oldest European nations seems to prove that the ancients were not ignorant of America. It especially proves that the Old World supplied men to the New. How would this similarity be explained otherwise? What a great resemblance there is in the religions, habits, and customs of the Indians and some of our ancient peoples! The most daring explanations of the origin of the American population will never account for these similarities. If the original inhabitants were a group of people who escaped from the flood—some argue in vain that the flood did not cover the whole world—they would have brought with them to America antediluvian customs. Are the nations which came into existence after the flood similar to those which perished in its waters? We do not have enough knowledge to make this comparison. There likewise is no answer to those who say that the Almighty hand that sowed plants and fruit in all parts of the world could have placed men there, too. An ingenious phrase does not always make a reasonable argument. No one denies that the Creator has this power, but he has deigned to tell us himself that he did not want to do things that way. He created only two human beings, who are the ancestors of all mankind.

All conjecture must take into account the path followed by the migrants who first came from the Old to the New World. Most of those who have written on this subject are primarily concerned with

[2] Not everyone will agree with this Jesuit on the effect of a mother's imagination on her children. The problem of why men of different places are of different colors is far from resolved. Nothing that has been written on the subject has explained this phenomenon. A combination of many causes must have been responsible for turning men from their original white color to black, red, and brown.

this problem, which will be solved once we have more precise knowledge of our globe. It would appear very likely that there is a link between Asia and America. I have already spoken to you about this, sir, when I mentioned the elephant bones which were found in one of the territories I visited. This is not a new idea. Father Lafitau says: "America could have been reached at different points and, thus, could have been populated from any direction. There is no doubt about it. The Old and the New Worlds are not very far from each other in the south. In the north, Greenland, which perhaps borders on the New World, is not very far from Lapland. The lands of Asia near Hokkaido may perhaps form a single continent with America. At least the distance between them may not be very great if the straits that are believed to be there open into the Tatary Sea. This ocean which surrounds America almost entirely has many islands, both in its northern and its southern regions. Because they had been shipwrecked, or through mere chance, the migrants could have crossed over from island to island."

This writer gives several reasons for the belief that North America is connected to Tatary or to some adjoining land. Here is a strange one. You know, sir, that the ginseng plant is really native to Manchuria. The Tatar, or Chinese, name of this plant means "man's thighs." The Americans, who have known and have used this plant for a long time, call it *gareul-oguen*, which has the same meaning. If North America is not connected to Tatary and if the Americans did not originally come from Asia, how did the inhabitants of both continents come to give the same name to the same plant? We are not talking here of the etymology of corrupted words which cannot be forced back into their old form; we are concerned with the meaning of the words.

Captain William Rogers considers it quite likely that some Tatars crossed over to America. He states that every year ships that leave the Philippines for Mexico are forced to sail northward to find favorable winds, since they meet only head winds in the tropics. He says that after they pass forty-two degrees North latitude, they often find they are in shallow water, which would seem to indicate that land is not far off. He imagines that there may be a continent, unknown to Europeans, which connects California and Japan. But would not this more likely be the coast of Kamchatka or that new stretch of land to the east of it which Captain Bering discovered?

To these observations I shall add the synopsis of an account found in the *Mercure Galant* of November, 1711. I shall simply cite the facts without making any favorable or unfavorable comments. The author claims to have taken this from a manuscript found in Canada.

Ten men, seeking their fortune, went up the Mississippi in three canoes. After traveling for a long time, they came to another river flowing south-southwest. They carried their canoes to it and continued their trip. Some time afterward, they came to a country extending two hundred leagues, which was inhabited by a people called the Escaanibas.

The Frenchmen (these ten travelers were of our nation) found a great deal of gold in this land. Agauzan, the king of the Escaanibas, who claimed to be a descendant of Montezuma, maintained an army of one hundred thousand men. The women were as white as Europeans. All of these people could be distinguished by their very large ears, in which they wore gold hoops, and their long fingernails. This polygamous nation rarely worried about its daughters, who were given great freedom and had no supervision. The country produced tobacco, various fruits of Europe and India, and some which were peculiar to this particular area. The rivers were full of fish, and there was a great deal of game in the forests. Parrots were particularly abundant. The capital was six leagues from the Missi River, the river of gold. They cared so little for this metal that they permitted the French adventurers to carry off as much of it as they wanted. You can well imagine what advantage they took of this permission. Each one of them took as his share 240 pounds of gold. The mines were in the mountains, and the metal was brought down on small streams, which were dry during part of the year.

The Escaanibas carried on a great deal of trade with a far-off people. To explain to the French just how great the distance was, they told them that the trip took six months. The French adventurers were among the Escaanibas just at the moment that a caravan was leaving for this distant land. It consisted of three hundred oxen loaded with gold; an equal number of men armed with spears, bows and arrows, and daggers led and protected these animals. In exchange for their gold, they would receive iron, steel, spears, and other arms.

I do not know how reliable this report is. Some explorers think that the land to which the Escaanibas traveled was Japan. If that is so, there must be a land passage between Asia and America. Some English writers, without stopping to consider whether or not the report is authentic, think that these Indians went off to trade with the inhabitants of Kamchatka or some other island or continent to the east of that peninsula. Only discovery of such a passage can prove its existence. Conjecture proves nothing; it merely tells what is within the realm of possibility. In any event it seems likely that such a passage exists. Even if there are several straits separating the two continents, they would not have prevented men from passing from one side to the other. Let us hope that our present lack of knowledge will not last forever. The discoveries that men will try to make in the Southern Sea, or the Pacific, will cast much more light on this question.[3] If, after exploration, it is found that there really are straits, that is still no reason to believe that they were always there. Earthquakes could

---

[3] At the very moment that these letters are being printed, the English have already discovered ten islands in this ocean. There has been an account of this in Commodore Byron's report of his travels, which has caused quite a stir. This account proves the existence of giants, believed in without proof by the ancients, rejected as purely imaginative by the moderns, and verified by the new discoveries. The very next voyage the English make in the same area will give us further details. This undertaking will certainly encourage others, and a more exact knowledge of the Southern Sea will answer the remaining questions on the passage between Asia and America.

have cut in two the isthmus which connected the two continents. Many writers believe that that is how the Strait of Gibraltar was formed. They say that the Mediterranean formerly had no outlet to the Atlantic. Some people think that England at one time was joined to France, even though the sea now separates Calais from Dover. Why could not the situation have been the same in the case of America and Asia?

Determining the period in which this migration took place presents as many problems as discovering the manner in which it was accomplished. Problems which are difficult to solve naturally excite the curiosity of men. They want to see something new and to speak of it. Sometimes they present their fancies as truth. Among the singular opinions to which this subject has given rise is the one offered by Marc Lescarbot in his *History of New France*. Father Lafitau will be my source once again, and I shall cite from his work on the customs of the American Indians: "Lescarbot had no trouble advancing in a most strong and irrefutable manner the claim that Noah was aware, if only by hearsay, of the existence of the western lands, Lescarbot's own birthplace. During the 350 years which he lived after the flood, Noah himself populated or repopulated those lands. This great worker and pilot, who was ordered to restore the desolated earth, could have led his children to those regions. If, after all, admitting that the secular writers are correct, Noah was able to go from the mountains of Armenia to Italy, where he placed Janiculum on the banks of the Tiber, and his children were able to settle in Japan, why could he not just as easily have passed through the Strait of Gibraltar to New France, Cape Verde, and Brazil?"

I doubt that we have to go back to the time of Noah to find when America was populated. If, as it appears, the Tatars migrated, it must have been some time after Noah. The inhabitants of a vast country do not migrate when they are few in number. They remain together until they have multiplied to such a point that they are forced to leave their native country. There may, of course, be other reasons. Such research should not be pursued, since it is of little importance and is based on idle curiosity, which is very difficult to satisfy. All that can be said for certainty is that America appears to have been settled just a few centuries ago.

The English writer, Powell,[4] reports in his *History of Wales* that in 1170 there was a war of succession over the Welsh throne after the death of Prince Owen Gwynnedd.[5] When a bastard son seized the crown, one of the legitimate children, Madoc,[6] went off on a voyage of discovery. He sailed westward and found a wonderfully fertile and beautiful land. Since the land was uninhabited, he settled there. Hakluyt[7] assures us that Madoc made two or three trips to England, where, upon telling of the charm of this new country, he recruited settlers who were willing to go back with him.

The English believe that this prince discovered Virginia. Pierre Martyr seems to furnish the proof that this opinion is correct when he says that the peoples of Virginia and Guatemala celebrate the memory of one of their ancient heroes named Madoc. Several recent explorers have found ancient British words used by the North Americans. The famous English bishop, Nicholson,[8] believes that a considerable part of the American languages comes from Welsh. Some students of antiquity claim that the Spanish got their double *l* from the Indians, who in turn owe the sound to the Welsh. There is no end to the arguments given as proof that the Welsh prince Madoc visited America. The Dutch have brought back from the Strait of

[4] David Powell, c.1552–98, British historian, translated and edited *Caradoc's History of Cambria* (1584).—Ed.

[5] Twelfth-century prince of North Wales.—Ed.

[6] Second son of Owen Gwynnedd.—Ed.

[7] Richard Hakluyt, c.1553–1616, British geographer. *Voyages Touching the Discoveries of America* (1582); *A Particular Discourse Concerning Westerne Discoveries* (1584); *The Principal Navigations, Voyages and Discoveries of the English Nation* (1589–1600).—Ed.

[8] William Nicholson, 1655–1727, archbishop of Cashel, Ireland, and bibliographer. *English Historical Library* (1696–99); *Scottish Historical Library* (1702); *Irish Historical Library* (1724); *Leges Marchiarum* (1705).—Ed.

Magellan a white-headed bird called a penguin by the natives. This is an old British word meaning "white head." It has been determined that the word came originally from Wales.

According to Roman historians, the English were not the only ones to settle and populate America. Bayer claims that the Normans were the first Europeans courageous enough to sail to the New World.

Doctor Lochner assures us that Martin,[9] a Bohemian of a very distinguished family, went to Brazil and discovered the Strait of Magellan. Several German writers, who would prefer America to bear the name of Martin instead of that of Americus Vespucci, have espoused this cause.

Whether one accepts or rejects these stories, whether they are true or false, we must admit that we and the Americans are of the same origin. Despite all their mistaken notions, they have kept several ideas which are rather similar to those which have been handed down to us in the Scriptures. I shall quote, sir, part of an English dissertation on the people of the New World. This work compiles American ideas that go back to the truths set down by Moses.

> The Peruvians believe that there was a flood at one time in which all the inhabitants of their continent perished, with the exception of a small number who hid in caves at the tops of the highest mountains. Their descendants repopulated the earth. Similar ideas were held by the inhabitants of Hispaniola, according to Gemelli Carreri.[10] In the old Mexican stories, too, there is mention of a flood which wiped out the entire human race with the exception of one man and his wife. These two had many children, all of whom were mute until a pigeon granted them the gift of speech. The legend goes on to say that the immediate descendants of this couple spoke different languages and were unable to communicate with each other. It was for this reason

[9] Martin Behaim, c.1436–1507, German navigator and geographer in the service of Portugal, sailed to the coast of Guinea.—ED.

[10] Gemelli Carreri, a Neopolitan traveler who lived in the second half of the seventeenth century. After a trip around the world, he published *Giro del mondo* (Naples, 1699). A French translation appeared in 1719.—ED.

that they separated and went off to different lands. Another American belief is that all of mankind is descended from four women. This is very much in line with Mosaic history which claims that all people have as their ancestors Noah and his three sons. All these stories prove that Noah was the ancestor of the Americans and that even they have heard some of the accounts contained in Mosaic history. This completely demolishes the peculiar claim that the ancestors of the Indians antedate Adam.

Does not this quote, sir, answer all the arguments and theories of those writers who want to substitute their absurd imaginative ideas for the truth? Where could the Americans have received these ideas if they were not a post-deluge people descended from nations which had the story of the flood within their tradition? It is easy to explain that, with the passage of time and through ignorance and the lack of serious thought, the Indians would drown the few facts that remained etched in their memories in a sea of fables. The lack of monuments and of an alphabet with which to record events in writing destroys the trustworthiness of their traditional stories. Traditions which are passed on orally from father to son must be greatly changed after several generations.

The wars which the Americans have always fought against their neighbors have been partly responsible for preventing population growth. They obviously lead a nomadic life because they are so few in number. They wander from forest to forest hunting for game, settle wherever there is enough food, and leave to go elsewhere as soon as there is not enough to eat. If they were more numerous, their needs would increase. The difficulty of providing for everyone would force them to think of new ways to find food and to depend less on mere chance. They would find use for many of the things provided by the earth and would learn to grow crops. In many regions they already cultivate corn; they would soon learn to grow other grains, and one discovery would lead to another. They would settle in the country which they farmed and would give up their nomadic life.

Several of the Indian nations have found it beneficial to move close to the European settlements in the north country. In exchange for furs, which the Europeans are so eager to have, the natives can easily obtain brandy and arms. They hunt and trap over a two-hundred-league area in order to get supplies which they now consider necessities. They appear to have settled down, while in reality they continue to enjoy their nomadic life. It will take a long time for them to become civilized. Perhaps they will destroy each other before then.

There, sir, is what I think can be said with some degree of accuracy about the people of America. My letter would be too long if I tried to repeat only one-hundredth of the things which have been said on this subject. Entire volumes could be written about the conflicting ideas and opinions which have been published for many years. I have tried to limit myself to several curious observations. I believe that those who come closest to the truth are the ones who believe that the Americans are of Tatar origin. You have no idea of the similarity between the customs of the Americans and those of the ancient Scythians. This is evident in religious ceremonies, habits, and diet. Hormius is full of stories which can satisfy your curiosity in this matter. I urge you to read him.

I shall not continue all these discussions, which, perhaps, should have come at the end of the account of my travels. I shall speak to you of something more important to humanity, something which can be more readily understood through experience and observation. Since it is natural for man to want to live a long time, I think that it would be appropriate for me, with my experience, to indicate briefly the way to conserve and prolong life in America.

I shall finish my letter with a little dissertation on cures. I remember reading in the April 3, 1687, issue of the *Gazette de Hollande* that a noble Venetian, Frederick Gualdus, lived to be four hundred years old. It is claimed that he discovered a universal panacea. When he left Venice on March 7, 1688, he brought along a portrait of himself done by Titian, who had died 130 years before. I am certain that you will agree with me, sir, that perfect health is brought about by exercise and sobriety. When Europeans first came here 260 years ago, the Indians had neither wine nor brandy. The natives, as I have already said, lived on dried and smoked game, roasted or boiled with corn ground in a hardwood mortar. This food, called chili, is very tasty and healthful. When I went up the Mobile River with the Indians, I lived for about two months on this food. I can assure you that I never felt better than I did during that period. The best of all the Latin proverbs is: *Plures gula occidit quam gladius.*[11] Voluptuousness and intemperance in eating and drinking kill more people than the sword. You should lead a life of moderation, especially in the warm regions of America.

First of all, you must allow yourself to become slowly accustomed to the climate, and you must avoid all fruit and liquor until your body gradually becomes adjusted. People with a great deal of blood should have some drawn from time to time to prevent apoplexy, and gentle laxatives should be taken occasionally. You should avoid exposing yourself to the burning heat of the sun and to the wind.

When you have drunk too much wine, eat things with acid in them, such as lemons, which are plentiful here. This will clear your head and keep the vapors from getting you drunk after meals. If you become overheated because you have drunk too much liquor, take something refreshing and be careful not to eat hot food. Spirits should be drunk as little as possible because they burn the blood and cause high fever.

When you have eaten too much, strong liquor is good for fortifying the stomach and aiding digestion, but if, on the other hand, you are overheated because you have drunk too much, alcohol can become very dangerous.[12] Those who drink to excess are almost always tormented by fantastic dreams which tire them so much that their minds

---

[11] "The gullet kills as many people as the sword."—Ed.

[12] I should mention that since the Americans have begun to drink wine and liquor, they have shortened their lives, just as we have.

become disturbed. The wine fumes in their bodies excite their imagination. We know from experience that sober people, especially those who drink water, sleep peacefully, without waking too easily or falling into a stupor. In the second chapter of Philostratus' *Life of Apollonius*, we learn that in Athens those who were afflicted with bad dreams went to be cured by the priests of the false gods. The priests prescribed abstinence from wine for three or four days. This privation cleared the patients' minds and brought about a cure which was attributed to the gods.

After overeating, if you feel so stuffed and lethargic that the nutritive juices bloat and exhaust your entire body, I believe you would do well to imitate the Indians, who find sweating an infallible cure. Increasing the heat of the body is a certain cure, if done at the first signs of discomfort. Europeans who use the perspiration cure lie between two blankets and cover themselves completely, except for their faces. They do not get up until they have perspired for a full hour. When this treatment is continued for several days, the patient's recovery is so remarkable that he regains his strength and his appetite. He is surprised to find himself agile and alert once again. Perspiring purifies the internal organs painlessly and naturally. Ordinary medicines cannot do this. In order to remain healthy, one should undergo this treatment three times a year: in spring, summer, and winter. My conclusion, sir, is that diet and sweating are general cures.

I would say that nature ought to be our guide in everything and should teach us the true means of remaining in good health. Otherwise, we are condemned to great suffering and even to death. I have already mentioned that the North American Indians' great physical activity, such as dancing, ball-playing, hunting, fishing, and fighting, overheats them so that they perspire and thus eliminate body waste. Why do the peasants live so long and remain healthy without the aid of doctors? It is because of their work and exercise that they do not have the gout, kidney stones, and other infirmities to which wealthy Europeans are prone because they eat rich food and walk as rarely as do sick old men. I have known some of them who have turned their stomachs into a drug store.

It has been observed that young people who migrate from Europe to the warm regions of America die more quickly than the old. This is because the young eat all kinds of fruit which cause diarrhea. Very little fruit should be eaten until the body becomes accustomed to the climate of the country. After one year there is no further inconvenience of this sort.

If these precautions are taken, I am sure that one could live longer in the New World than in the Old. There are at present a number of people in Louisiana who have been there since the founding of the colony. I have met a settler named Graveline who is 118 years old. He came here with Monsieur d'Iberville in 1698 and served as a soldier in Canada for about thirty years during the reign of Louis XIV.

I am, sir, . . .

Letter XXII

To the Marquis de l'Estrade.

The author's return to France; the narrow escape off the Cape of Florida; the origin of a supposed fountain of youth; the ship's escape from the English; a fight with an English privateer; the ship is almost burned; plans for a raid on the New England coast; the capture of an enemy ship; the author's arrival at Corunna.

Sir:

When I got to Corunna November 1, 1762, I learned that Monsieur de Kerlérec had used a Spanish schooner to send to the Minister charges against Monsieur de Rochemore, commissioner general of the navy and finance and quartermaster officer for Louisiana, who was recalled to France by a *lettre de cachet*. Charges were also brought against the officers who accompanied him. I was among them, although I was unaware of it. As far back as June, the Governor of Louisiana had notified Monsieur de Belle-Isle, of whom I have written you, and the Chevalier d'Erneville, commander of the naval troops in Louisiana, the unpleasant news that they were being recalled. These are the words he used: "I am notifying you that I have received a letter, dated January 1, from the Duke de Choiseul, stating that the King, dissatisfied with your work, has demoted you and has relieved you of your duties."

You can imagine the astonishment of these two officers, who had served their king and their country with such great honor and distinction. This misfortune affected Monsieur de Belle-Isle even more than did his sad captivity among the cannibalistic Indians. Despite his age, this worthy officer, who had hoped to die peacefully in the colony which owes him so much, was not afraid to risk the dangers of the sea in time of war.

He sailed back with us in order to seek justice from the King. Because of his illness and the suffering caused him by the Court's disfavor, I am very much afraid that he will never reach the court of our glorious kings. This last unexpected bit of misfortune, coming at the end of his sad life, will kill him.[1] You will see in the story that I am going to tell you that, without this old officer's experience, all 150 of us would have gone down with the *Médée*, a ship carrying 12 guns and commanded by Captain Cochon. The English fleet, which had just taken Martinique, was attacking Havana, Cuba. As everyone knows, ships going from Louisiana to France must come within sight of this island.

I feel that this observation is a very natural one to make. Should not the Governor of Louisiana have communicated to Captain Cochon the same information which he himself had received so that our captain would not have run the needless risk of stopping at Havana? Information concerning a situation which could lead to such grave consequences should have received much more serious consideration.

We sailed from Balize on August 10, 1762. In order to avoid Cuba, we sailed within sight of the Tortugas, or the Turtle Islands.[2] We were sailing before a good strong wind, but our pilot, who was

[1] Monsieur de Belle-Isle, overcome with grief and fatigue, died in Paris, May 4, 1763, and was mourned by all men of integrity. Although he had spent his youth among the most barbarous people, his kindness gained him the respect and friendship of all servicemen. His home was a center of piety, and his family set a good example for the entire colony. Monsieur de Belle-Isle was related through his wife to the illustrious Duguay-Trouin, whose memory will always be cherished by the French. Monsieur de Belle-Isle's grief-stricken wife and his daughter, Madame Dorville, did not long survive him.

[2] Turtles hatch their eggs in the sand of these islands. The Tortugas are so flat that they cannot be seen until you are quite close to them.

unfamiliar with these waters, missed the entrance of the channel to the Bahamas in the dusk and headed into a bay on the cape of Florida. Taking his bearings and finding that we were at exactly the same latitude as we would have been on the other side of the cape, he assumed that we had gone through the channel and out to sea. We would have been lost were it not for Monsieur de Belle-Isle, who had been familiar with the North American coast for forty-five years. Suspecting that the Captain was incompetent, he kept a sharp lookout against danger. As a matter of fact, this experienced officer, noticing at dawn that the color of the water had changed, awakened the soundly sleeping Captain, who was convinced that we were out at sea. When soundings were taken and the Captain, much to his surprise, found only five fathoms of water, he realized beyond any doubt that he had wandered off the route. We turned about and continued to take soundings until we were out of those waters.

Before going any further, sir, I should like to digress a bit to speak of that famous Florida Fountain of Youth which caused so much stir in Europe. The attempt to discover it was the reason for almost as many voyages as was the greed for gold. The Spaniards would very much have liked to own the Fountain, in addition to the rich mines of Peru. If these details please you, that in itself will be sufficient reason for my telling you this story.

In Spanish, the Florida cape is called the *Cabo de los Corrientes*, because the water here flows so fast that it more than counteracts the wind and keeps ships from advancing even when all the sails are used. Sometimes the current forces ships onto the rocks. This almost happened to us as we came close to being smashed against the little islands which Columbus called *los Mártires* because their pointed rocks looked from afar like tortured men. There are eleven of these islands. The Tortugas got their name because the Spanish caught six thousand tortoises on them. The Bahama Islands are so flat that they seem to be submerged. The current runs through a channel which, at its narrowest point, is twenty leagues wide from Albana to the Martyrs and then another fourteen leagues wide from the Martyrs to the Florida coast. All these islands are situated 25 degrees, 15 minutes, North latitude.[3] We sailed about in these waters for twenty-seven days. It took almost a miracle to get us on our way again.

It is known that Florida was discovered by Juan Ponce de León, who was looking for Bimini, the island which had caused so much talk because it was, according to the Cuban Indians, the site of the River Jordan and the Fountain of Youth. Juan Ponce de León believed this fable and looked for the Fountain without ever finding it. Not at all discouraged, he sent Pérez de Ortubia and the pilot, Antonio de Alaminos, in search of it. He was going to land in a bay at Puerto Rico, when he discovered Bimini, but he did not find the Fountain or the River Jordan. Juan Ponce de León died shortly afterward without ever having succeeded in his task.

In an attempt to get rid of their troublesome gold-seeking Spanish guests, the Cuban Indians told them that the island of Bimini contained not only gold but also a river and a fountain which rejuvenated old men who bathed in their waters. This report was immediately sent to the Castillian court. As a result, several Spaniards set sail from Cádiz to the New World to see this wonder, which, had it really existed, would have been worth more than all the gold in the world.

When the Spaniards returned to Cádiz everyone was convinced that the hopeful, cheerful report had been false. Those who had gone in search of the Fountain had grown old, and they were laughed at for having undertaken such a long, painful voyage. During their search for the imaginary fountain, they did discover the Florida cape. In an attempt to grow younger, all visitors to the island of Bimini tested every river, fountain, lake, and pond, by swimming in them and drinking the water. It has not been so very long since people have

[3] In the vicinity of the Florida keys, according to an eighteenth-century French map reproduced in Justin Winsor's *Christopher Columbus* (Boston and New York, Houghton, Mifflin and Company, 1892), 559.—ED.

given up looking for the Fountain. In the same way, people in Europe looked for the philosophers' stone until recently.

We agreed that if the English privateers captured us and took us to Bimini, we would bathe in all the rivers and fountains. Bimini, which now belongs to the English and is called Providence Island, was formerly a haven for the pirates who infested American waters for a long time.

This is what gave rise to the fable of the Fountain. The climate of Florida is so temperate that it is said men have lived to be 250 years old. The most beautiful women in North America supposedly lived in Bimini at one time. Even old men from the continent retired to the island to ease the miseries of life. All these innocent pleasures ended with the arrival of the Europeans who took over the lands of these people. The inhabitants of Cuba have settled all these islands. Accounts tell us of how bravely the Florida Indians resisted the Spaniards. Armed with bows and arrows, these Indians went out in eleven canoes to stop the invaders and were bold enough to cut the cables of Ponce de León's ship. The explorer was forced to sue for peace. (These Indians are governed by *paraoustis*, or chiefs.)

While I am on the subject of the so-called Fountain of Youth, let me add that the natives of Darien, like those of Cuba, wanted to get rid of the Spaniards because of their constant search for gold. The natives told them jokingly that since they were so greedy for this metal, they ought to go farther south where it was plentiful enough to be fished up in nets. When Vasco Núñez de Balboa included this in his report to the Court, the Spaniards were overjoyed. Balboa discovered the Southern Sea and Peru at this same time, but it turned out that the story of fishing for gold in nets was false.

You probably know that during the period of John Law's famous system, which almost overturned the entire kingdom, Parisians were shown a picture of an Indian from the Mississippi Valley exchanging a gold ingot for a Frenchman's knife. Everyone at that time was mad enough to spend his hard cash on worthless stock in an imaginary

El Dorado. It must be admitted that if New Orleans Indians had been in Paris at that time, they would have correctly surmised that the French had gone mad or that they were all magic-working medicine men. We have been told that those imaginary mines are what ruined La Salle, when he missed the mouth of the Mississippi in 1684. He did not stop to think that the interior of this great continent contained much more valuable treasure in the cultivation of the land, which nurtures all men and creates the true riches of nations.

We were forced to sail along the coast of Florida, and on the thirty-seventh day of our voyage we were near Louisiana. To make matters worse, a strong wind came close to sinking us and forced us to head towards Cuba. Since we did not see the fleet, we assumed that the English had lifted the siege, but we were heading right into a trap, as you will see from what follows.

We decided to stop at Havana to take on necessary provisions and to get a pilot familiar with the coastal regions. We approached the harbor on September 8, 1762, Our Lady's feast day. We were surprised that no one came after we had hoisted a flag and fired several cannon shots in an appeal for help, but upon entering the port, we discovered that Morro Castle was almost completely destroyed. We then decided that some of the officers should take the launch and go out on reconnaissance. The launch accidently came upon a barge which was leaving the port with several Spanish families aboard. They had been issued passports by the English governor, Lord Albemarle. We learned from the captain that the city and all the forts had been surrendered to the English on August 12, 1762.

We veered about immediately, but an English frigate pursued us. Providence, looking out for our safety, sent a very thick fog through which we escaped in the dark of night to the Bahama Channel.

Several days later we saw a ship preceded by two boats. We soon recognized that she was a privateer from Providence Island and that the two boats had been captured from our compatriots. She came in to attack us, and we put up a good fight, despite the fact that we had four cannons less than the enemy.[4] Not relying on the officers and cannoneers of the merchant fleet, each one of us made good use of his talent and experience in firing artillery pieces. We fought so well that after about three hours of fierce combat the English ship was almost destroyed. No longer able to withstand our fire, she was forced to retire. We were very happy to find that no one among us had been killed or wounded. Our ship, however, had been shot through, and our sails and rigging had been so badly damaged that we had to replace them after the battle.

During the fight we were exposed to the greatest danger imaginable. The wind blew back into our ship some burning oakum, which set fire to a case of cartridges on the deck. Fortunately, it did not spread to the magazine, or we would have been blown up.

The winds were against us so that we had to remain at sea without having any idea of when we would be able to land. Every day the danger of starving to death became more real; we were already reduced to eating only one-quarter of the essential minimum ration each day. We held a meeting and decided to attack the first enemy ship that came along or to raid the coast of New England, off whose shores we were sailing. We were determined to get supplies or to die sword in hand. The plan was bold, I might even say foolhardy, but we have a proverb that says, "Hunger drives the wolf out of the woods." We were just about to take this extreme measure when, through the goodness of Providence who watched over us, we saw a large ship and headed toward her. We were eager to board her even though she seemed to be much better armed than we. At first we raised English colors, but the ship began to sail away from us anyway. The wind was against her, however, and she prepared for combat with such determination that anyone but starving men would have

---

[4] I must remark here that Monsieur de Kerlérec took two cannons away from us before we left New Orleans. When it took the staff officers of the Angoumois Regiment to Louisiana, this ship had fourteen cannons. It is certain that if we had had the same number, we should have taken the privateer and her two prizes.

been frightened off. We fired a cannon as we hoisted our colors, in accordance with the law of the sea. When we were within range of the enemy, we fired a broadside which caused the English ship to surrender immediately. She was carrying a very rich cargo. We took her cannons as well as several cases of rifles, pistols, and sabres, which we added to our supply of arms, but we did not find much in the way of provisions aboard since she was almost at the end of her voyage. After having been paid a ransom for her release, we left her just enough supplies to reach her destination in the Carolinas about seventy leagues away.

Finally, we thought we were in a position to set out for Europe with the provisions we had and in the hope that, being well armed, we could capture another ship or land in the Azores.[5] Our expectations, however, did not materialize. The contrary winds kept us from reaching land, and we did not meet any other ships. For a period of fifty days we lived in the most horrible misery, reduced to three ounces of biscuit and half a bottle of water per day.[6]

Even these inadequate rations would have given out after our many dangerous experiences if a violent storm had not brought us to the coast of Spain on the ninety-fourth day of our crossing. We had come very close to being killed by the sea, the sword, fire, hunger, and thirst.

The first thing that we did upon arriving in port was to have Abbé Piquet[7] sing a *Te Deum* to thank the Supreme Being. This was accompanied by a salvo fired from all our guns.

In port we found the Chevalier de Ternay, the commander of the French fleet that had just returned from a glorious expedition to

[5] Islands in the Atlantic between Europe and North America.

[6] In the English ship we found thirty quarts of hulled barley, which helped us a great deal. We boiled the barley in water with moldy biscuits. This made a nourishing and tasty soup. It is true that hunger is the best of sauces.

[7] Abbé Piquet is the one who presented several Indians to the King in 1754. He is the nephew of Monsieur François Piquet, who died while he was the King's ambassador to Siam.

Newfoundland. He was very surprised to see the great number of soldiers on our ship who could have been used to good advantage in Louisiana in this time of war. He made some of them get aboard the ships of his fleet so that they could serve during the rest of the campaign. The others, who had leaves signed by Kerlérec and Foucat, joined the Spanish army which was going to Portugal.

We landed on All Saints' Day, November 1, 1762, and all of us went to visit the Marquis de Croix, a general in the kingdom of Galicia. This nobleman greeted us very cordially. From there we went to see Monsieur David, the French consul general in Galicia, who lives in Corunna. We asked him to advance us the money to take care of our most pressing needs, since we did not even have enough to take care of our trip through Spain. He answered that although he had no orders to do so, he would take it upon himself to help such worthy people. We thanked him for his kindness.

Then, having recovered somewhat from our voyage, we made ready to leave overland for France. We were hoping to arrive at the Court at the beginning of January, 1763.

I do not think that I have omitted anything important in my correspondence with you. I have tried to give an accurate account of my voyages, and I have tried to act like the bee who works for the benefit of others. I shall not speak of my success or lack of it, since my letters have informed you of the disagreeable situations I have been subjected to for disapproving of the terrible abuse of authority and for stubbornly trying to go against the current. I had asked for permission to go back to Europe aboard a neutral ship. The Governor used various pretexts not to grant my request. I was, therefore, forced to leave on a merchant ship, and as you have seen, I came close to losing my life.

As far as rewards are concerned, is it not enough for a citizen to have been loyal to his king and useful to his country? It is because of this that I dare hope that our very just and intelligent minister will be kind enough to inform the best of all kings of the ardent zeal of an officer who had the honor and satisfaction of serving him well in both Europe and America. I shall await respectfully and confidently the rewards due military valor. These rewards granted by our august monarch will be a thousand times more precious to me than all the riches of the New World. Until I have the honor of seeing you, I am, sir, . . .

Corunna
November 10, 1762

Copies of Letters and Certificates Sent to the Author
Which Concern the Various Missions
in Which He Served the King

A letter from Monsieur Rouillé, minister of the navy, to the Chevalier de Grossolles, brigadier of the army and His Majesty's commander at Belle-Île-en-Mer.

Versailles

June 15, 1750

Because of your recommendations concerning Monsieur Bossu, a former lieutenant in the Dauphine's Regiment, I shall suggest to the King that he grant him a commission in the colonial troops. In the meantime, you can use him at Belle-Île to train the recruits who are to be sent to the colonies. I shall leave it to you to pay him enough so that he can support himself. I am, ...

Rouillé

An extract from a letter written by Count d'Argenson to Monsieur Bossu.

FONTAINEBLEAU

October 1, 1750

I am writing to inform you, sir, that the King has just commissioned you lieutenant in the colonial troops. You must leave immediately for Rochefort, your point of embarkation. There you will receive the sum of three hundred pounds. Upon your arrival, you will report to the naval commander who will give you your papers. You will conform to the orders that you will receive. His Majesty hopes to hear nothing but good reports about your work and expects you to continue serving him with devotion and loyalty in the new post which he has offered you. I am, sir, . . .

D'Argenson

We, Chevalier of the Royal and Military Order of Saint Louis, the King's commanding officer in Illinois territory:

Certify that Monsieur Bossu, lieutenant in the troops on detached service from the navy in Louisiana, has served under us with all the zeal and diligence of a good officer who has scrupulously carried out all the duties of his office on all the assignments given him for the good of the service. Because of bad health, he has been granted our permission to recuperate in the capital. In view of his record, we have given him this certificate to be used in any way which may be of service to him.

Macarty

A letter from the Governor of Louisiana to the Minister of the Navy.

SIR:

I have the honor of informing you that I could not help but grant a one-year leave of absence to Monsieur Bossu, a lieutenant stationed in this colony. Since the conditions of war demand that I grant a leave only in case of absolute necessity, I had the doctors and surgeons give me a report on Monsieur Bossu's health. They deemed it necessary for him to return to France to take the waters at Bourbonne so he might recover from a wound that he received during the attack on Château-Dauphin. It is because of their certificates that I am permitting this officer to leave on a small ship, which is going to Santo Domingo where he will have greater opportunity to find passage to Europe. Since His Majesty does not want officers booked on merchant vessels because of the expense, I did not think it wise to take the responsibility of having the government pay for Monsieur Bossu's passage. In all fairness, however, I should tell you that this officer, who is penniless, is in no condition to pay his own fare to Europe, let alone the expense of getting to Bourbonne, where he is to take the baths. I should add that when he was on his way to the Illinois territory, his boat sank, and he lost all his possessions. Monsieur Dauberville was supposed to join me in asking you to reimburse Monsieur Bossu for his losses, but Dauberville is at present very ill and will for quite some time (if he recovers from this siege) be incapable of doing any work. We cannot wait, since Monsieur Bossu's ship is leaving.

Monsieur Bossu is a good officer, whose conduct, since I have been in this colony, has been beyond reproach. Moreover, he has always shown a great deal of enthusiasm in carrying out his military assignments. I believe that it would be an act of justice if you reimbursed him for his losses and paid his passage. I beg you to take this under consideration. I am, with profound respect, . . .

Kerlérec

NEW ORLEANS
March 12, 1757

233

*A copy of the letter of the Governor of Louisiana to Monsieur
Bossu on the mission which he accomplished at Tombigbee.*

New Orleans
October 14, 1759

I see, sir, from the details which you have given me of your mission to Tombigbee, that you have suffered all the hardship that is to be expected on such a trip, especially in this season. You arrived at your destination in good condition and without accident, and, knowing you the way I do, I am sure that you did all in your power to assure the success of the mission.

In regard to the ration allowance for officers of which you spoke to me, I cannot change anything for the moment, but in the Court's next communication to me, I hope to receive a reply to my strong and pressing requests in this matter. I regret, sir, that I cannot confer with the commissioner about the certificate that Monsieur Bobé must have sent him concerning the sum you turned over to the Alabama post. I shall, however, urgently request Monsieur Tudot, the assistant adjutant, to do so, and I shall let you know how things turn out. I am, sir, . . .

Kerlérec

We, Pierre Rigaud, Marquis de Vaudreuil, bearer of the Grande Croix of the Royal and Military Order of Saint Louis, former governor and lieutenant general of all of New France:

Certify that Monsieur Bossu, captain in the troops on detached duty from the navy in the King's service in Louisiana, served in the colony, while I was there, with the greatest distinction, efficiency, and devotion. In view of his record, we have given him this certificate to be used in any way which may be of service to him.

Executed in Paris
April 21, 1763

Vaudreuil

We, Pierre-Annibal de Velle, Chevalier of the Royal and Military Order of Saint Louis, King's lieutenant and formerly His Majesty's commander of the city and citadel of Mobile, in the province of Louisiana:

Certify that Monsieur Bossu, captain of a company on detached duty from the navy in the King's service in Louisiana, has served under me with all the enthusiasm and efficiency possible. Moreover, he has gone on several important and difficult missions among the Indian tribes.

In view of this, we have signed this certificate to be used in any way which may be of service to him.

Executed in PARIS

May 17, 1765

Velle

We, Pierre-Henri d'Erneville, Chevalier of the Royal and Military Order of Saint Louis, former commander of the troops on detached service from the navy stationed in Louisiana:

Certify that Monsieur Bossu, captain of the naval troops in Louisiana, has served with indefatigable devotion. Several of the events reported in his account happened in my presence among the Alabama Indians, in New Orleans, and on his last voyage to Corunna when we were fellow travelers. In view of this, we have signed this certificate in Paris, September 1, 1766.

Le Chevalier d'Erneville

INDEX

Index

of which *Jean-Bernard Bossu's Travels in the Interior of North America, 1751–1762* is Number 35, was started in 1939 by the University of Oklahoma Press. It follows rather logically the Press's program of regional exploration. Behind the story of the gradual and inevitable recession of the American frontier lie the accounts of explorers, traders, and travelers, which individually and in the aggregate present one of the most romantic and fascinating chapters in the development of the American domain. The following list is complete as of the date of publication of this volume.

1. Captain Randolph B. Marcy and Captain George B. McClellan. *Adventure on Red River:* Report on the Exploration of the Headwaters of the Red River. Edited by Grant Foreman. Out of print.
2. Grant Foreman. *Marcy and the Gold Seekers:* The Journal of Captain R. B. Marcy, with an account of the Gold Rush over the Southern Route. Out of print.
3. Pierre-Antoine Tabeau. *Tabeau's Narrative of Loisel's Expedition to the Upper Missouri.* Edited by Annie Heloise Abel. Translated from the French by Rose Abel Wright. Out of print.
4. Victor Tixier. *Tixier's Travels on the Osage Prairies.* Edited by John Francis McDermott. Translated from the French by Albert J. Salvan.
5. Teodoro de Croix. *Teodoro de Croix and the Northern Frontier of New Spain, 1776–1783.* Translated from the Spanish and edited by Alfred Barnaby Thomas. Out of print.
6. A. W. Whipple. *A Pathfinder in the Southwest:* The Itinerary of Lieutenant A. W. Whipple During His Exploration for a Railway Route from Fort Smith to Los Angeles in the Years 1853 & 1854. Edited and annotated by Grant Foreman. Out of print.
7. Josiah Gregg. *Diary & Letters.* Two volumes. Edited by Maurice Garland Fulton. Introductions by Paul Horgan.
8. Washington Irving. *The Western Journals of Washington Irving.* Edited and annotated by John Francis McDermott. Out of print.
9. Edward Dumbauld. *Thomas Jefferson, American Tourist:* Being an

Account of His Journeys in the United States of America, England, France, Italy, the Low Countries, and Germany.

10. Victor Wolfgang von Hagen. *Maya Explorer:* John Lloyd Stephens and the Lost Cities of Central America and Yucatán.

11. E. Merton Coulter. *Travels in the Confederate States:* A Bibliography. Out of print.

12. W. Eugene Hollon. *The Lost Pathfinder:* Zebulon Montgomery Pike.

13. George Frederick Ruxton. *Ruxton of the Rockies.* Collected by Clyde and Mae Reed Porter. Edited by LeRoy R. Hafen.

14. George Frederick Ruxton. *Life in the Far West.* Edited by LeRoy R. Hafen. Foreword by Mae Reed Porter.

15. Edward Harris. *Up the Missouri with Audubon:* The Journal of Edward Harris. Edited by John Francis McDermott.

16. Robert Stuart. *On the Oregon Trail:* Robert Stuart's Journey of Discovery (1812–1831). Edited by Kenneth A. Spaulding.

17. Josiah Gregg. *Commerce of the Prairies.* Edited by Max L. Moorhead.

18. John Treat Irving, Jr. *Indian Sketches:* Taken During an Expedition to the Pawnee Tribes (1833). Edited and annotated by John Francis McDermott.

19. Thomas D. Clark (ed.) *Travels in the Old South, 1527–1860:* A Bibliography. Three volumes. Volumes One and Two issued as a set (1956); Volume Three (1959).

20. Alexander Ross. *The Fur Hunters of the Far West.* Edited by Kenneth A. Spaulding.

21. William Bollaert. *William Bollaert's Texas.* Edited by W. Eugene Hollon and Ruth Lapham Butler.

22. Daniel Ellis Conner. *Joseph Reddeford Walker and the Arizona Adventure.* Edited by Donald J. Berthrong and Odessa Davenport.

23. Matthew C. Field. *Prairie and Mountain Sketches.* Collected by Clyde and Mae Reed Porter. Edited by Kate L. Gregg and John Francis McDermott.

24. Ross Cox. *The Columbia River:* Scenes and Adventures During a Residence of Six Years on the Western Side of the Rocky Mountains Among Various Tribes of Indians Hitherto Unknown; Together with a Journey Across the American Continent. Edited by Edgar I. and Jane R. Stewart.

25. Noel M. Loomis. *The Texan–Santa Fé Pioneers.*

26. Charles Preuss. *Exploring with Frémont:* The Private Diaries of Charles Preuss, Cartographer for John C. Frémont on His First, Second, and Fourth Expeditions to the Far West. Translated and edited by Erwin G. and Elisabeth K. Gudde.

27. Jacob H. Schiel. *Journey Through the Rocky Mountains and the Humboldt Mountains to the Pacific Ocean.* Translated from the German and edited by Thomas N. Bonner.

28. Zenas Leonard. *Adventures of Zenas Leonard, Fur Trader.* Edited by John C. Ewers.

29. Matthew C. Field. *Matt Field on the Santa Fe Trail.* Collected by Clyde and Mae Reed Porter. Edited and with an introduction and notes by John E. Sunder.

30. James Knox Polk Miller. *The Road to Virginia City:* The Diary of James Knox Polk Miller. Edited by Andrew F. Rolle.

31. Benjamin Butler Harris. *The Gila Trail:* The Texas Argonauts and the California Gold Rush. Edited and annotated by Richard H. Dillon.

32. Captain James H. Bradley. *The March of the Montana Column:* A Prelude to the Custer Disaster. Edited by Edgar I. Stewart.

33. Heinrich Lienhard. *From St. Louis to Sutter's Fort, 1846.* Translated and edited by Erwin G. and Elisabeth K. Gudde.

34. Washington Irving. *The Adventures of Captain Bonneville.* Edited and with an introduction by Edgeley W. Todd.

35. Jean-Bernard Bossu. *Jean-Bernard Bossu's Travels in the Interior of North America, 1751–1762.* Translated and edited by Seymour Feiler.

The text of *Jean-Bernard Bossu's Travels in the Interior of North America* has been set on the Linotype in twelve-point Granjon, with two points of leading between lines. The large twelve-point size, which was selected primarily for easy readability, nicely displays the beauty of Granjon, which George W. Jones derived from the elegant sixteenth-century French Garamond design.

University of Oklahoma Press

Norman